COUPLES

An Eclectic View

cou-ple (kup-il), n. (ME < OFr *cople* < L *copula*, a tie, link: see COPULA) **1.** a combination of two things; a pair **2.** two partners in a romantic or sexual relationship **3.** a man and a woman who are engaged, married, or joined as partners, as in a dance or game: (*They are such a handsome* couple.)

COUPLES

An Eclectic View

PHOTOGRAPHS by Max James Fallon

INTRODUCTION by Jeffrey Goodby

Published by

MustSeeBooks®

San Francisco

www.mustseebooks.com

COUPLES
An Eclectic View

Publisher's Cataloging-in-Publication
(Provided by Quality Books, Inc.)

Fallon, Max James, 1946-
Couples : an eclectic view / photographs by Max James Fallon ; introduction by Jeffrey Goodby.
p. cm.
Includes bibliographical references.
LCCN 2009910218
ISBN-13: 978-0-9766893-1-7
ISBN-10: 0-9766893-1-6

1. Portrait photography. 2. Couples--Pictorial works. 3. Couples--Anecdotes. I. Title.

TR681.C68F35 2010 779'.2
QBI09-600187

Printed in China by Oceanic Graphic Printing

10 9 8 7 6 5 4 3 2 1

Inquiries and correspondence should be addressed to:

info@mustseebooks.com

MustSeeBooks®

San Francisco

www.mustseebooks.com

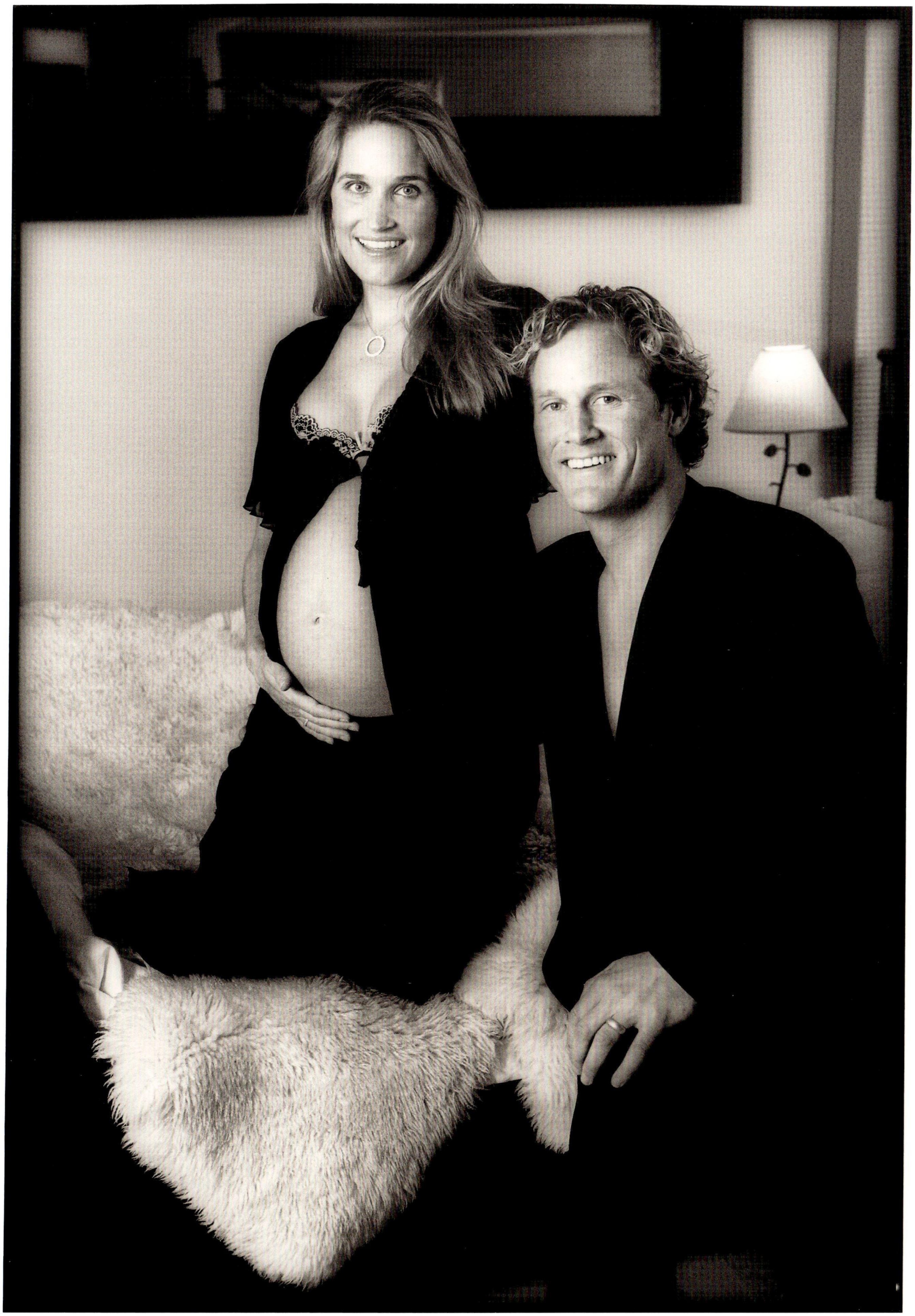

"The flight of 'Haaken' (our baby) is eternal love in the purist form."

COUPLES
An Eclectic View

In *The English Patient*, one of Michael Ondaatje's characters suddenly asks her lover: *"If I gave you my life, you would drop it. Wouldn't you?"* Max Fallon's couples don't answer that question. But when we look at these photos, we feel an urge to answer it for them.

This will never last, we hear our inner voice saying. How did she end up with him? Or: Look at how beautiful we all are. We are instantly caught up in the delicious universes that can be suggested by two people we don't even know, standing together for a quarter of a second.

I have known my friend Max for over two decades and only now realize how valuable, in fact lethal, his shy, unaffected nature would be in the facilitation of these photographs. We worked together in the world of making and printing beautiful images, and I watched as his apparently accommodating presence ushered along a deeper purpose. He is the perfect spark for this fire.

A picture of a couple is the momentary confluence of two rivers, a knot in the middle of two long pieces of string. It inevitably makes you wonder how the two of them got here and what will happen after this. The couples provide captions, but they're almost unnecessary, and maybe even distracting. We bring our own stories and conclusions to the photos for these characters. And in that sense, any photo of a couple is really a story about the three of us.

You find yourself building the story as you take in the details of these sometimes haunting shots. A lissome dancer twines her arms around a much larger, imposing partner. He's likable, smiling, and his bare feet mirror hers. Yet despite the dancer's physical beauty and affectionate bear hug, neither of the guy's hands is touching her. One is on his hip, the other clasping a cold iron fence.

A couple that appears to be ranchers has donned fringed outfits and posed with two horses. The man seems about to speak. What did he say?

A black man and white woman are intertwined, smiling beatifically beneath their Muslim head coverings. Their hands, like photographic negatives of each other, are posed with fingers and thumb at identical angles. Was that by chance? Do they always do that?

And then there is that transcendent older couple that glows from these pages – everyone who sees this book stops for them. Posed in front of what looks to be Mount Shasta in northern California, the woman in the wheelchair is swathed in black, yet with some effort reaches over her shoulder to clasp her husband's left hand. You look more closely and see that, inches from her serene smile, her index finger is pointed up his hand as if to say: Him. Yes. This is the one.

You want to get to the bottom of these stories, yet you know you cannot. And in that moment is captured the hope implicit in coupleness, the questionable promise that we might somehow be able to overcome our essential loneliness and separateness in life. So many of these couples seem to do just that, to be more connected, more close, more deeply sharing of each other's happiness and sadness and special moments than you'll ever hope to be. In this, one can't help feeling a twinge of jealousy, even a sense of longing. An ache for what they have that you don't have.

It's all an illusion, of course – both the positive and the negative interpretations. It's more about us than about them, in most cases. Susan Sontag warned us about the truth of photographs, but in the presence of these lovely images, it is so easy to forget. Coupleness is a highly respected thing, a church at which we are quick to worship. As Max himself told me, "It's an affirmation that our culture is working. Being part of a couple is viewed as such a positive state."

And yet it is also something of which we are deeply suspicious, and even afraid. Paparazzi chase down Charles and Diana in a desperate attempt to expose cracks and flaws. Supermarket weeklies trumpet the woes and perfidy of coupleness. We fear the intimacy of Sweeney Todd and Mrs. Lovett, and with good reason. Aren't you just a little worried about what Bill and Hillary talk about when no one's around? Maybe we shouldn't invite the Macbeths over after all.

Then there is the sexuality of these pairs, which is ineluctable. It seems to be everywhere, in every corner of the photographs. We see it in the looks of the people, the way they pose their bodies, and in their eye lines at the moment the shutter sounds. Your imagination runs wild with images, with what will happen after this moment. Again, it is a source of jealousy. But also of hope. The Greeks believed the two members of a couple were like bereft halves of a single animal that would be made whole when they made love. And why not?

All this is undeniably in these pages, and hovering above it all are the larger questions of fate and choice. Every photo here asks: What brought these people together today? Are there forces larger than we are that determine such things? Do our choices really matter at all? Is our fate, as Shakespeare wondered, to be found in our stars or in our selves?

In this sense, Fallon's photos seem to say two things at once. It was irresistible fate; it was a lucky and never-to-be-regretted choice. This is one of many things that could have happened; this is the only way it could have gone. We are thankfully together; we are alone in the same photo. In passing, Max told me that one of the couples had broken up shortly after the photo was taken. On the one hand, it didn't seem possible, what with this affectionate, seemingly timeless image looming in front of us. On the other, it was also somehow totally irrelevant to the power of the photograph.

Coupleness, in this way, represents a kind of hope. It is the hope that comes with spontaneous attraction and affection and passion that seems beyond our control, an undeniable faith in powers greater than ourselves. Each of these photographs represents immense potential energy in a form that convinces us we can reach across the distances between us, that this is in fact happening right this moment, all over the world. And could happen to you.

Therein, I suppose, is the gift Fallon has given us all with this book. He is, of course, the intrusive, instigative and invisible force in all these images. He has insinuated himself upon these people, asked and cajoled and wheedled until they posed for him, and the result is undeniably about his influence on the outcome of the photo, struggling against theirs, and against the momentum of their lives at this moment. The result is gorgeous and deep.

Like a priest, Max has herein married his subjects with the scepter of his camera. It is a very short ceremony. We are all happy attendants at this wedding and yet, turning our gaze to the couple at the center of the room, we find that we are looking instead at ourselves.

—Jeffrey Goodby

Attempting to Photograph a RELATIONSHIP

"You want to photograph us for a book on couples...
What makes you think we're so special?"

That was a fairly typical question that came up again and again as I searched for couples to photograph for this book. No matter what part of the world I found myself in, the questions were similar. Needless to say, it's not surprising that people would react quizzically to a stranger asking them to pose for a photograph that a lot of other strangers would be looking at! I had to convince them that this was a worthwhile project, and if they consented, they might find it rather interesting—and revealing. The more intrepid ones said yes! Here are a few other common questions that arose when I initially approached them:

"Okay, you can take our picture, but what do you want us to do?"

It's always interesting how couples relate to each other in front of the camera.

"Can you show us what we look like while you're shooting?"

There are passive couples, and then there are those who want to be really involved in the process—this is their relationship, and they want some control.

"I don't know—this could be a little too revealing. What do you think, dear?"

Others are rather shy about making a single-image statement about their relationship.

"Do you have a secret way to get us to relax? We don't take good pictures."

At some point, the couple usually forgets about the camera and starts to enjoy the image-making process.

"Yes, we're proof-positive that opposites attract – don't you agree?"

Many are very proud that they are slightly outside the culturally accepted "norm" of a typical group.

"No pictures! Our culture has very strict rules about pictures. Do you understand?"

In certain cultures, a photographer has to deal with a great deal of rejection!

"You've traveled a long way to find us – you think we're worth it?"

Finding great couples in various parts of the world and interacting with them can be a very rewarding experience, for all three of us!

"How can you possibly capture the love we share in a single photo?"

There will be that one shot, among the dozens, that will say it all! Ever the optimist.

In most cases, the couples were very protective of how their relationships would be portrayed visually. They wanted to maintain a certain degree of privacy, but with a little coaxing, they were willing to share a bit of that relationship – that they were obviously so proud of.

As you peruse the following photographs, you'll no doubt have questions of your own – after all, you're looking at a mystery. How did they come together, and what's kept them together? I know how I felt while I was making them: impressed and moved by the relationships I was privileged to observe and record. I attempted to capture the essence of their relationships (probably impossible), or at least a significant gesture, mood or expression that might reveal a bit of the unique bond they share. We should all be so lucky to have what they have: a committed partner who is such a significant part of their past, present and future.

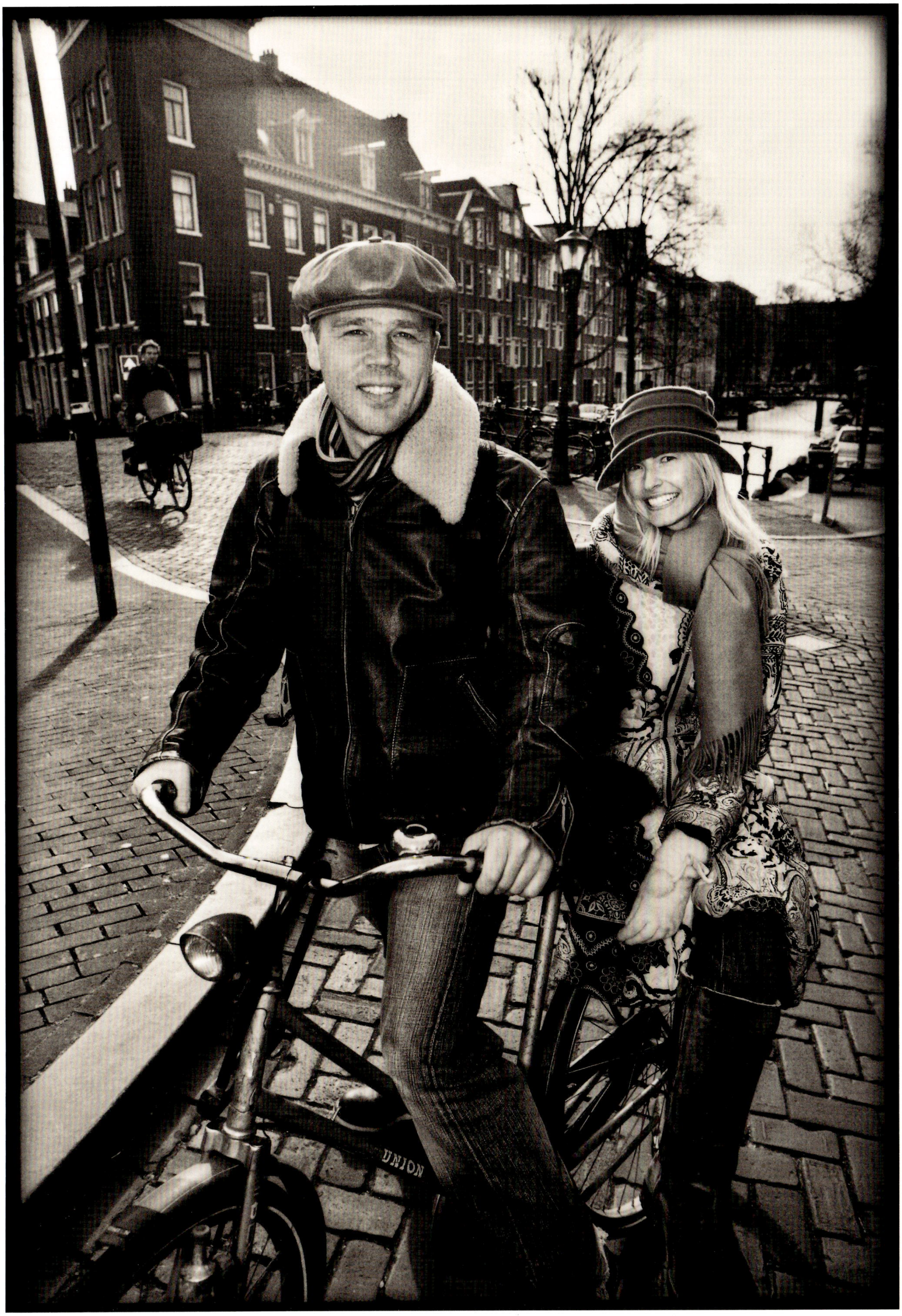

"Met mijn schatje door weer en wind, door steeg en straat, zij is het allemaal meer dan waard."

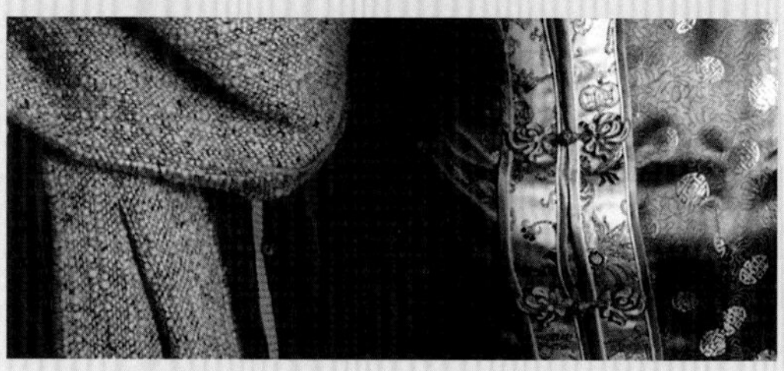

"After much searching, we finally found the perfect wedding and reception location for a Chinese-American woman with a quasi-Buddhist background and an Irishman with a Catholic background: a Moroccan restaurant with floor cushions, a belly dancer and no eating utensils."

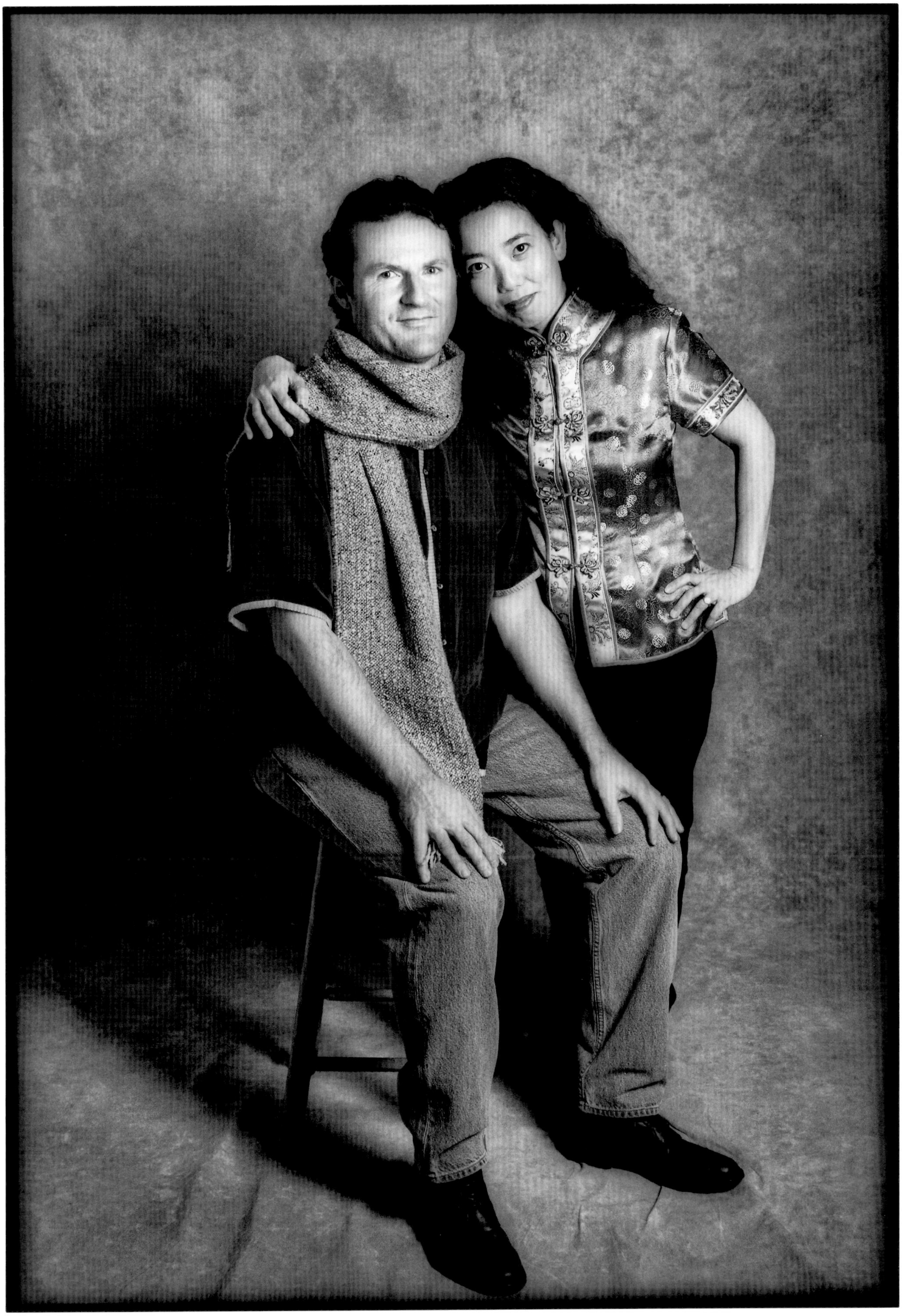

LOCATION

Australian Outback

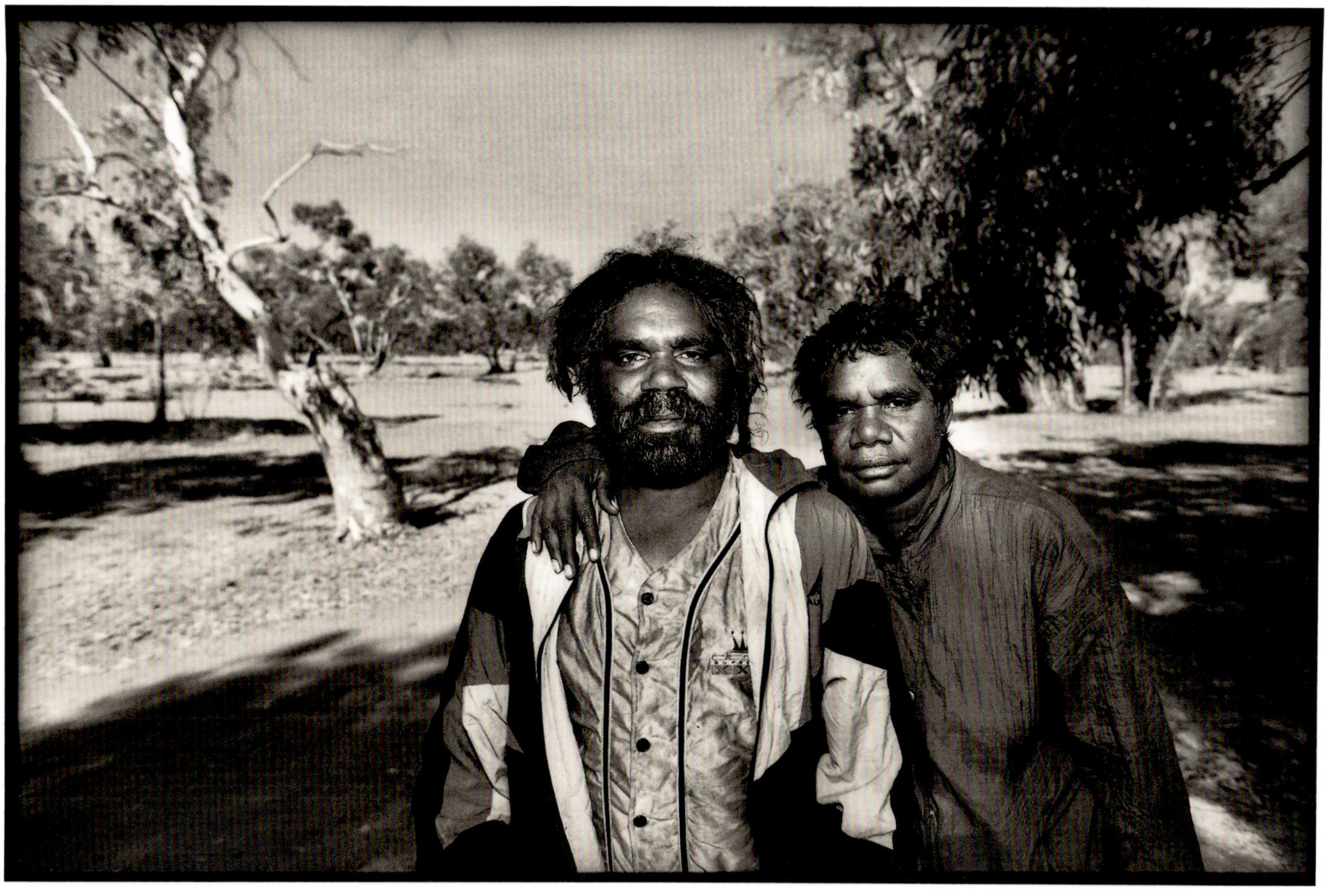

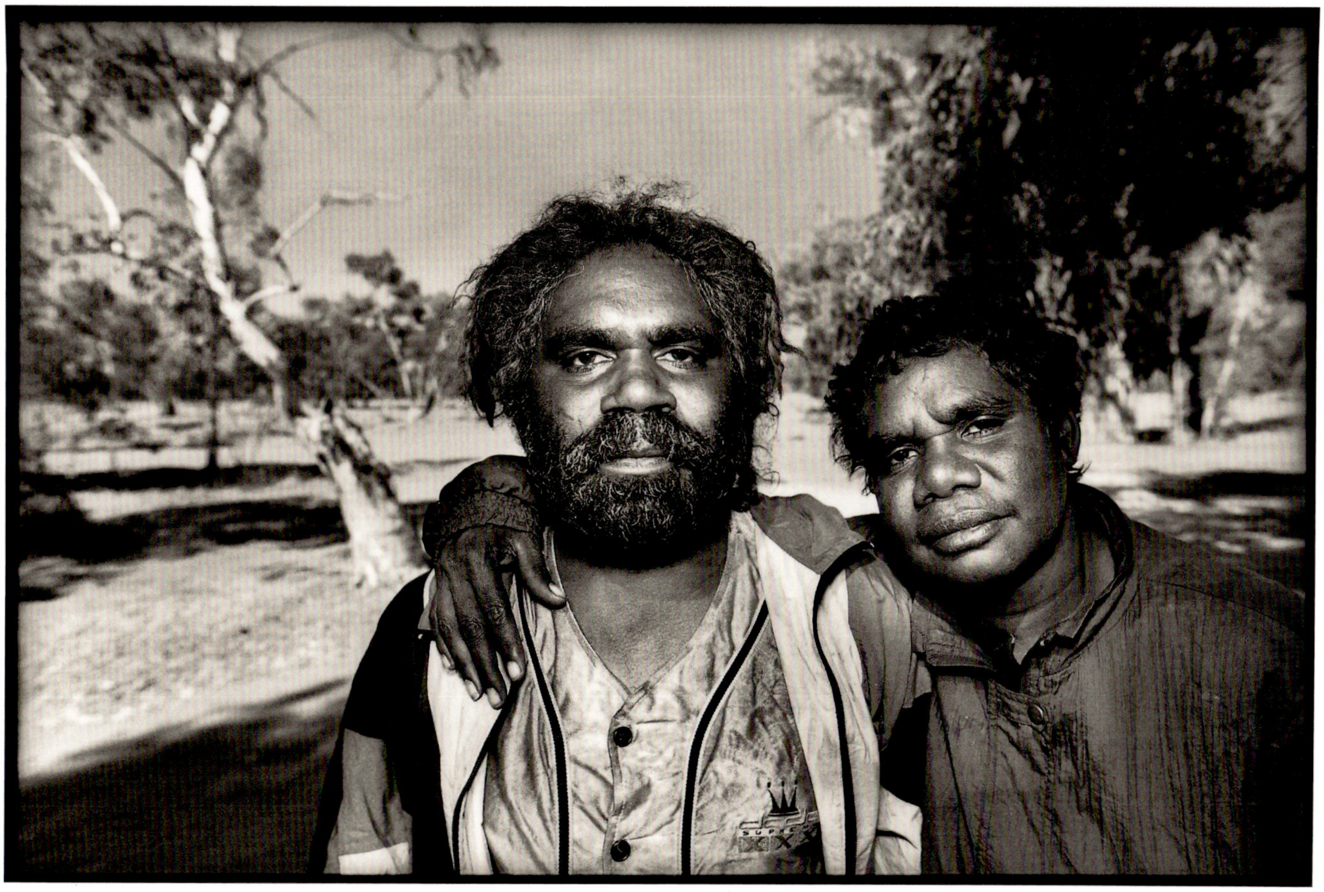

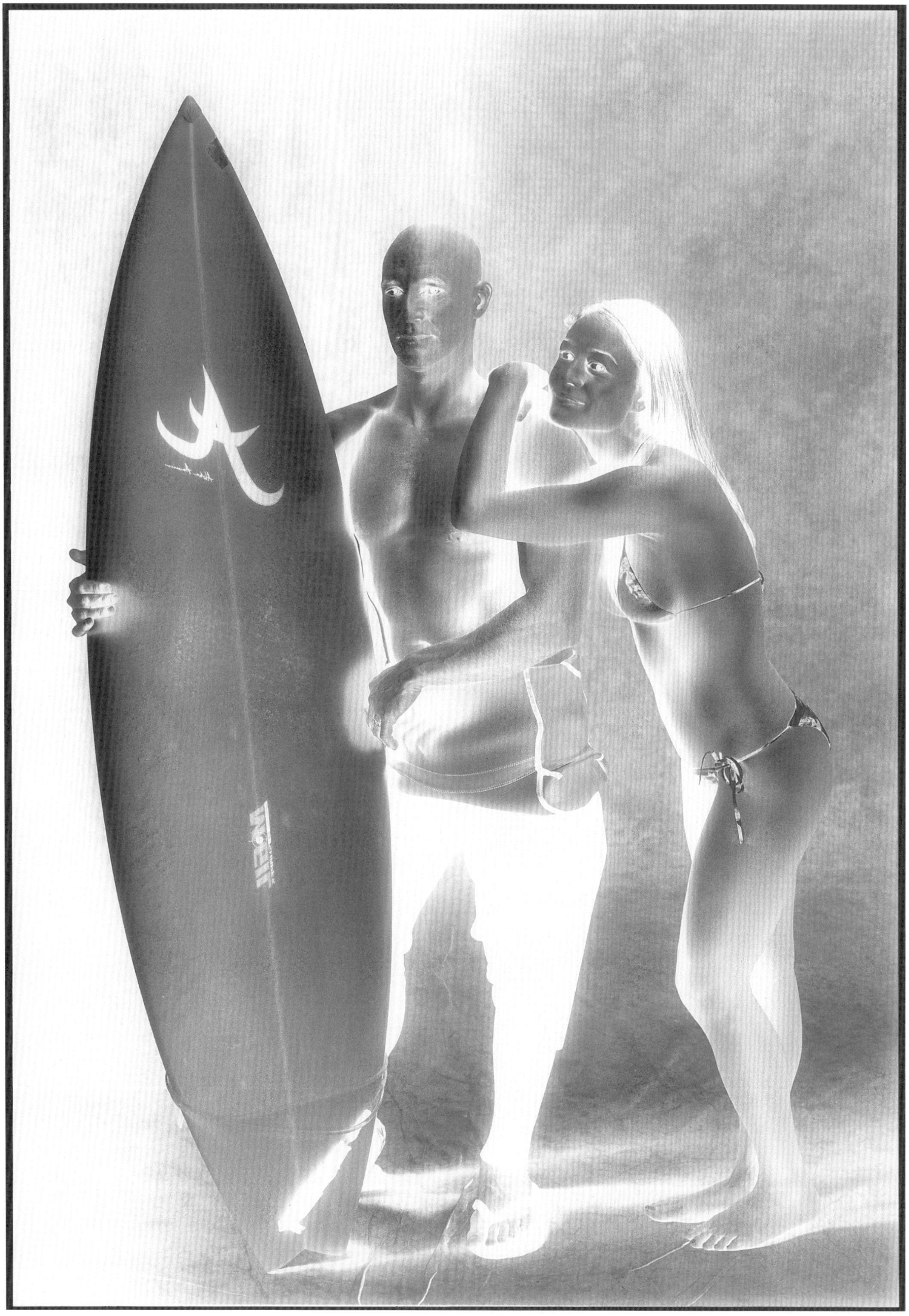

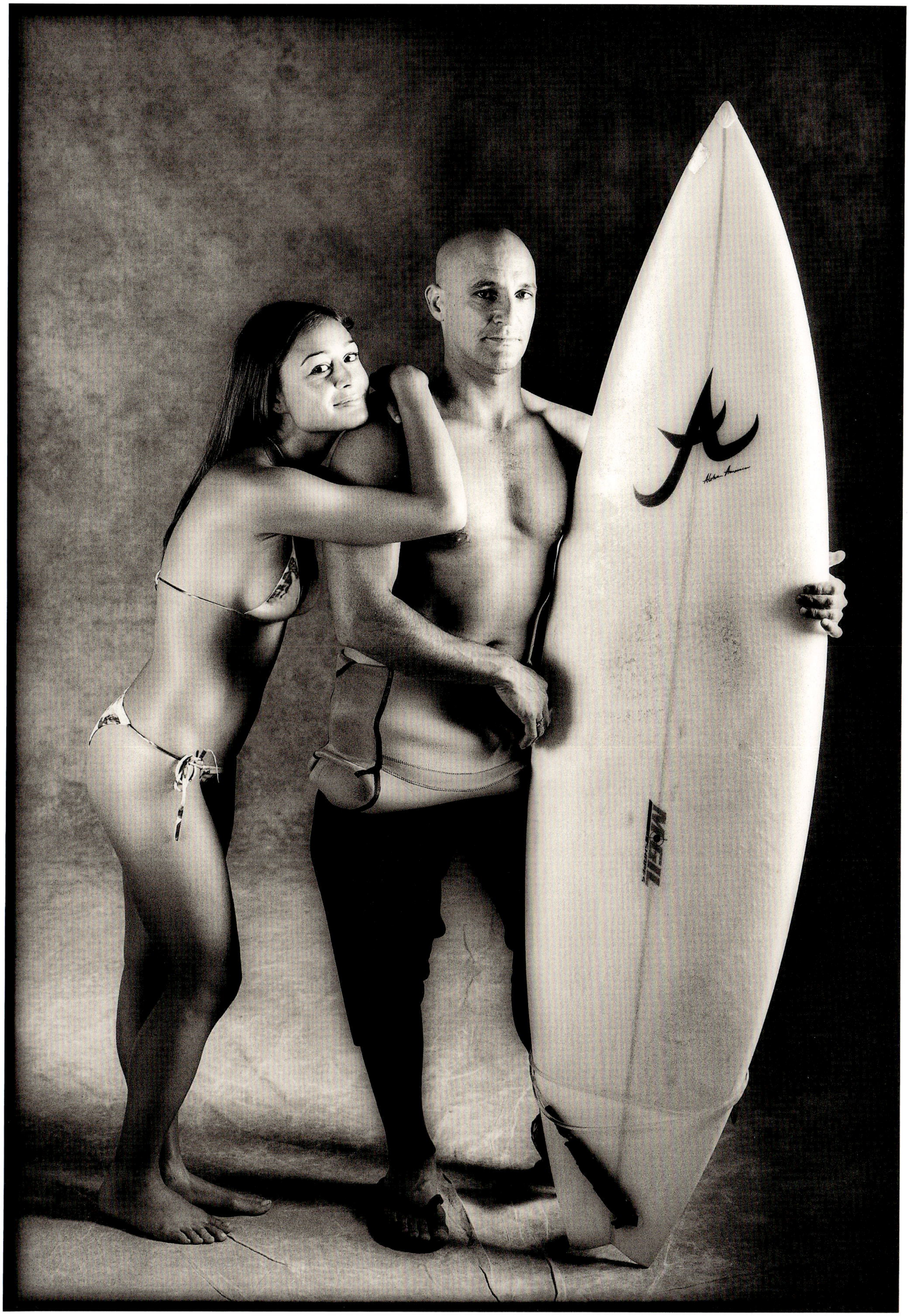

"My mom told me, never marry a Sicilian – my sister told me, never marry a surfer."

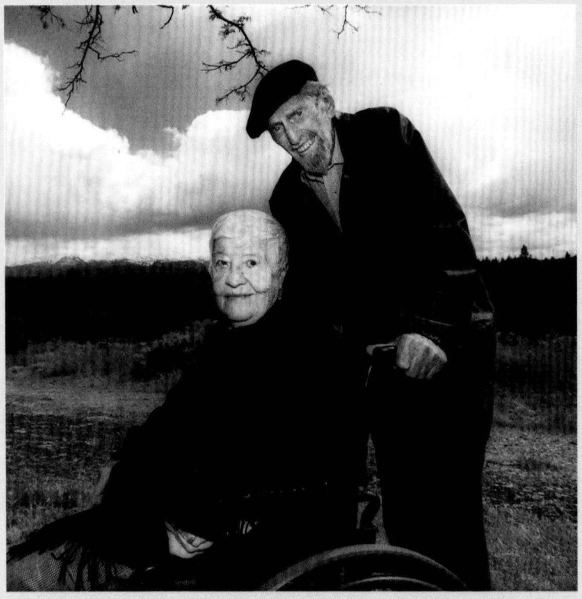

"Our 68th anniversary is coming up, but who's counting."

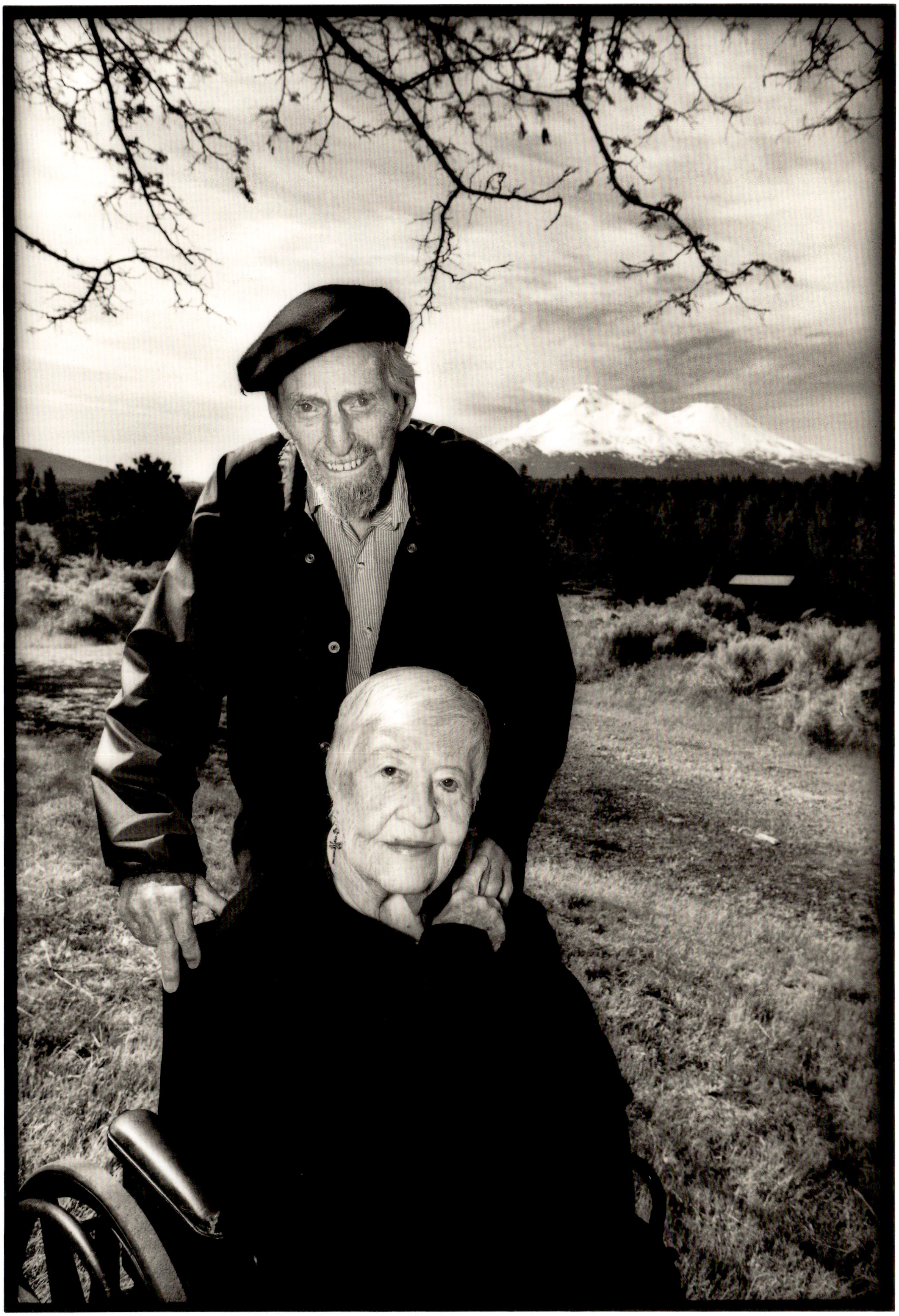

LOCATION

A Sun-dappled Pond

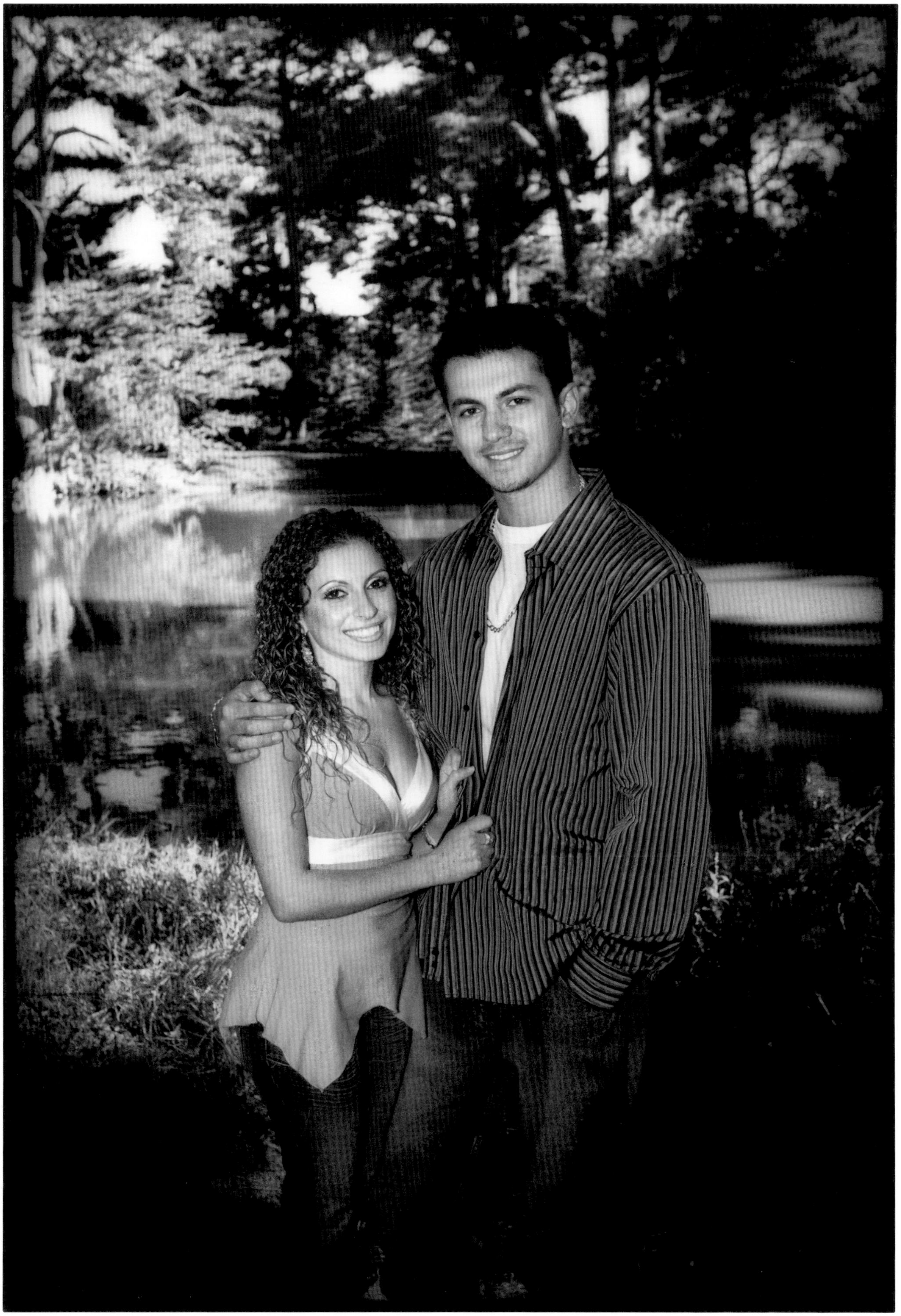

"Two ducks from the same pond, Nona and Arsen found each other."

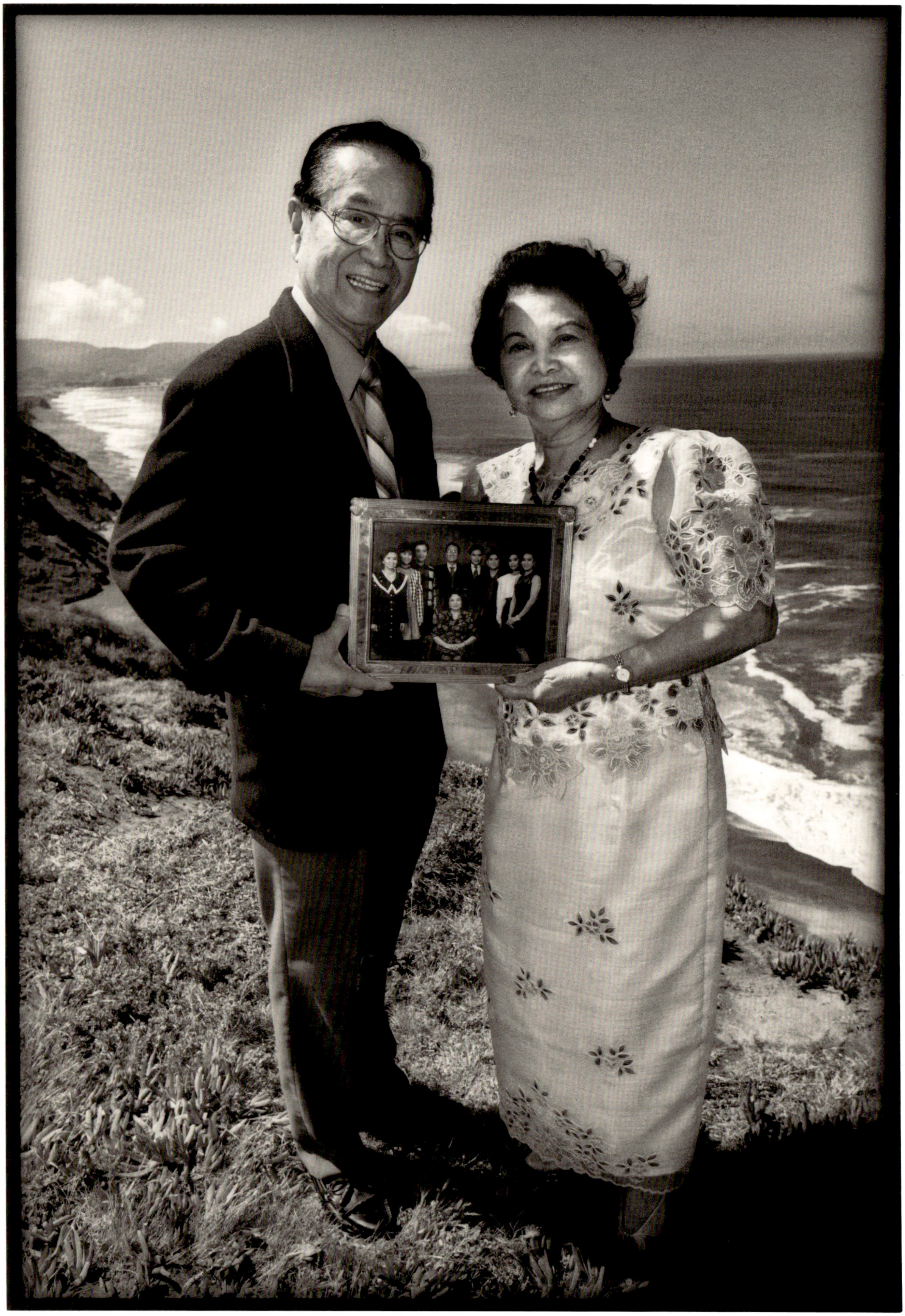

"God's loving breath moves the waters and fans the whole universe."

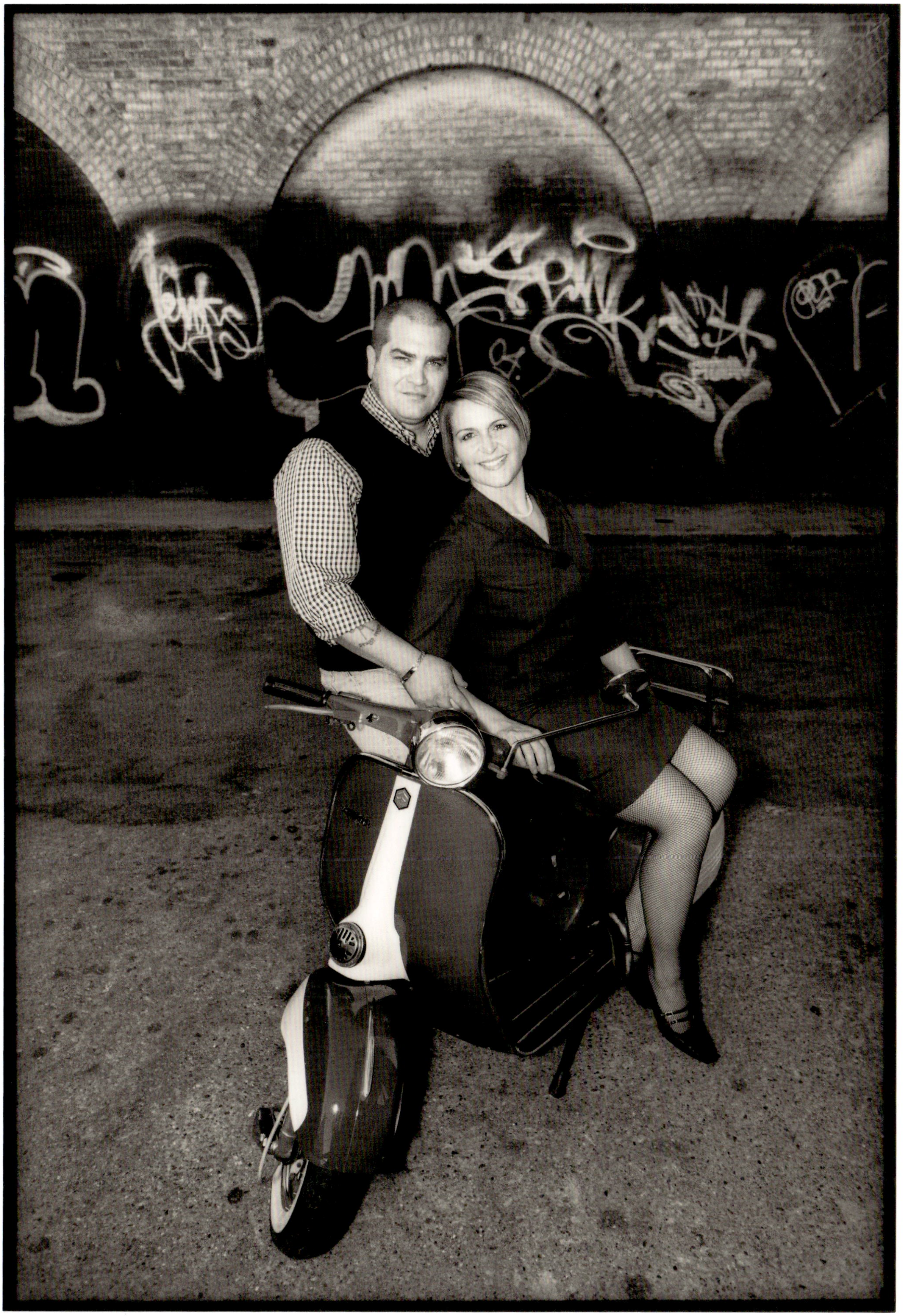

"Mi Corazon." ("My Heart.")

"...we were set up."

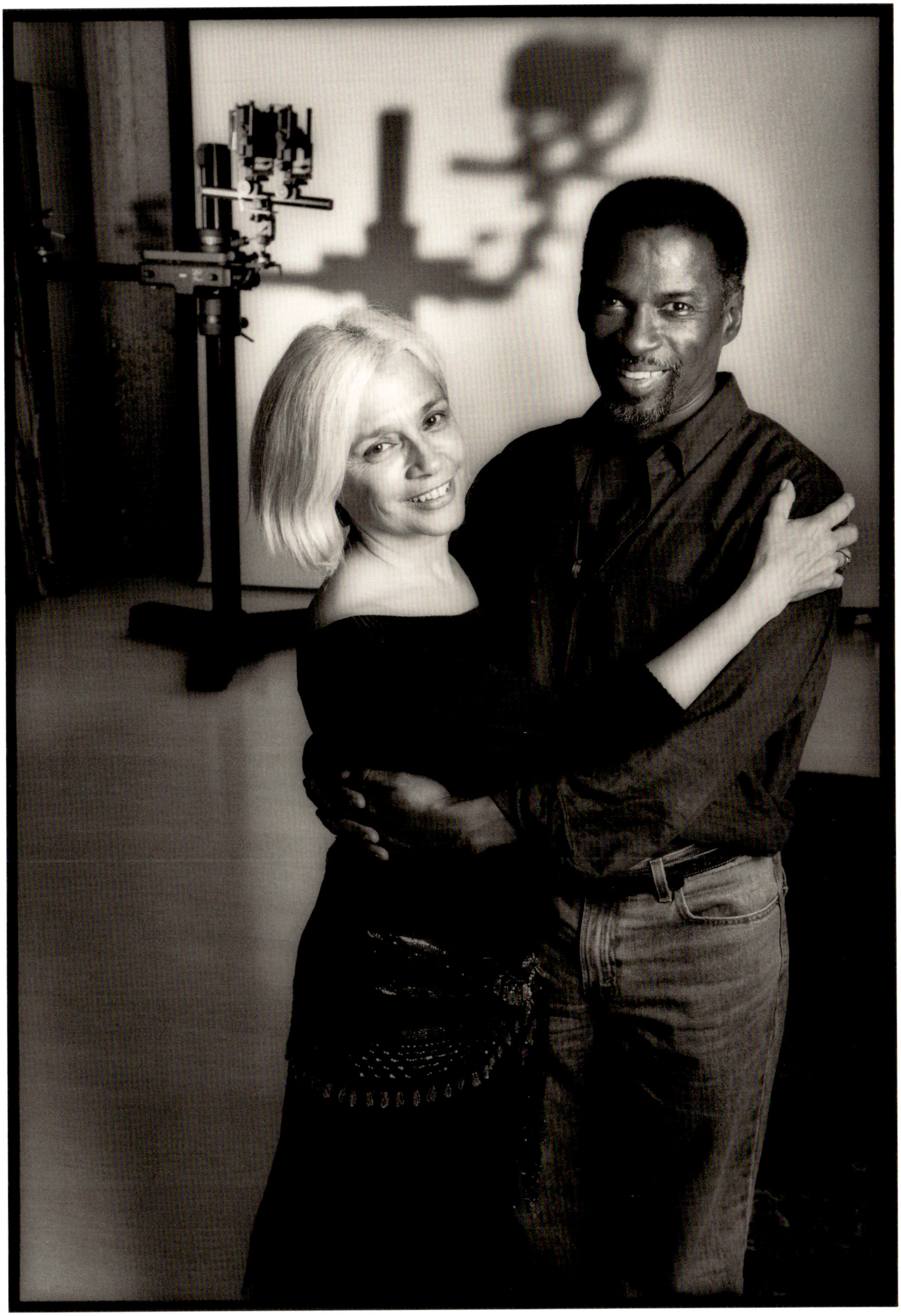

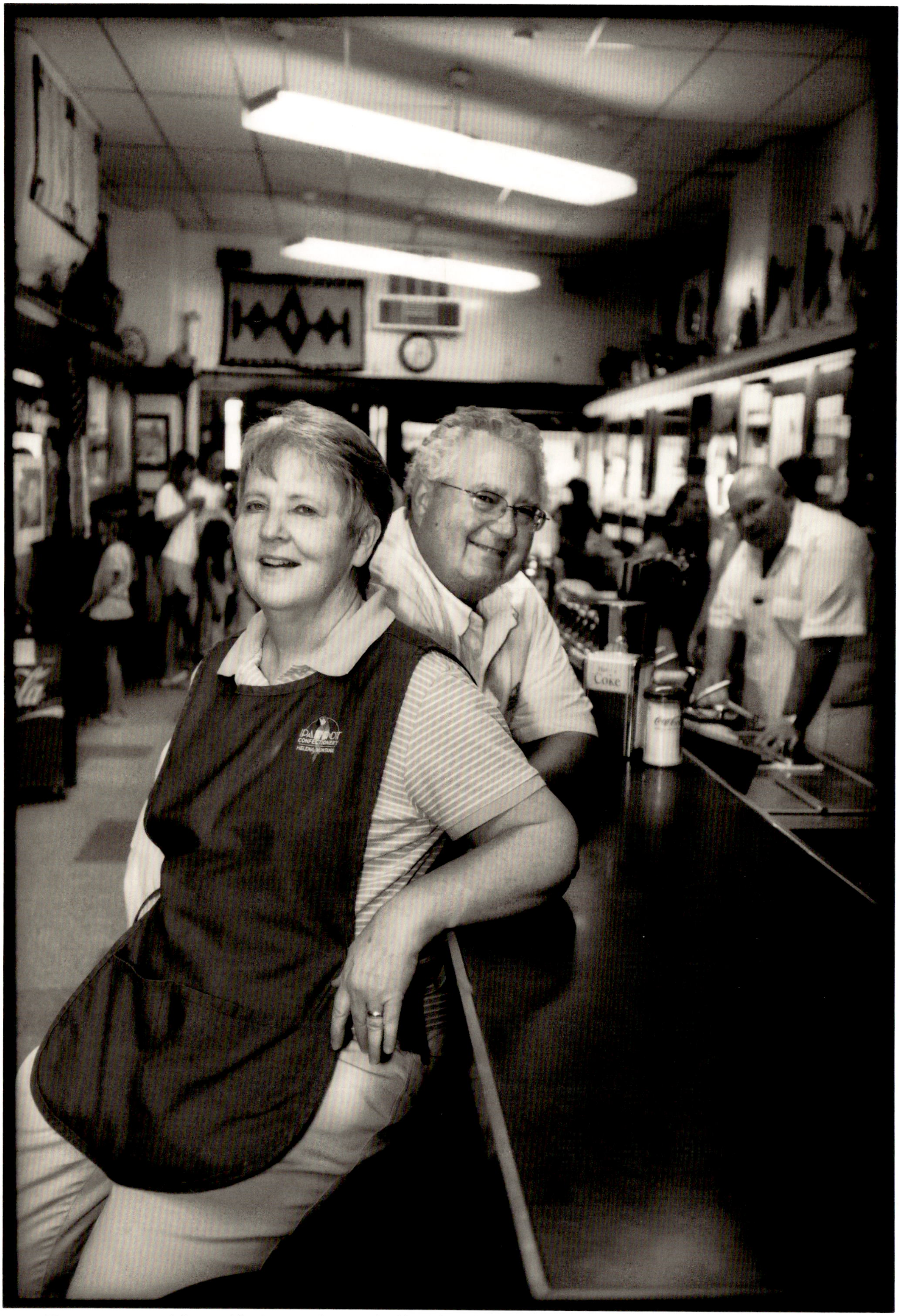

"We met 38 years ago in idyllic times, fell in love, married, grew comfortable with each other and worked together in our family-owned business for the past 30+ years."

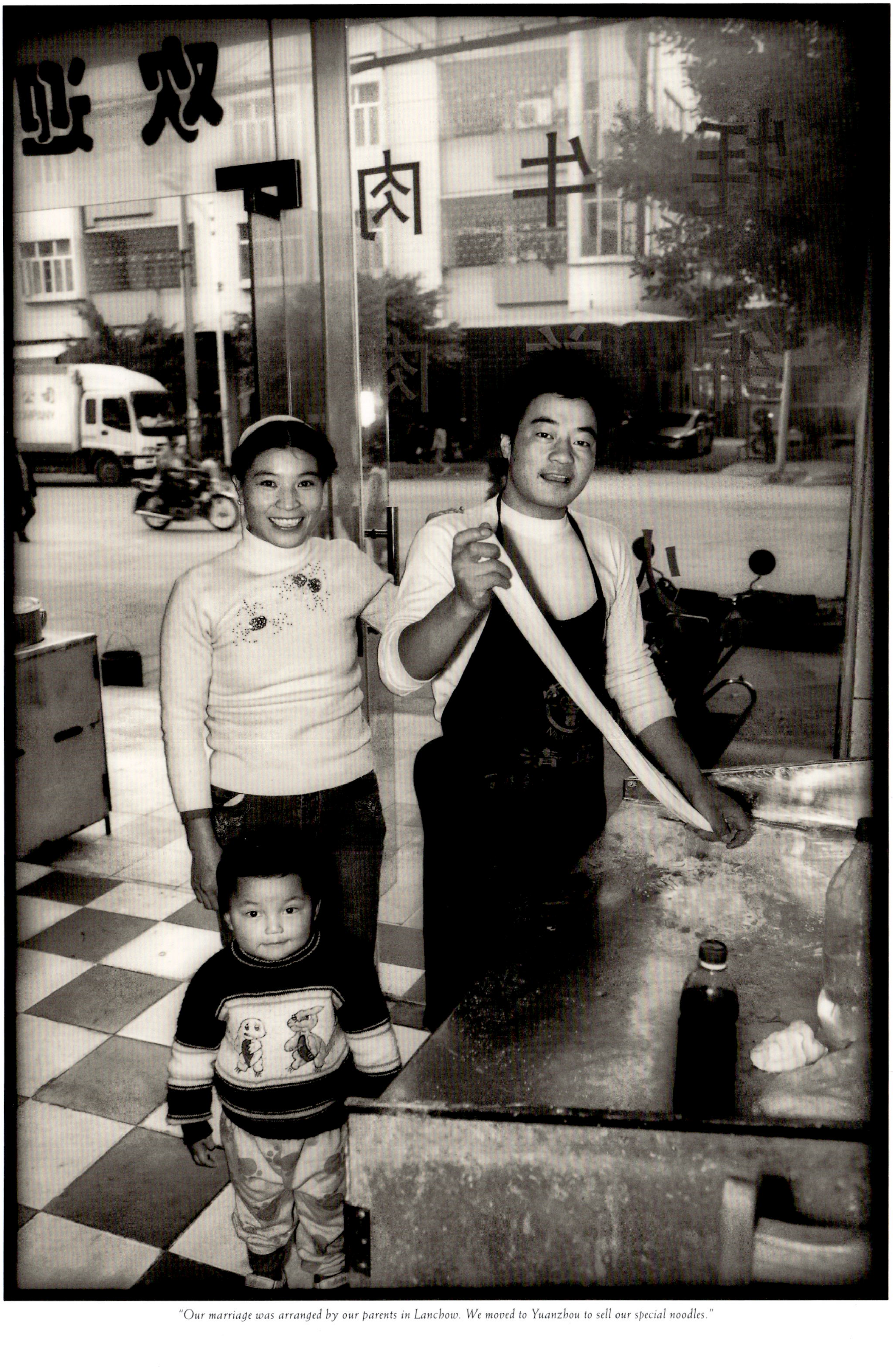

"Our marriage was arranged by our parents in Lanchow. We moved to Yuanzhou to sell our special noodles."

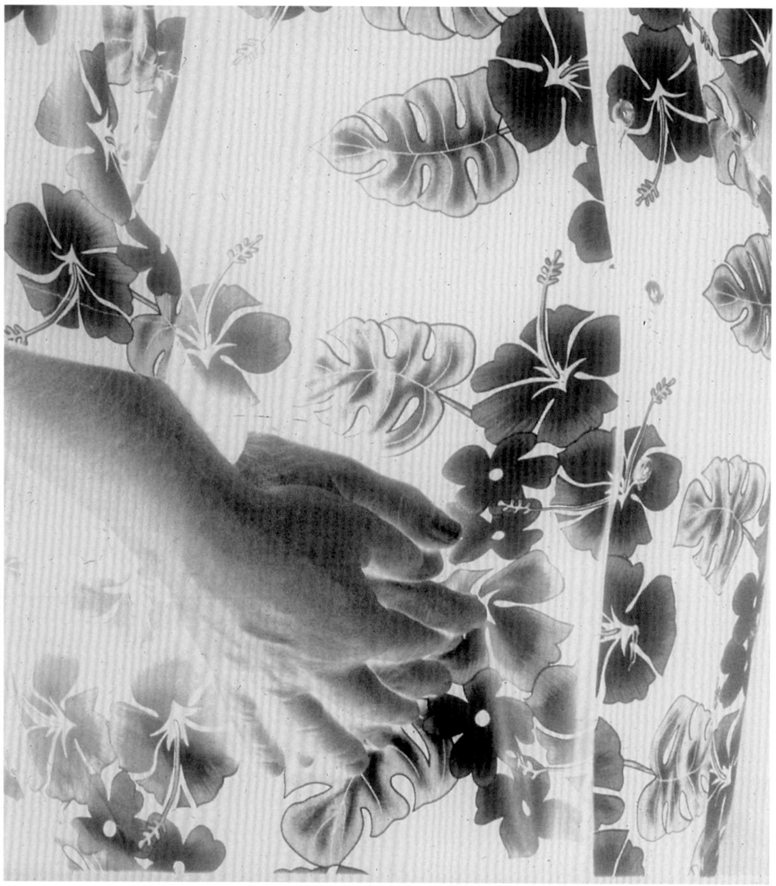

"An unlikely pairing that's lasted 30 years."

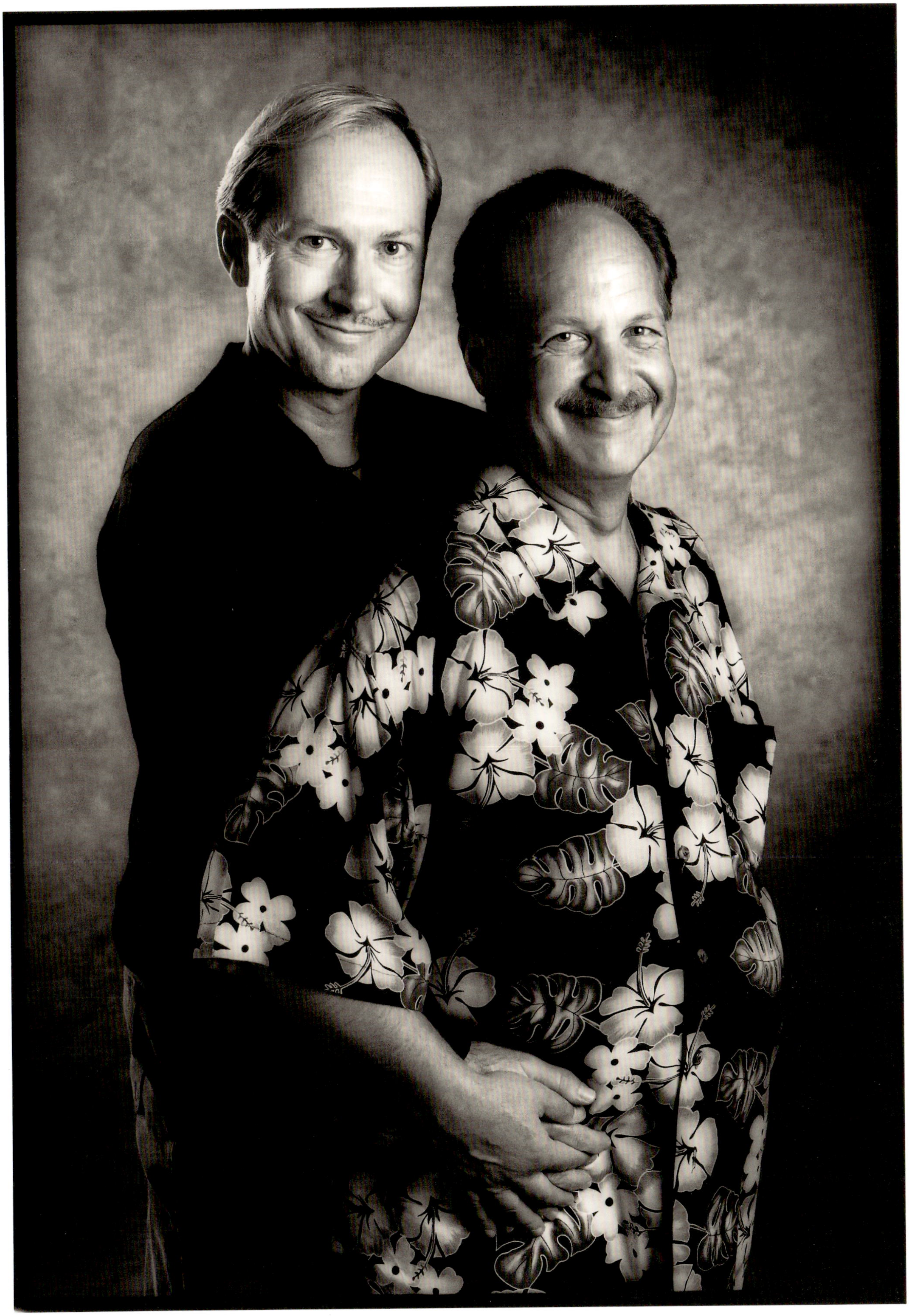

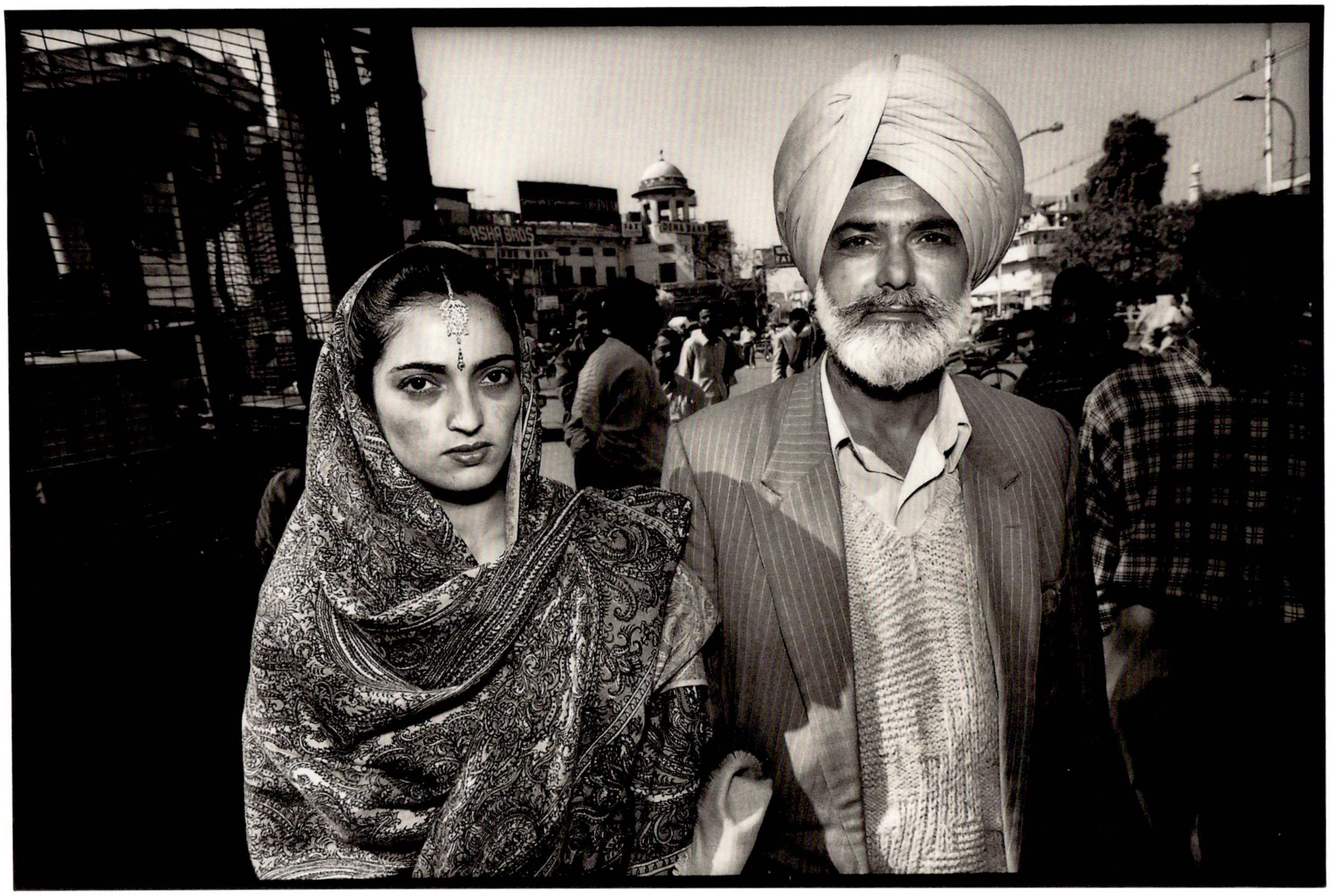
ASHA BROS

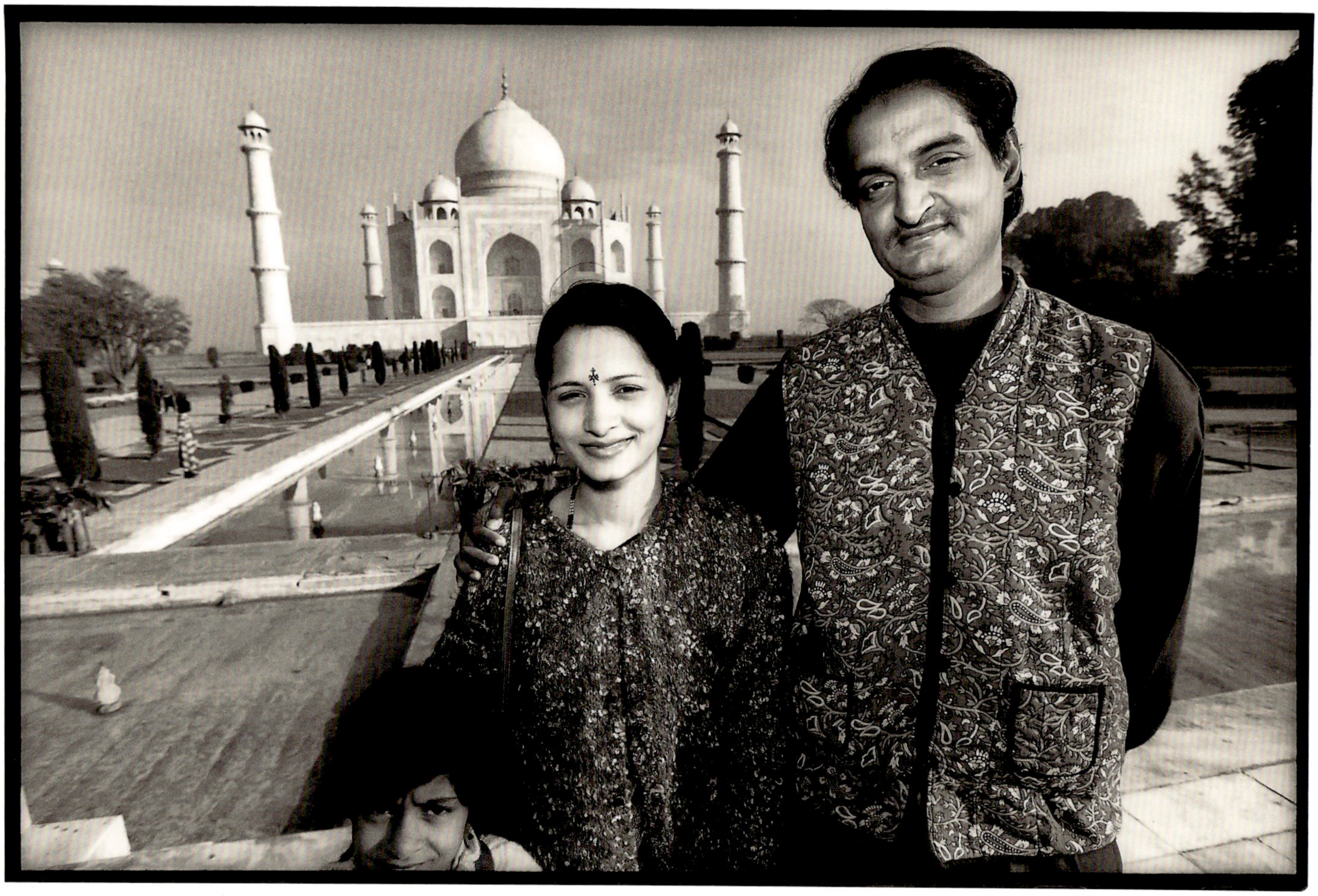

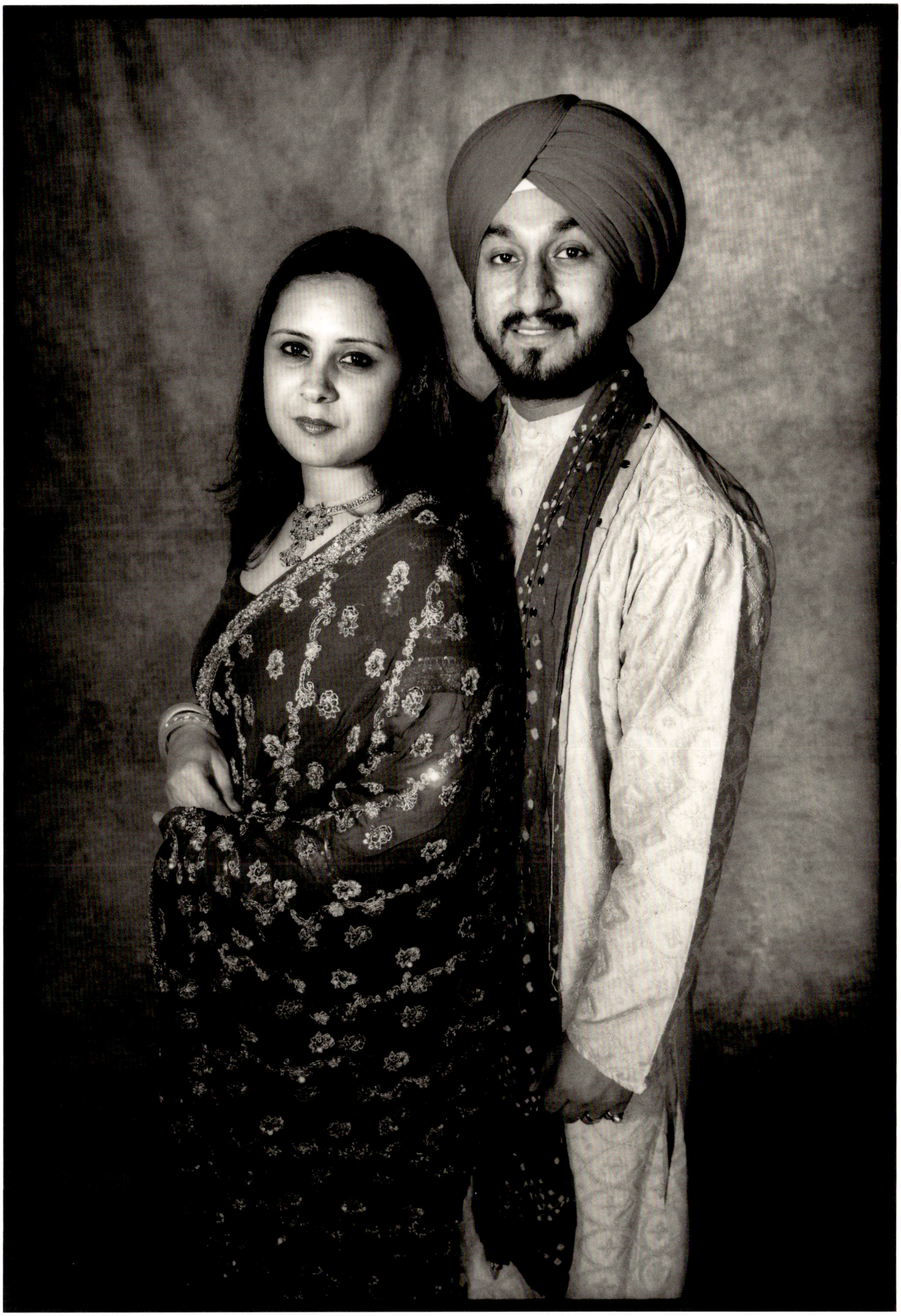

"God destined our lives together in Heaven, but the Internet made it possible on Earth."

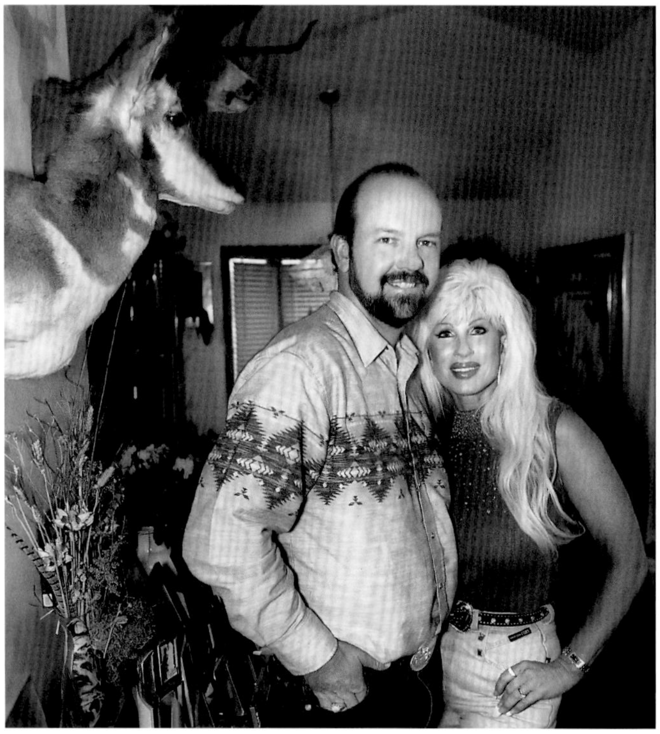

"I bagged the blond in Las Vegas."

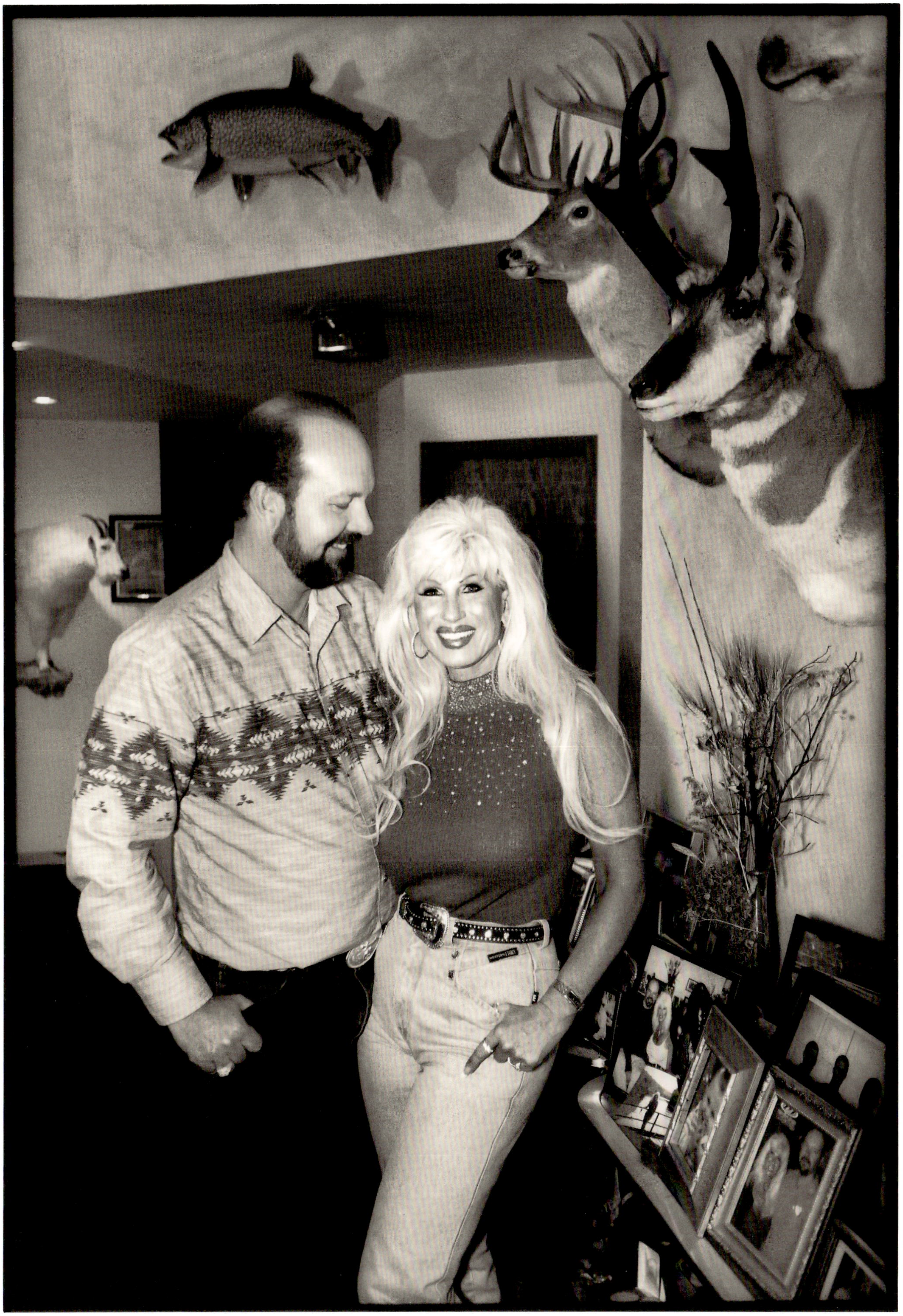

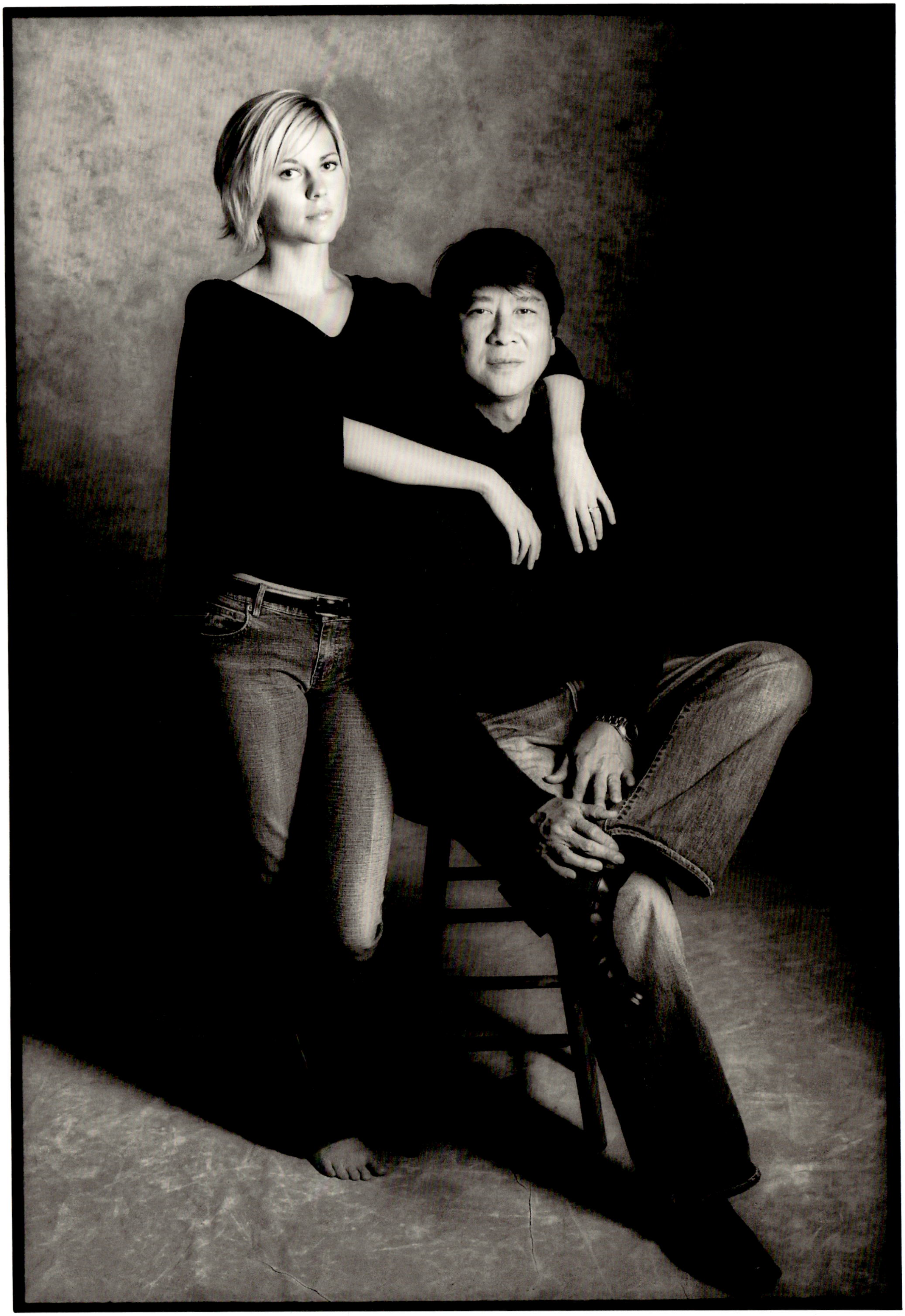

"It is only with the heart that one can see rightly; what is essential is invisible to the eye."

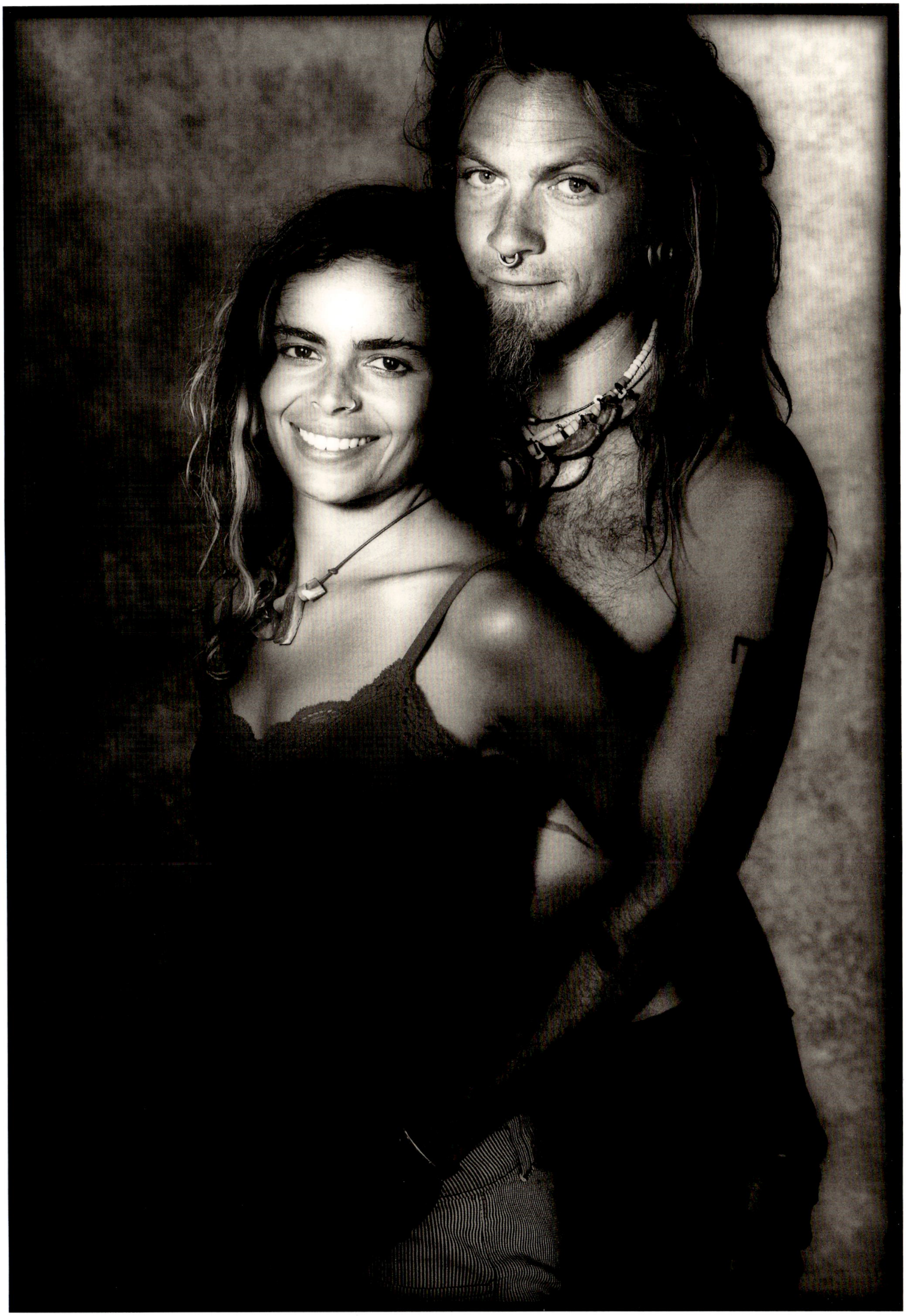

"Welcome home love, let's take it with us wherever we go."

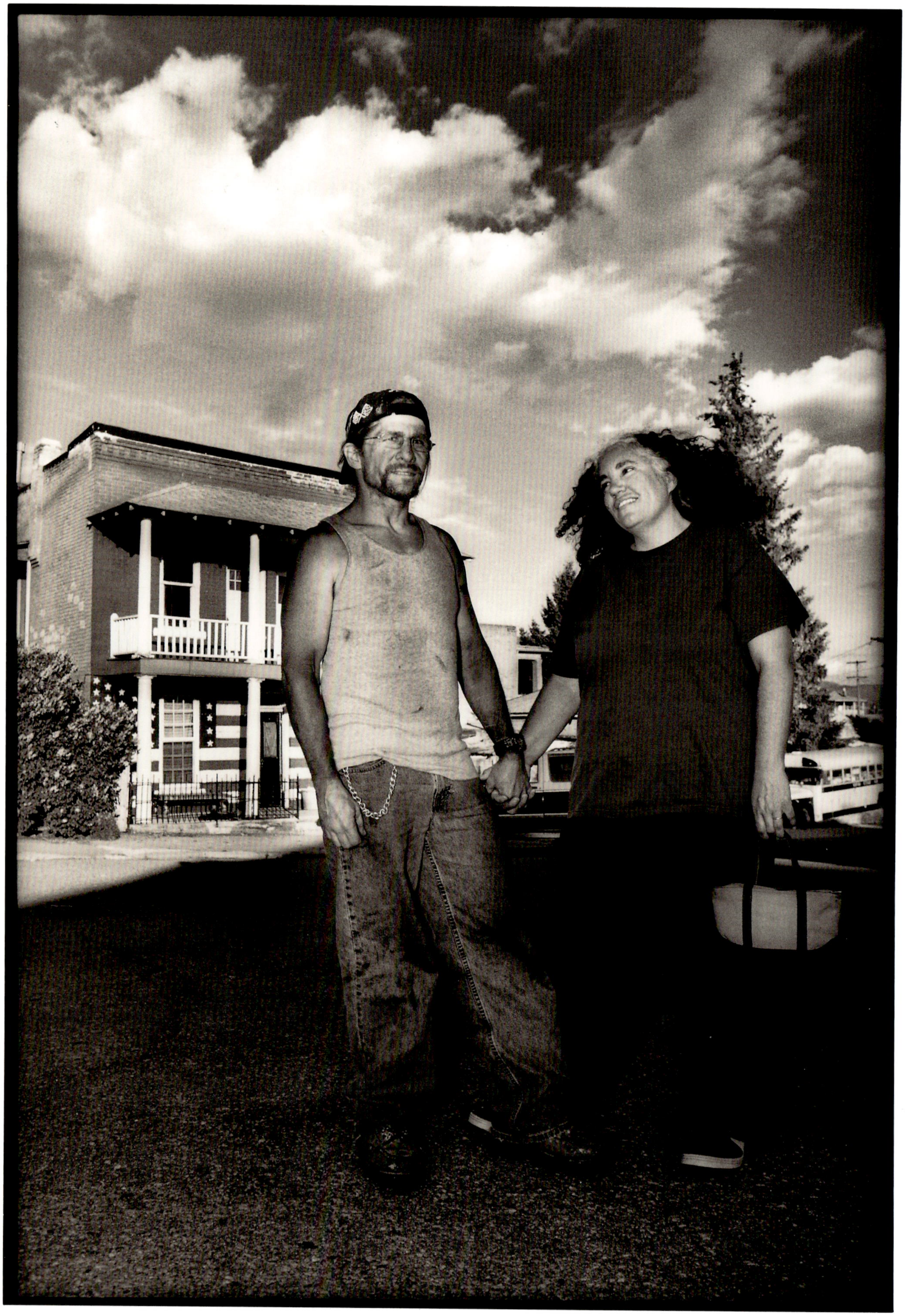

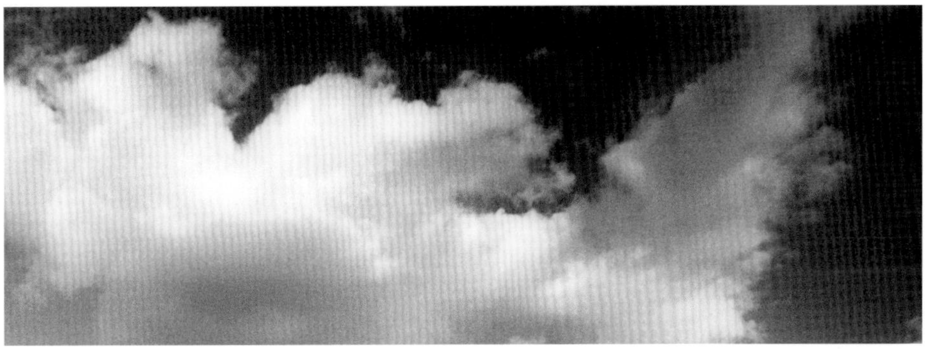

"I was the new cashier and he was the new volunteer.
Soon our coworkers were teasing us badly because we'd fallen in love, hard!"

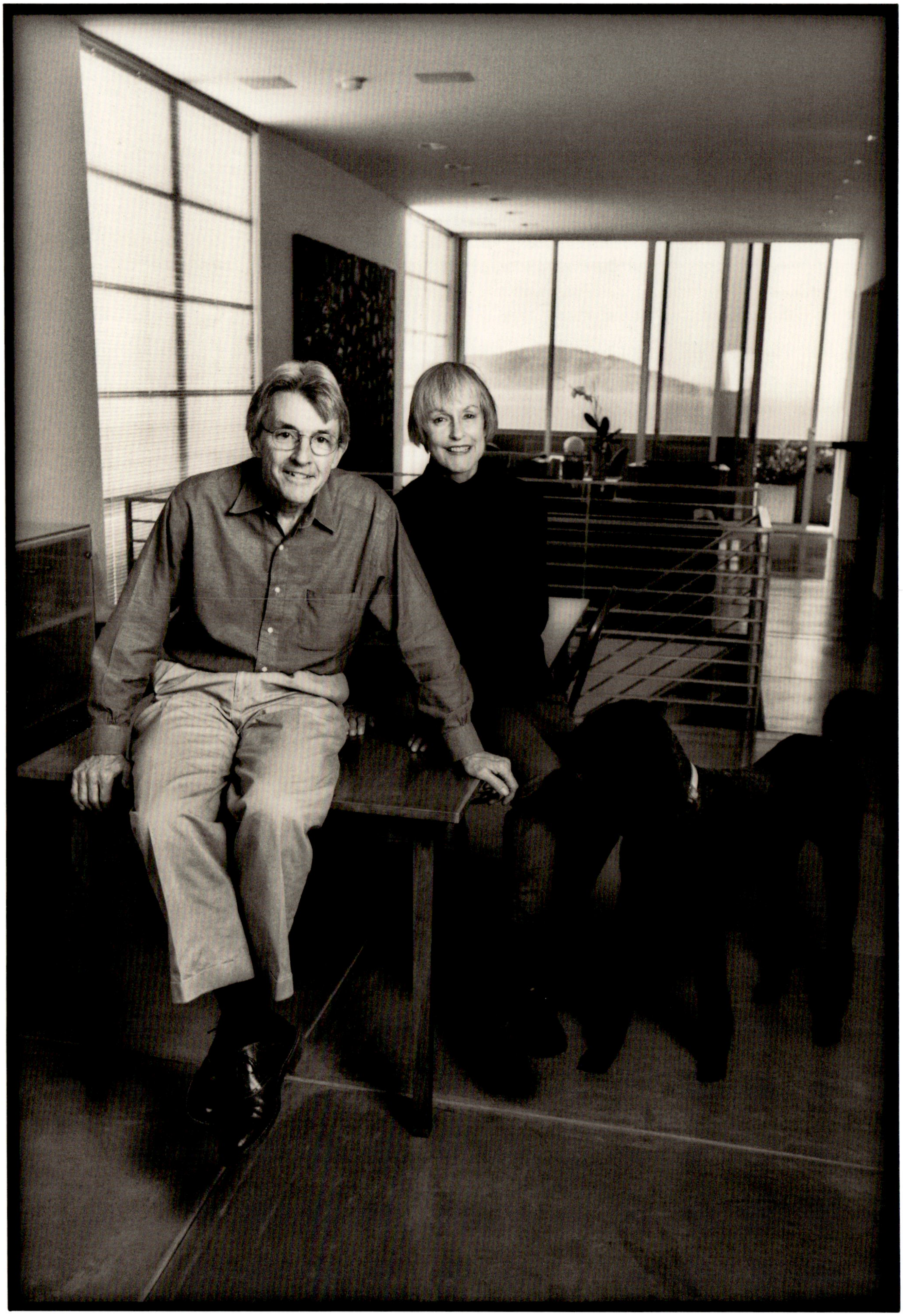

"Together 41 years. Life is not dull."

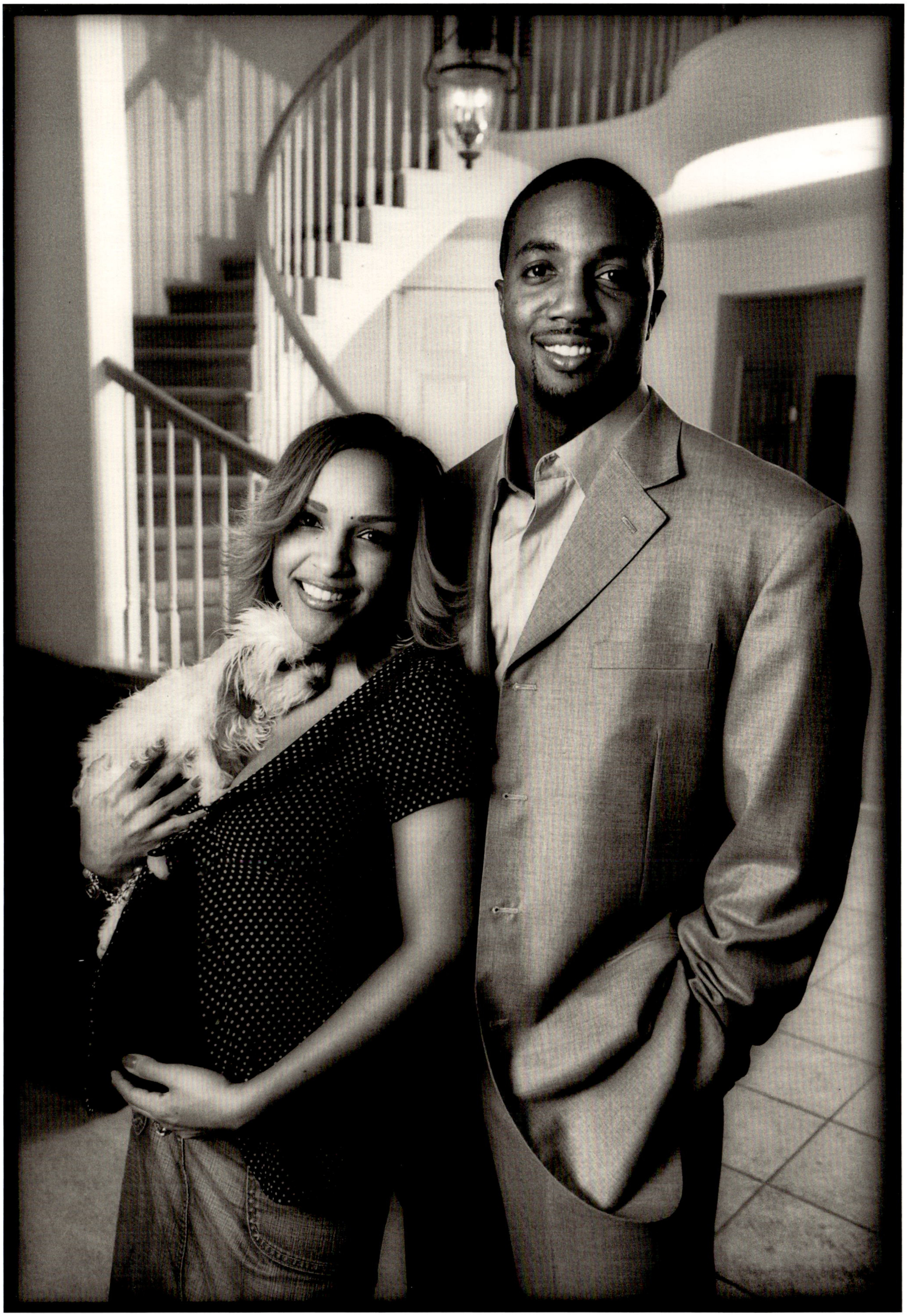

"Young love at its best!"

4th of July

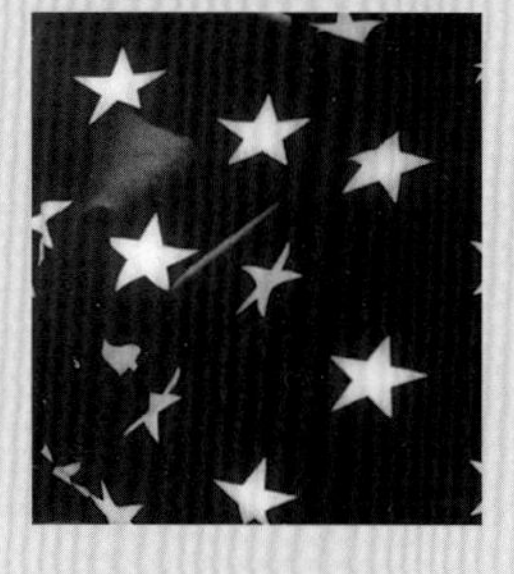

"My husband was born in Butte, Montana – and that's where his roots are.
It wasn't till I went to Butte that I really understood who he really is."

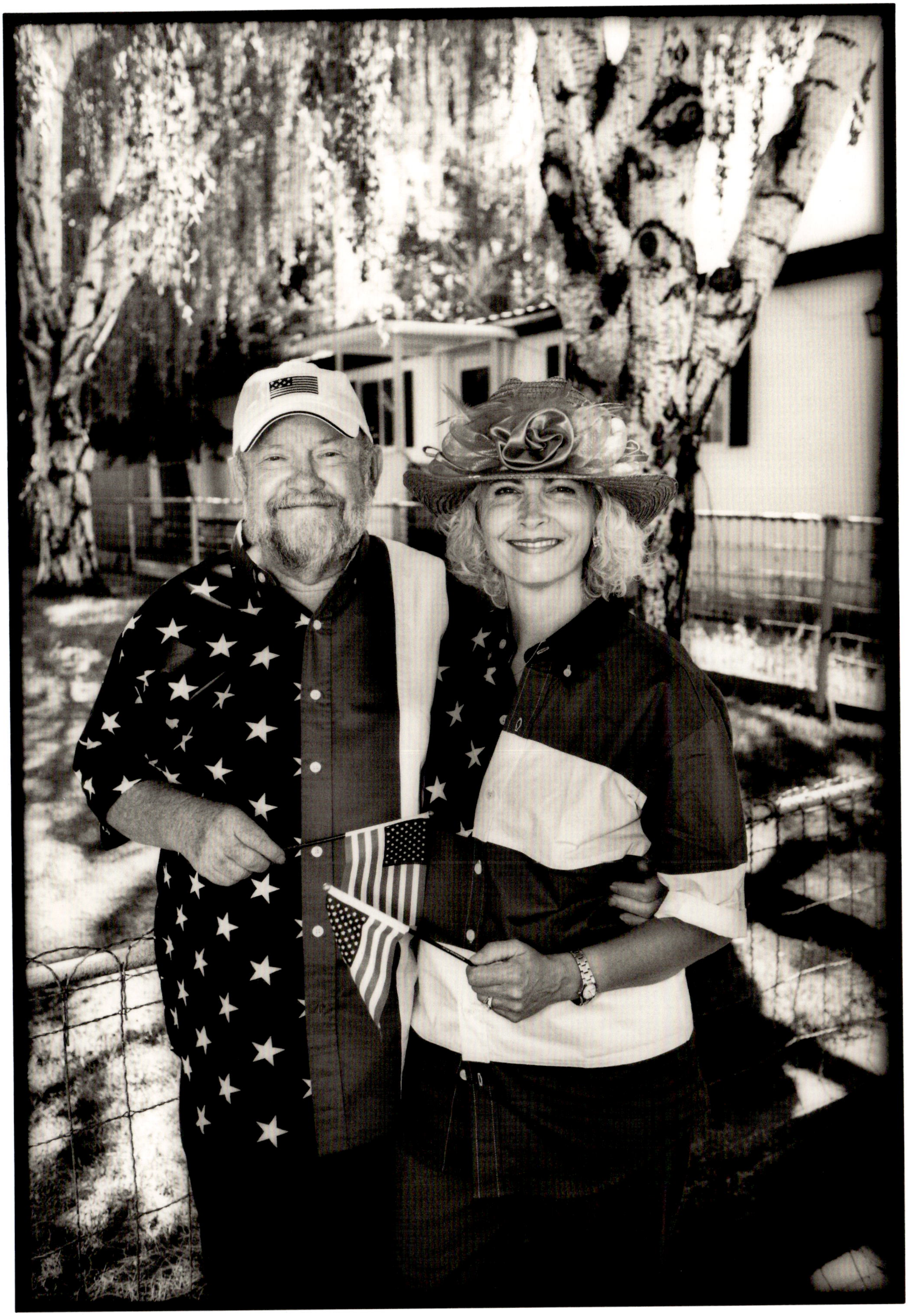

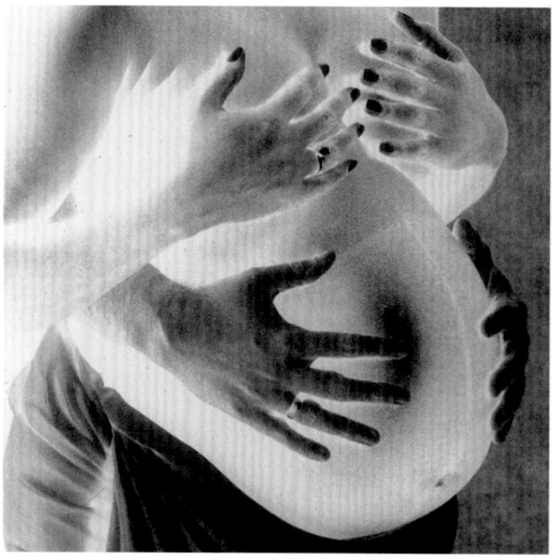

"Mene wo yebewu akonno ba."

A Ghanaian phrase, meaning:

"You and I are going to have beautiful children together."

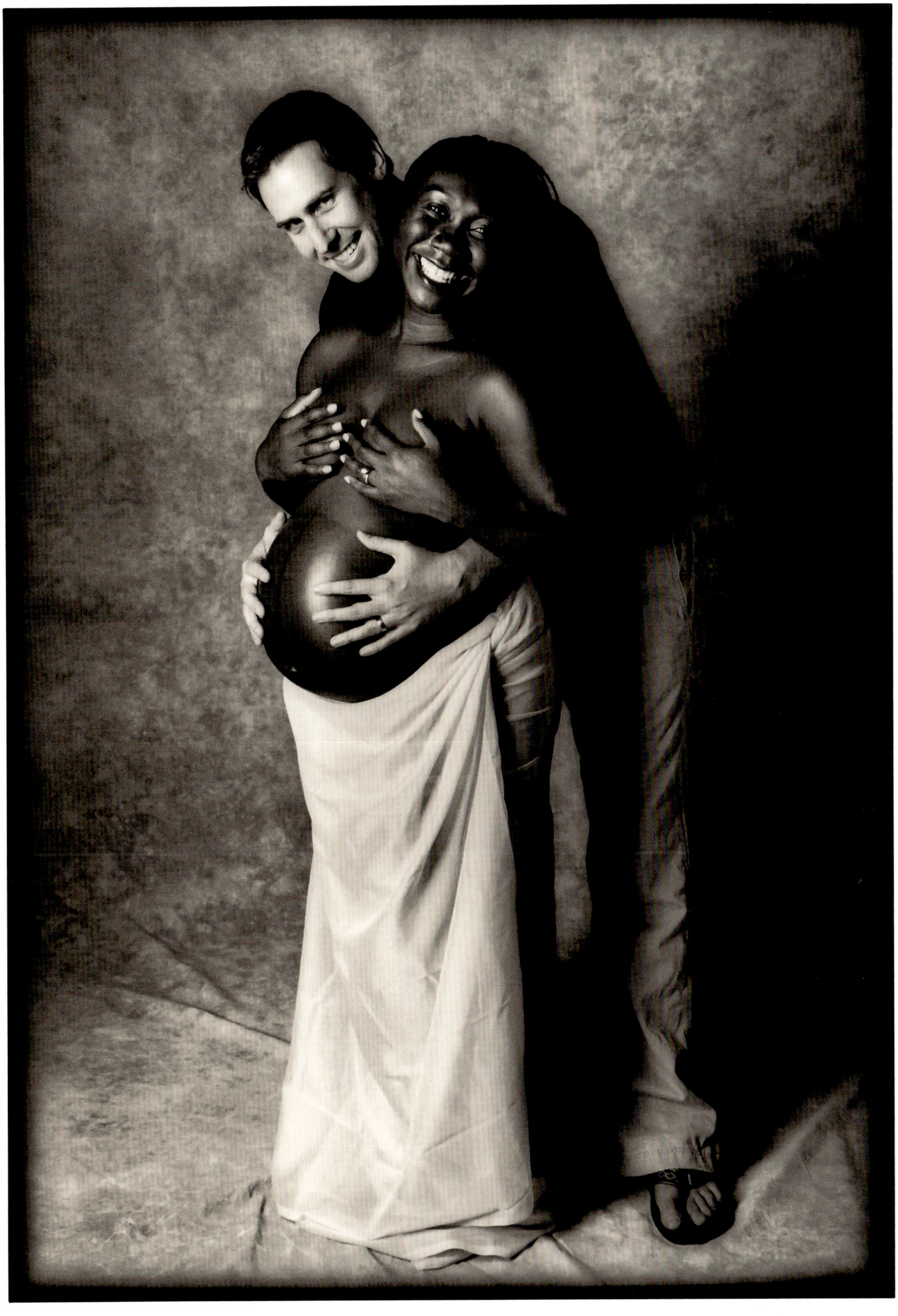

*"Years after AIDS took him, he remains the love of my life.
It's been hell letting go—my heart remains closed. Pain and suffering aside,
I'd do it all over again… his fried chicken was to die for!"*

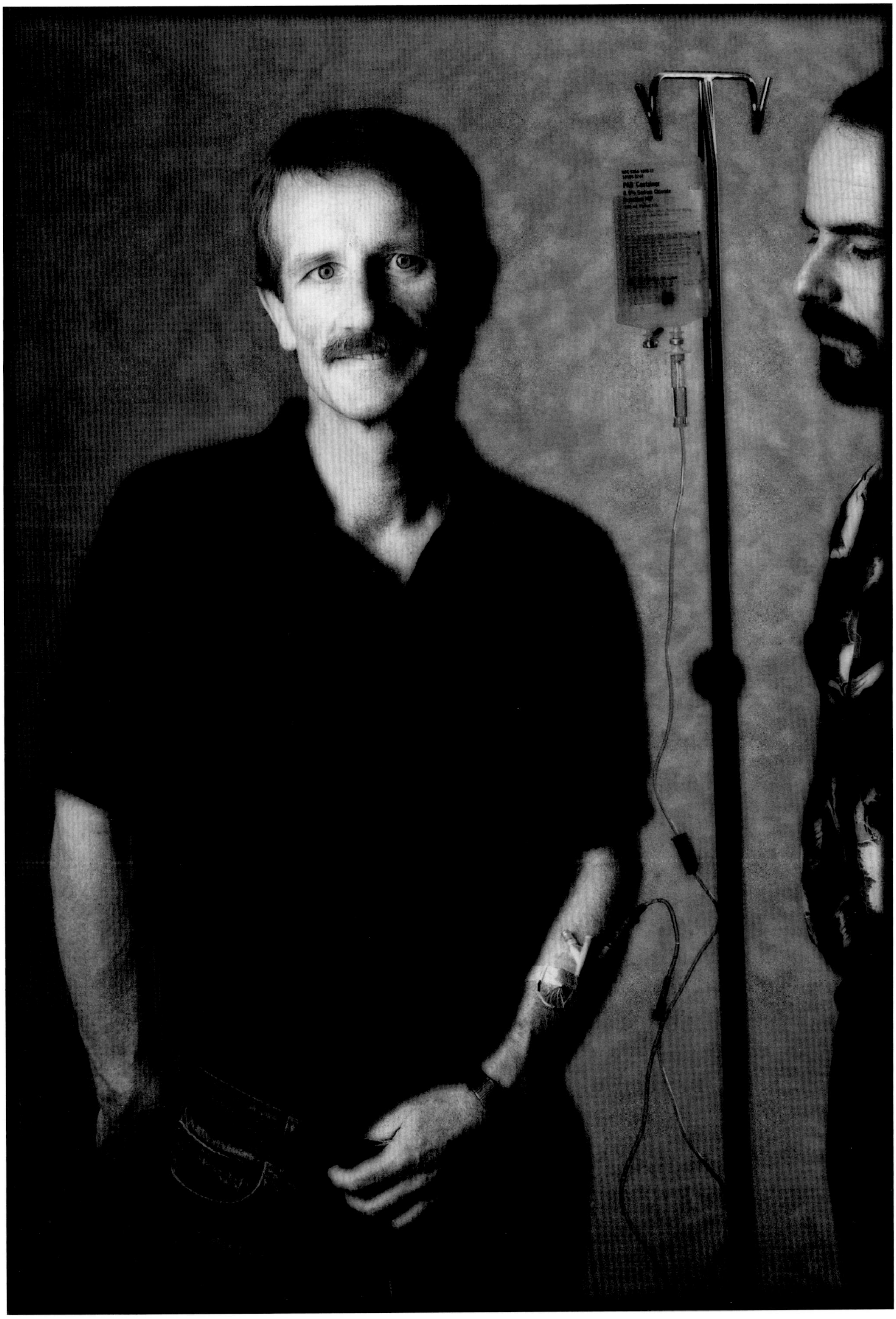

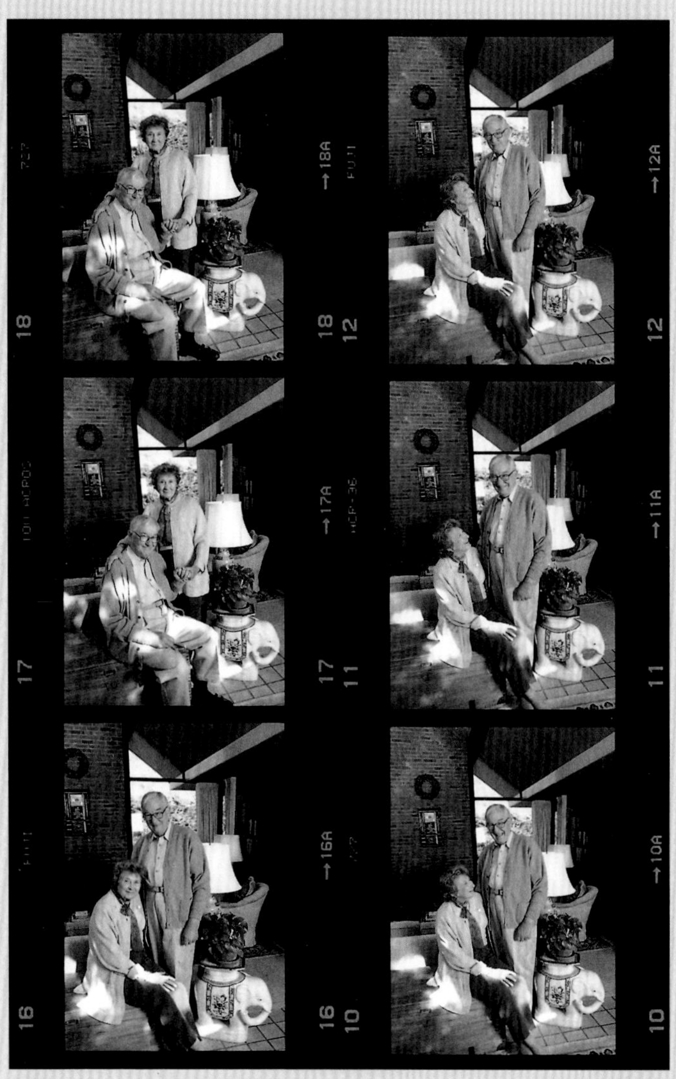

"Spaces… for family, for friends, for common interests and for individual pursuits."

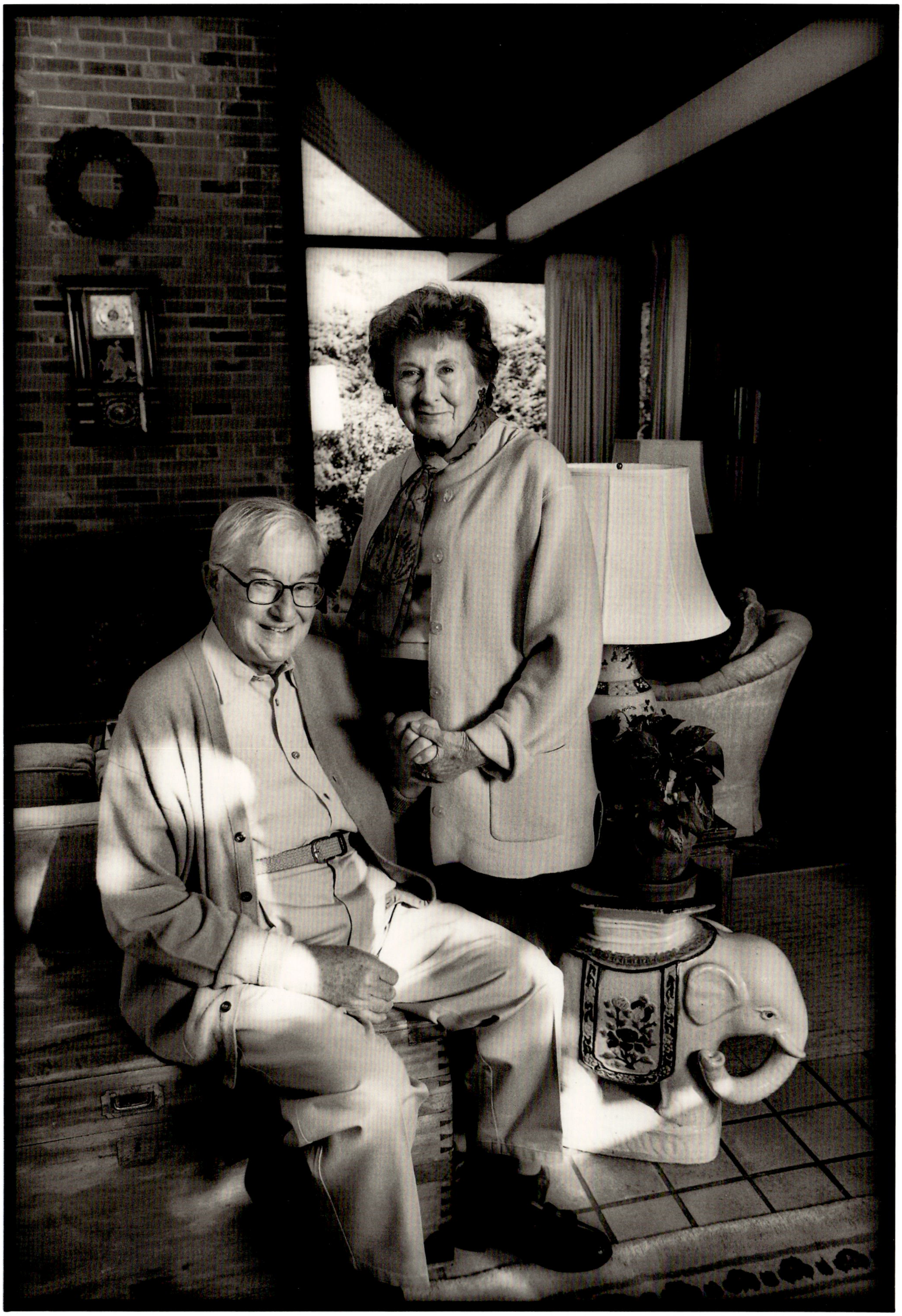

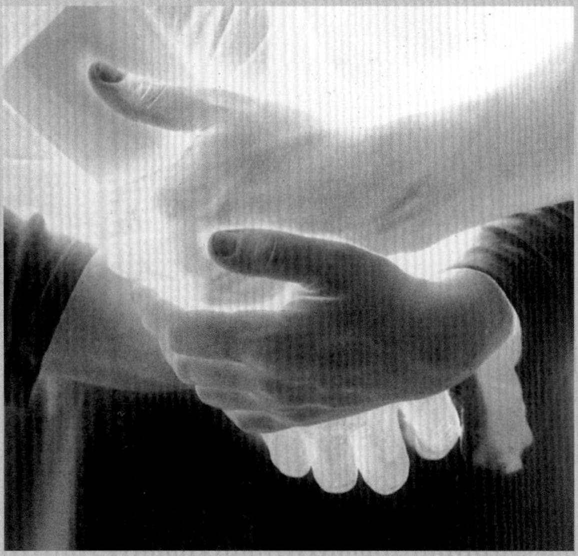

"Truly created beings are meanings set up in images."

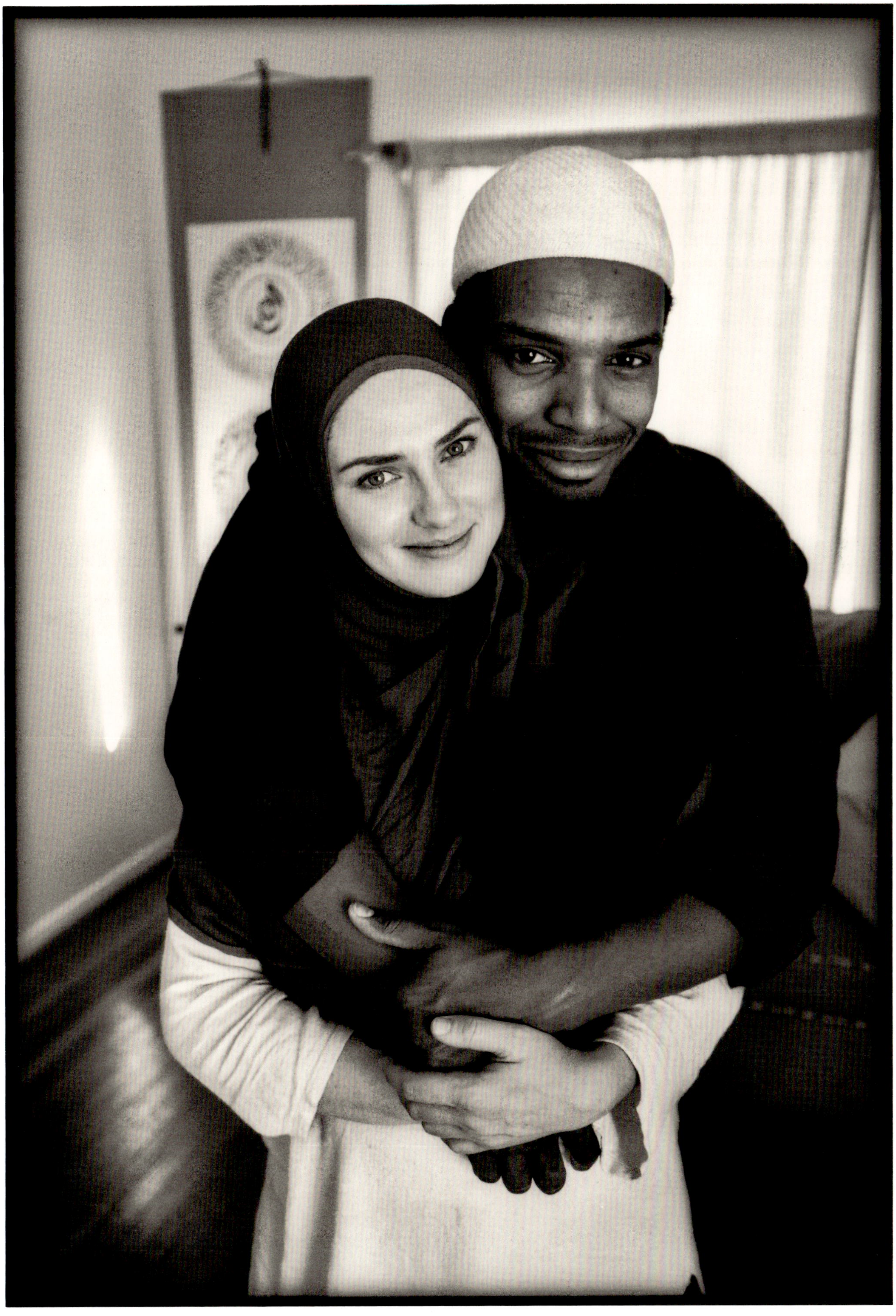

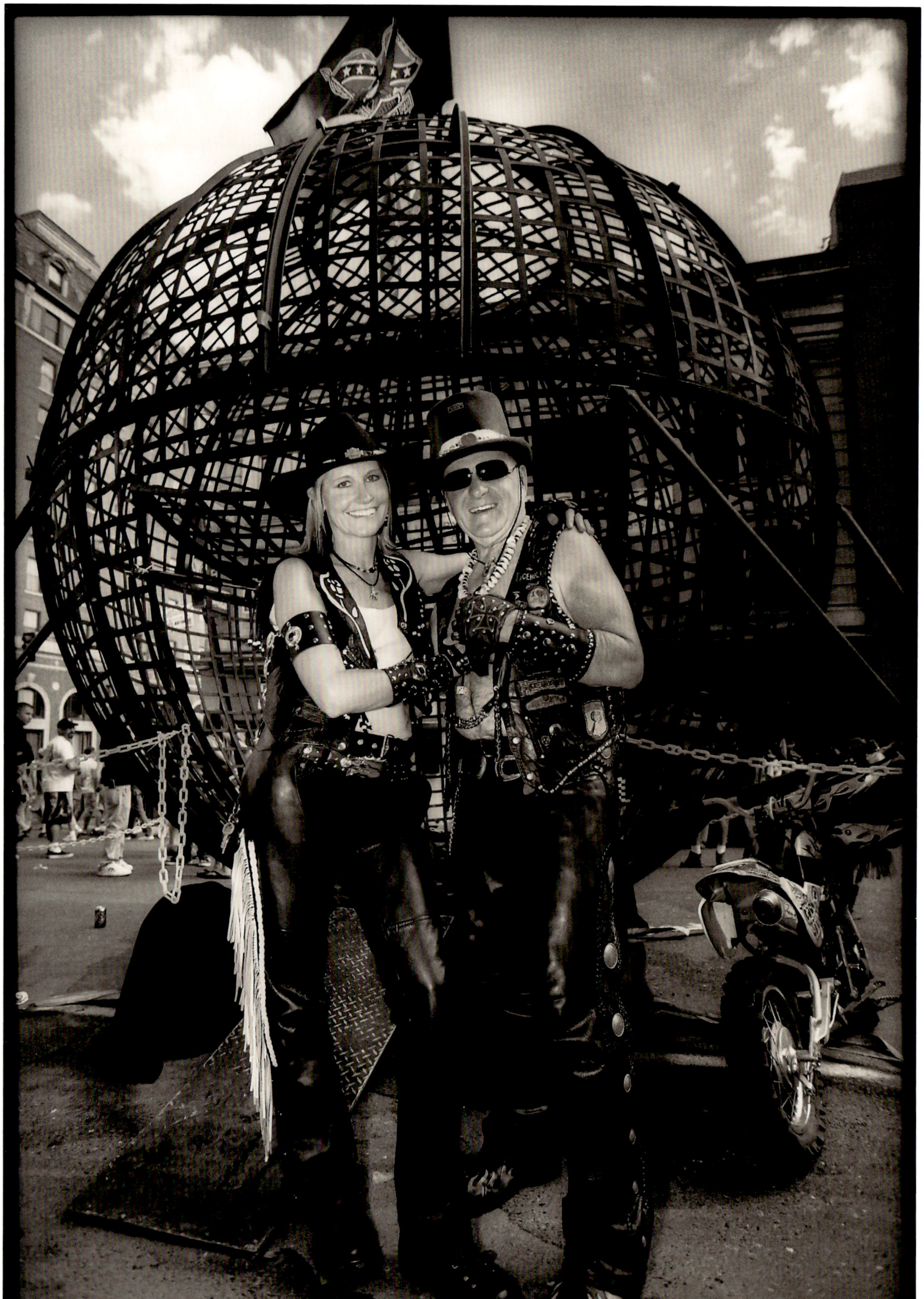

"With 120 years between us, life and love are good!"

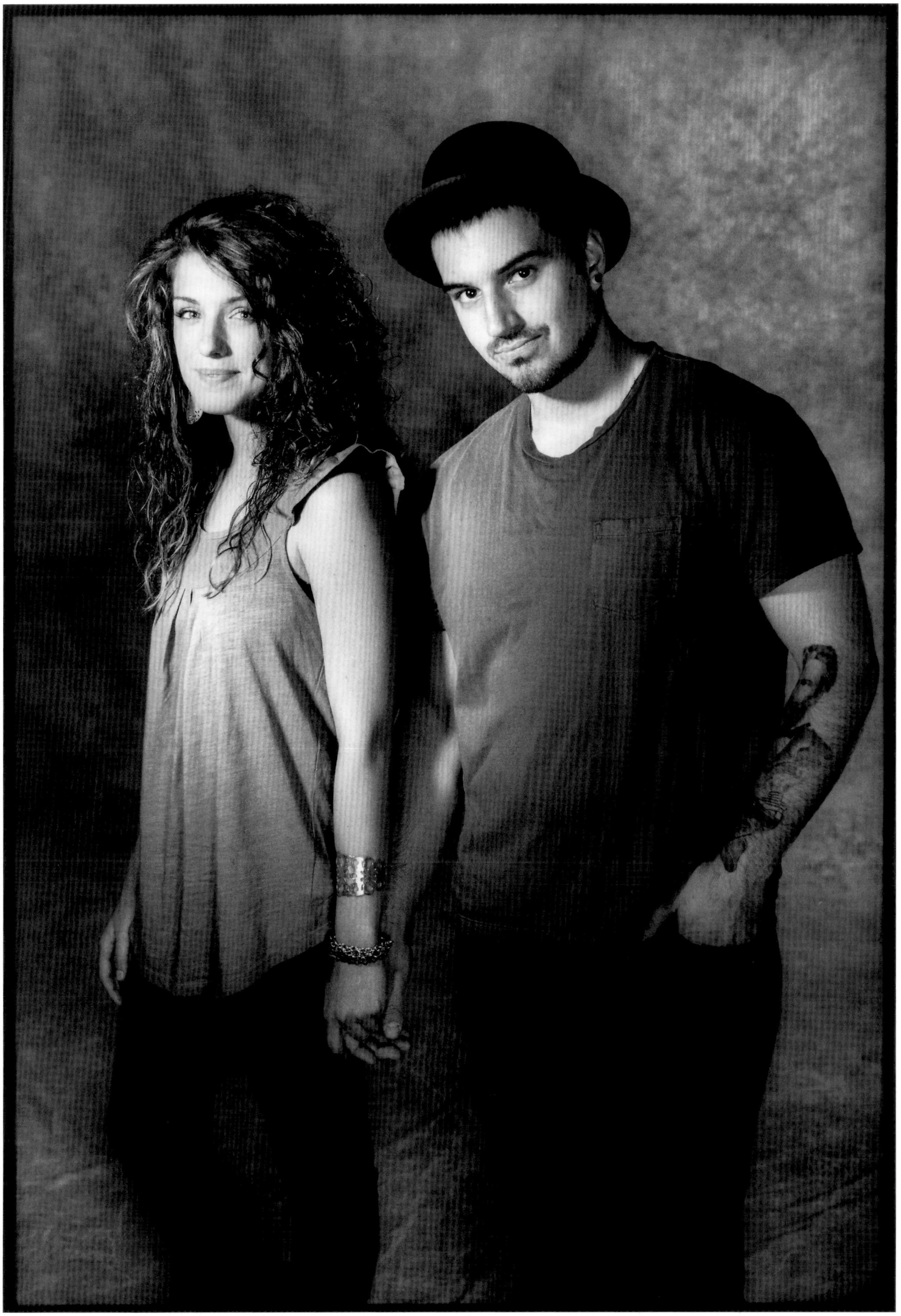

"When we first met, I told her to make me an Italian submarine and she said, 'make your own damn sandwich.' I fell in love."

"Many novocaine Octobers of intravenous love."

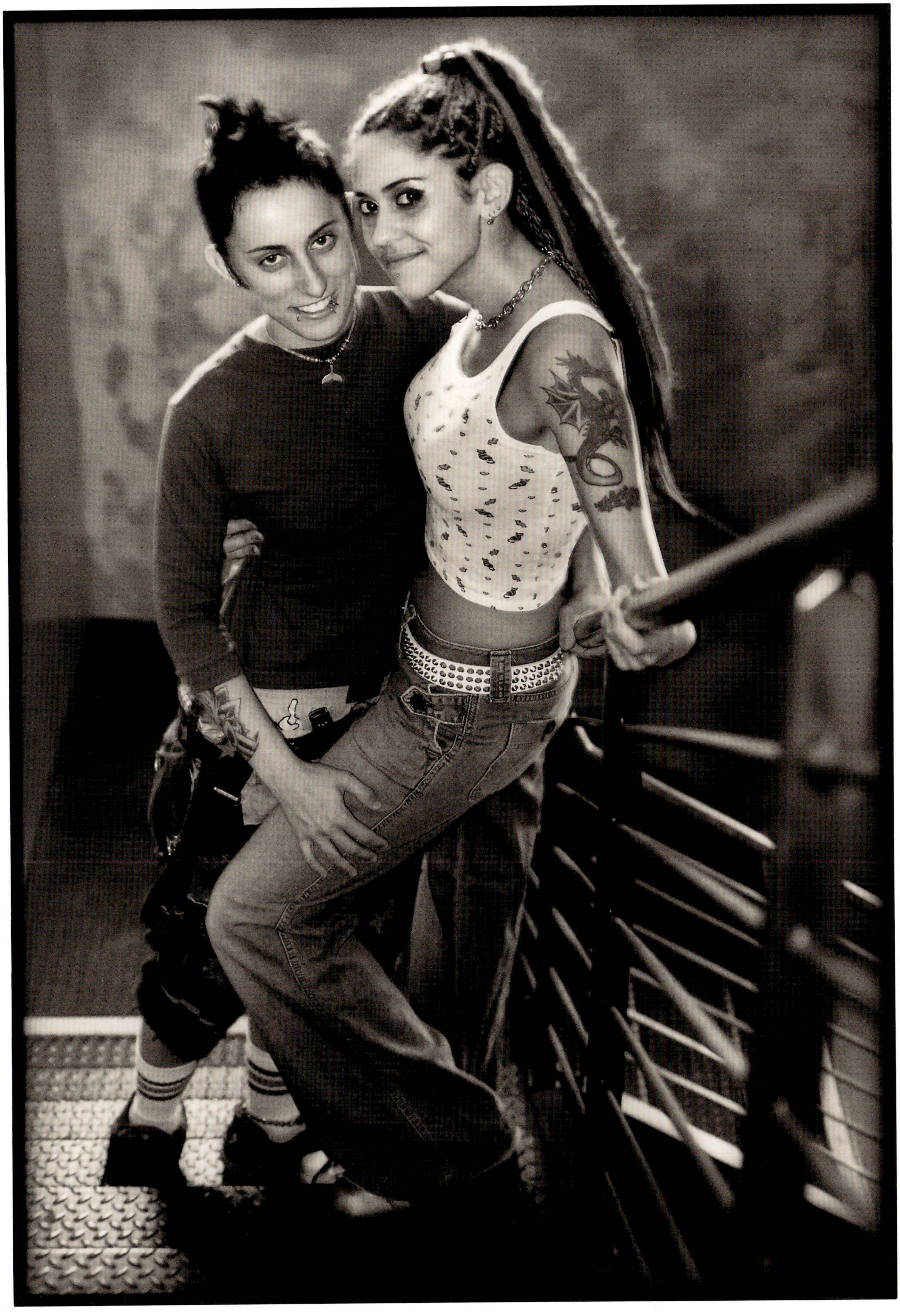

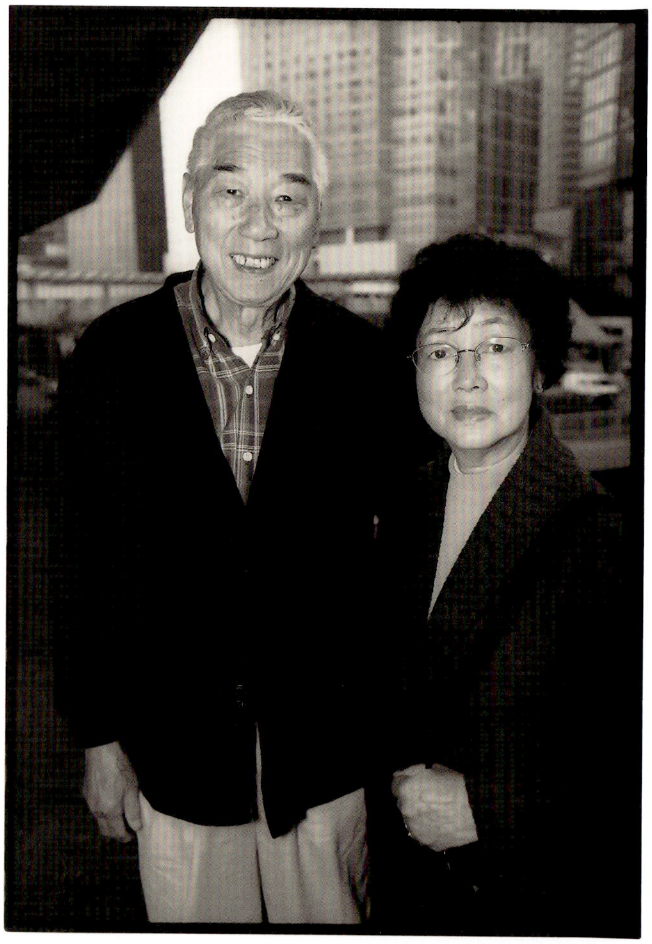

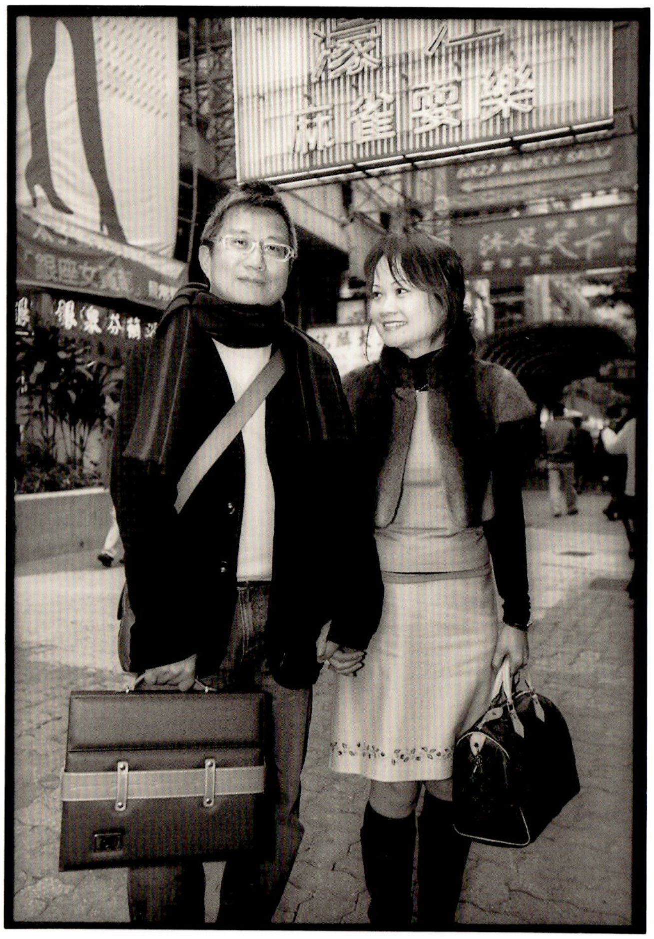

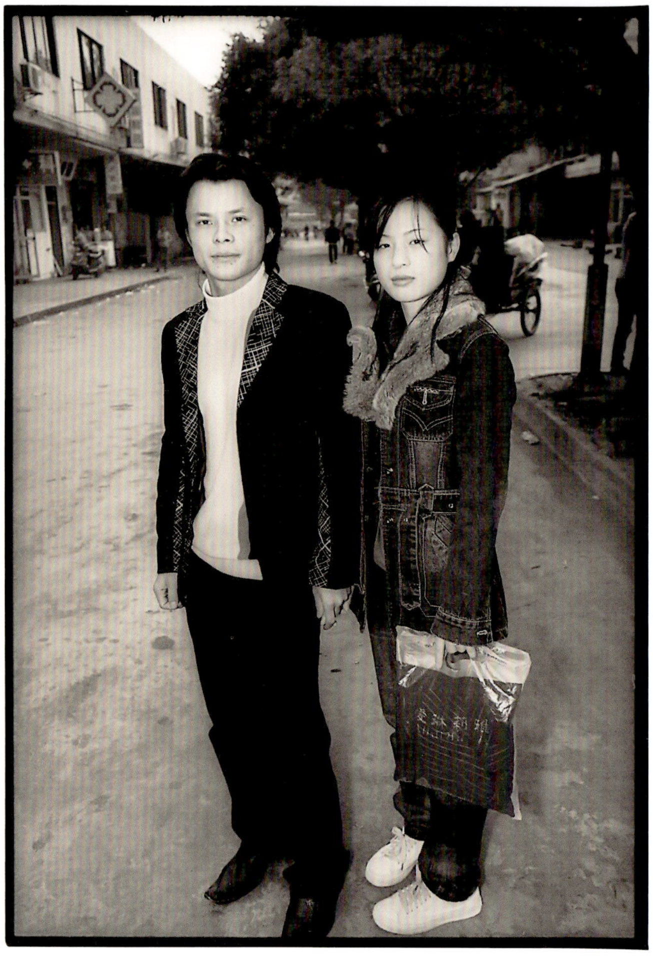

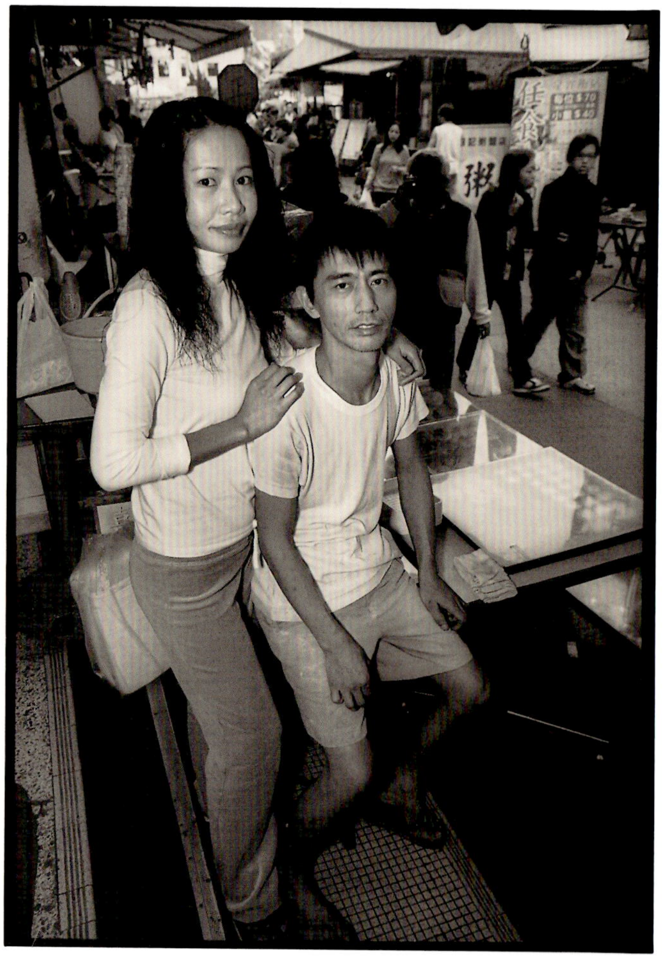

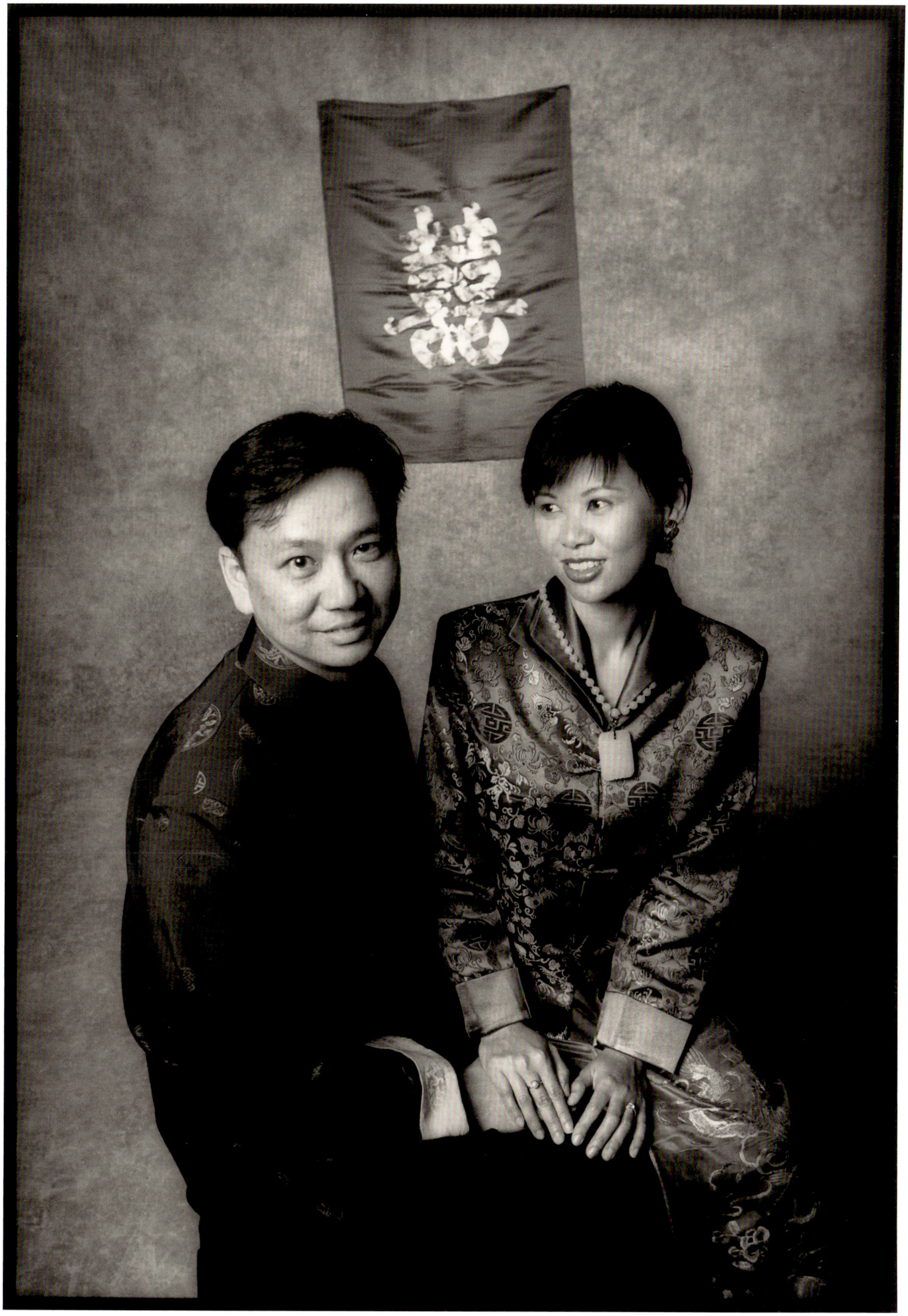

"Anything worth having is worth waiting for. If it is worth waiting for, it is worth having now."

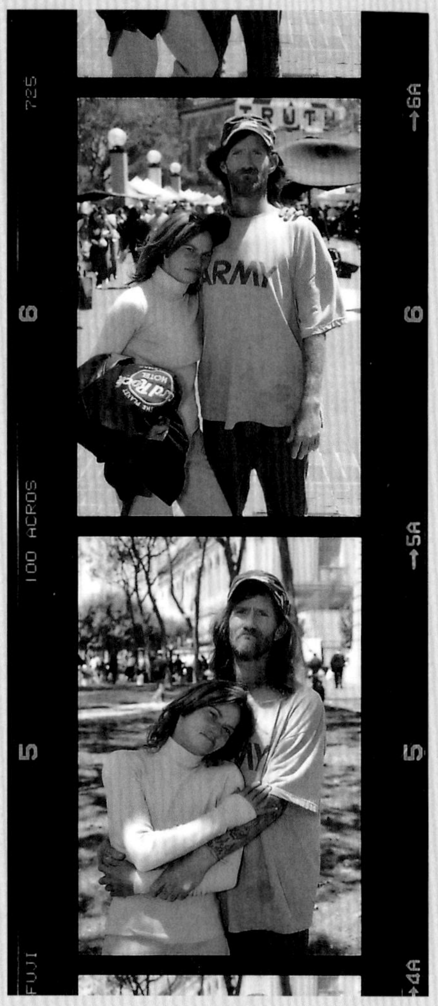

"We've been through a lot together, but tomorrow is another day."

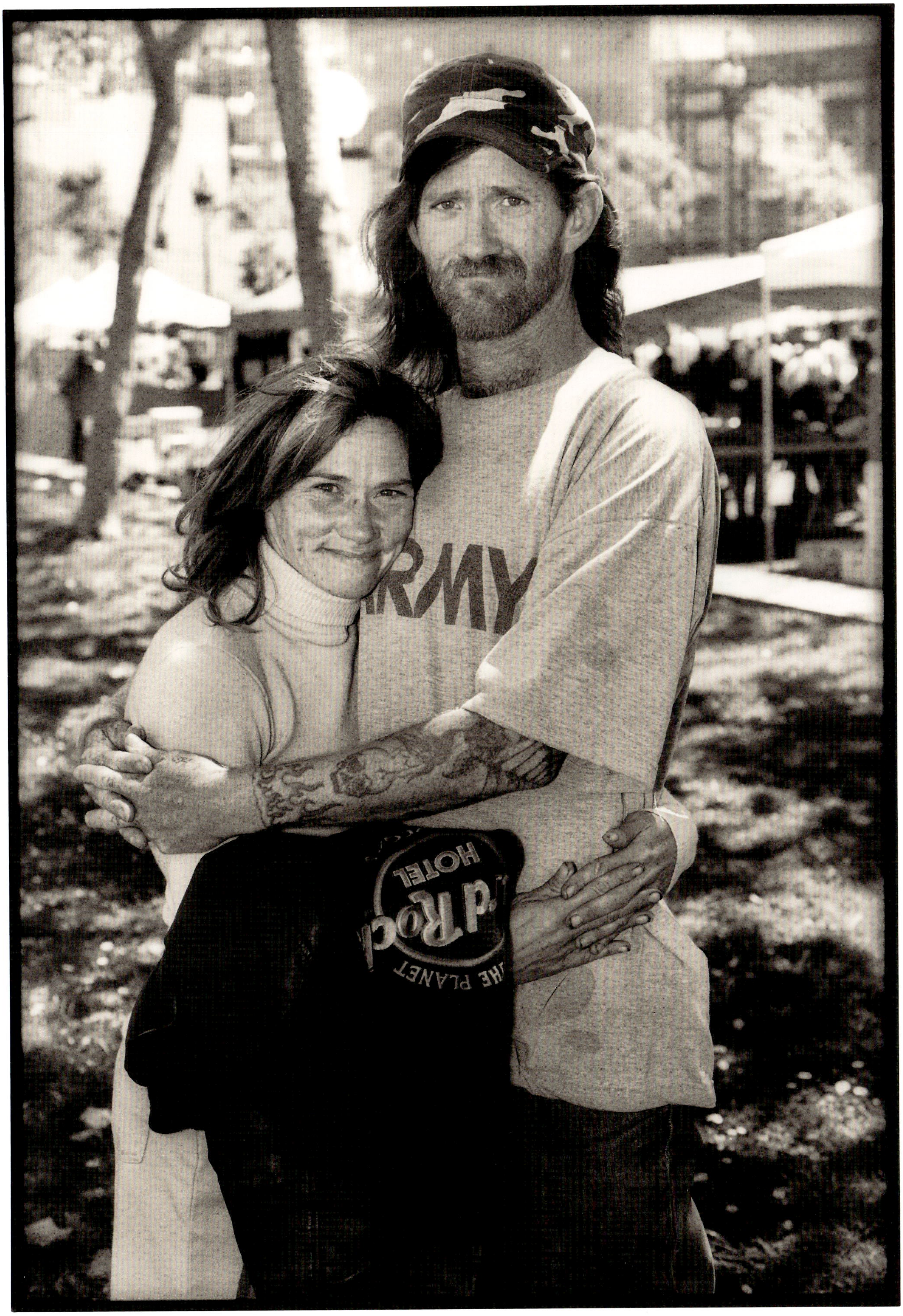
HOTEL
PLANET

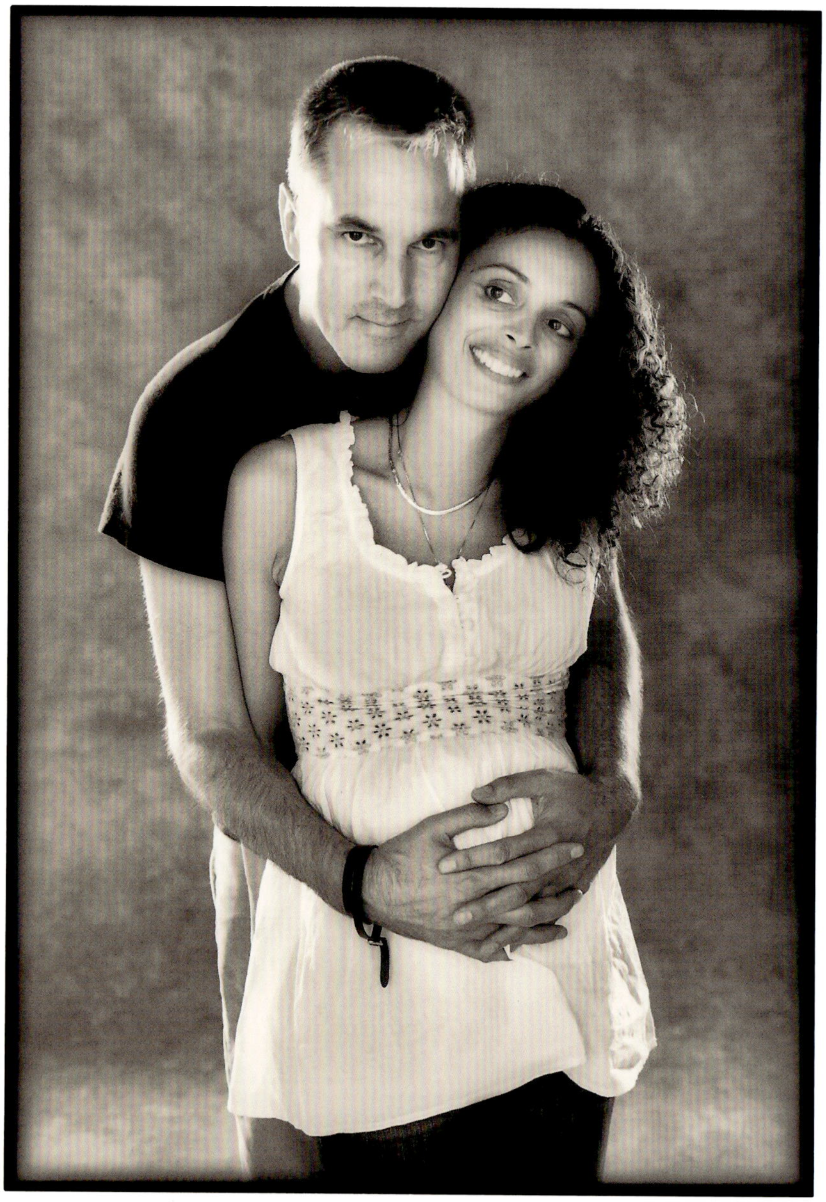

"Of all the Pastry Shops in all the world..."

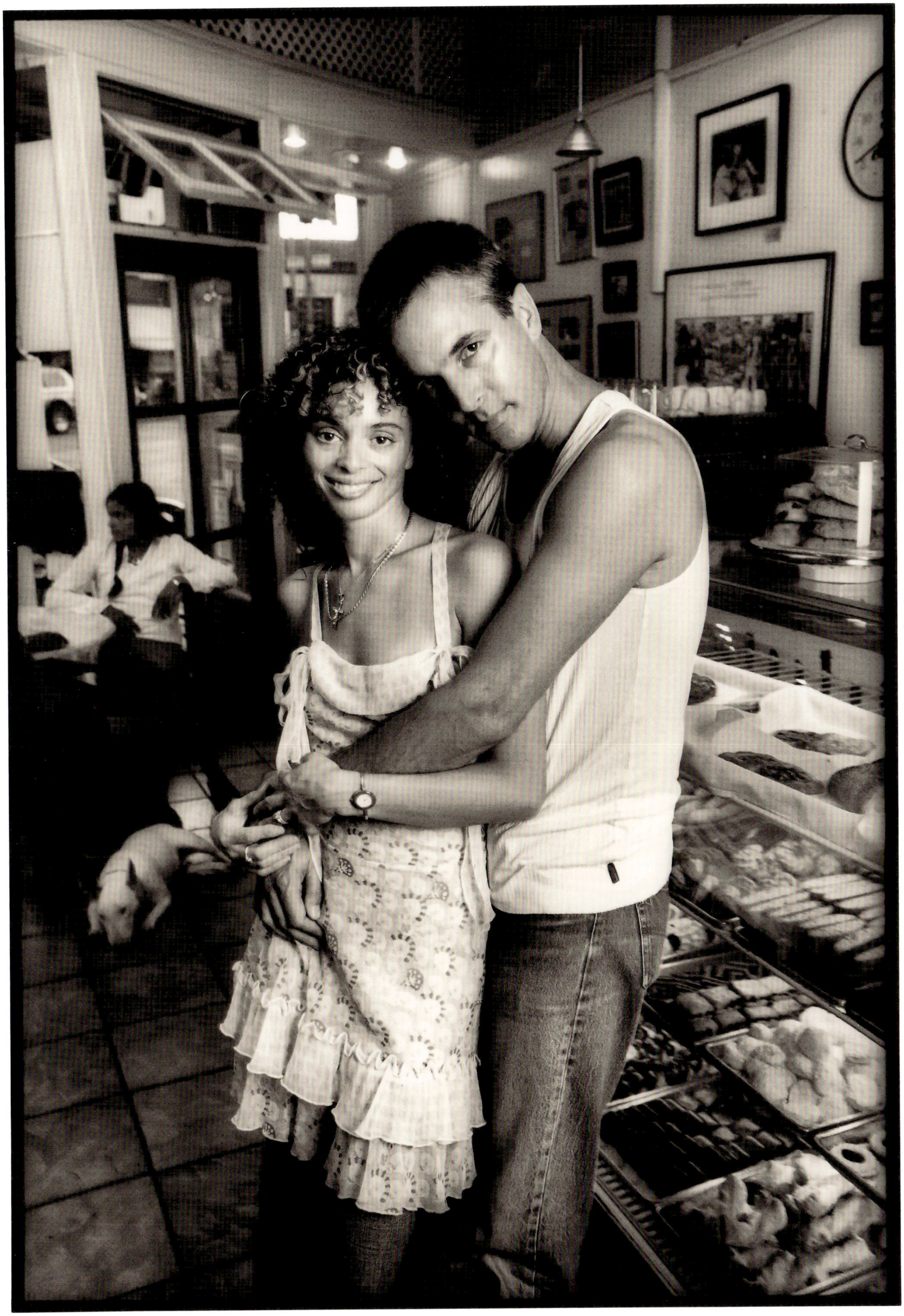

LOCATION

Dubai, UAE

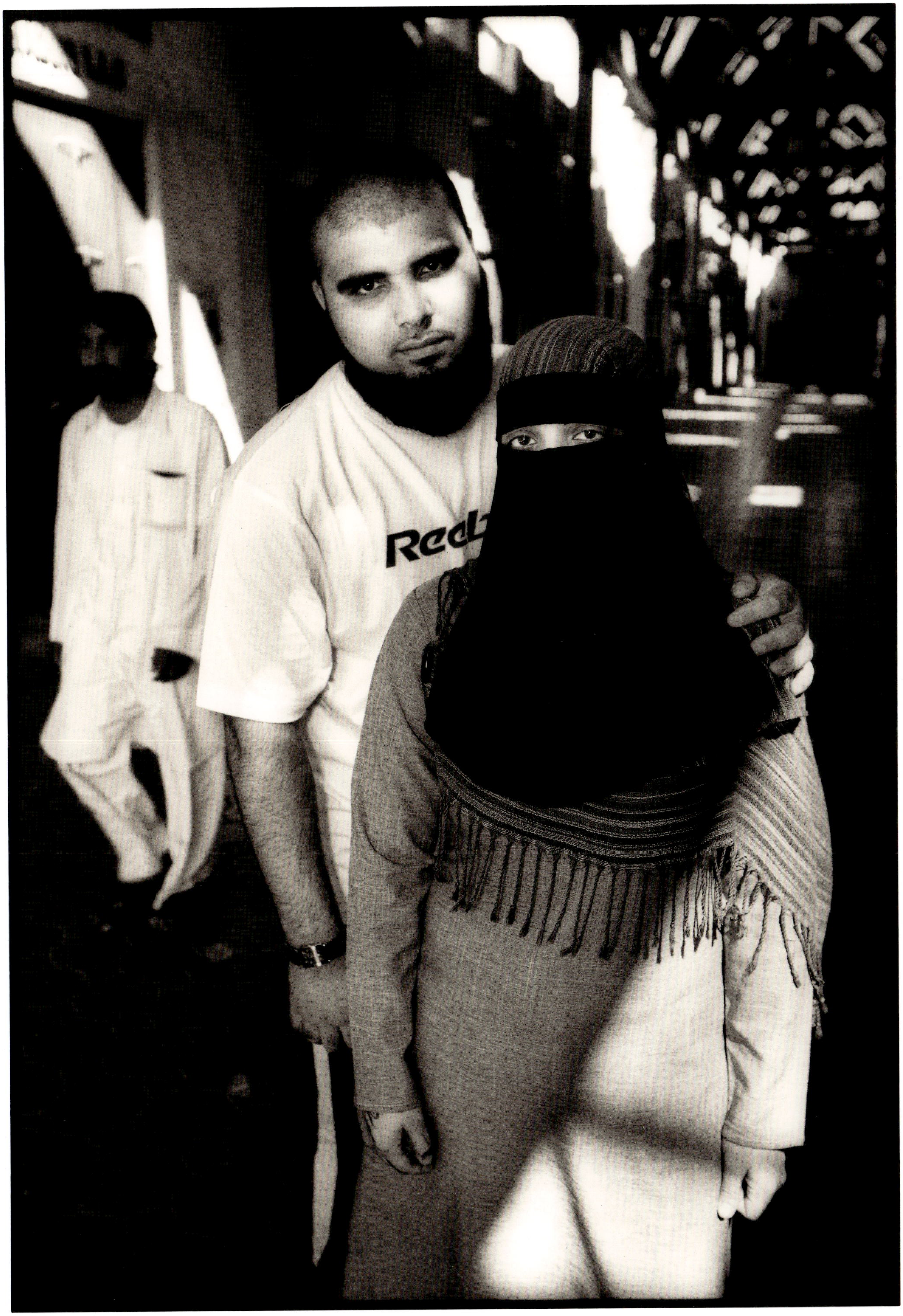
Reeb

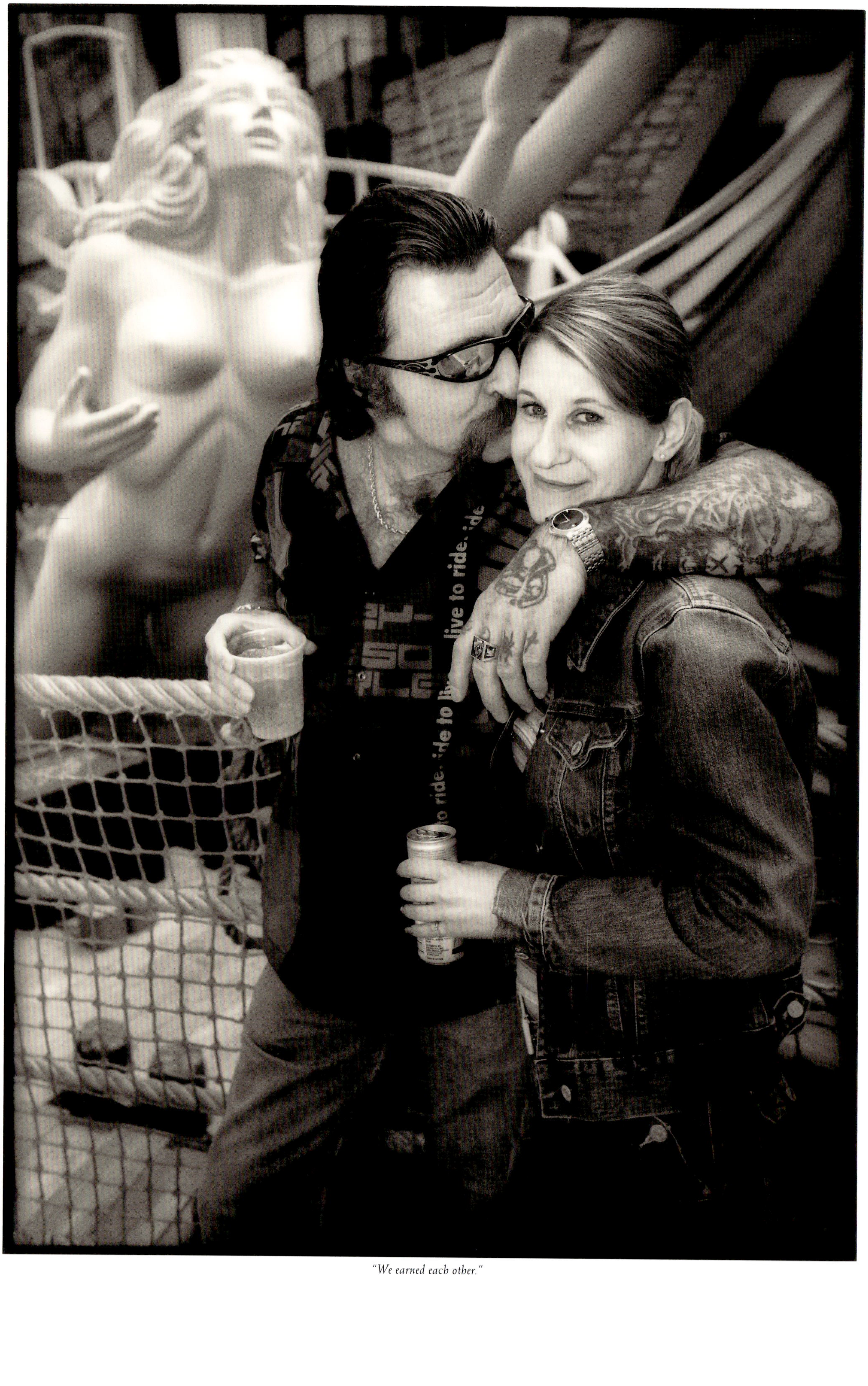

"We earned each other."

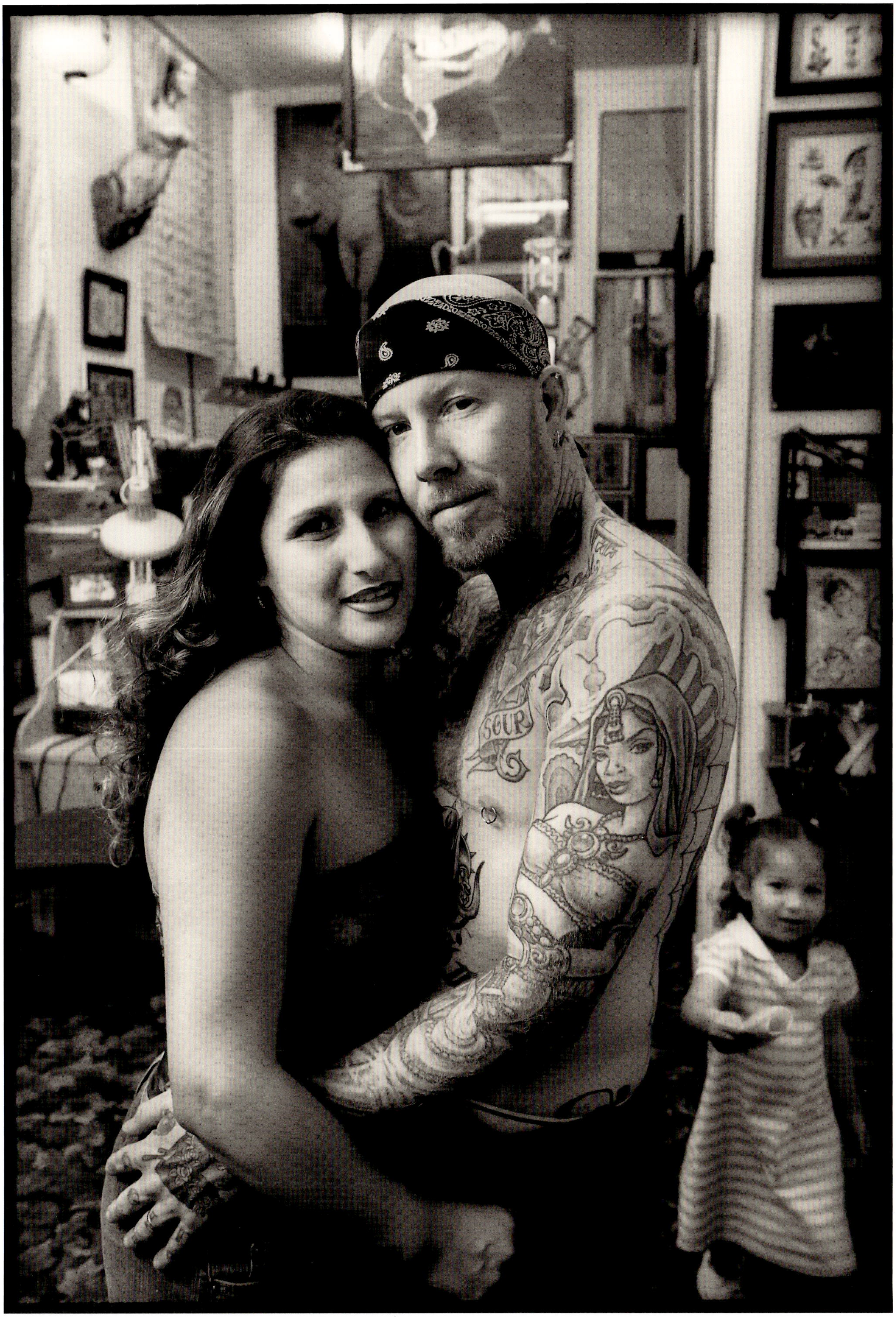

"Just like a tattoo, our love is forever."

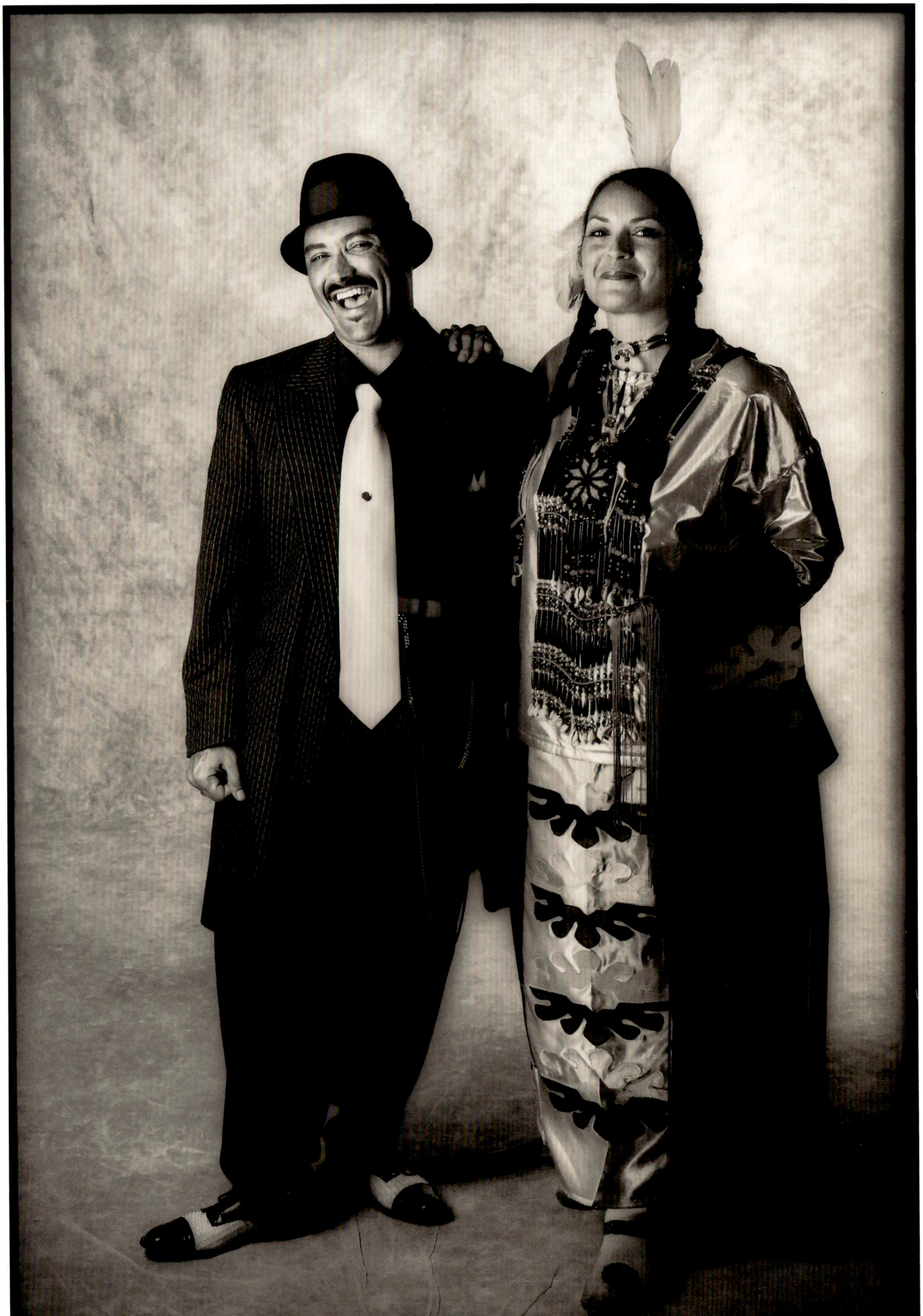

"I love his clean press, cool Vato style – it drives me wild."

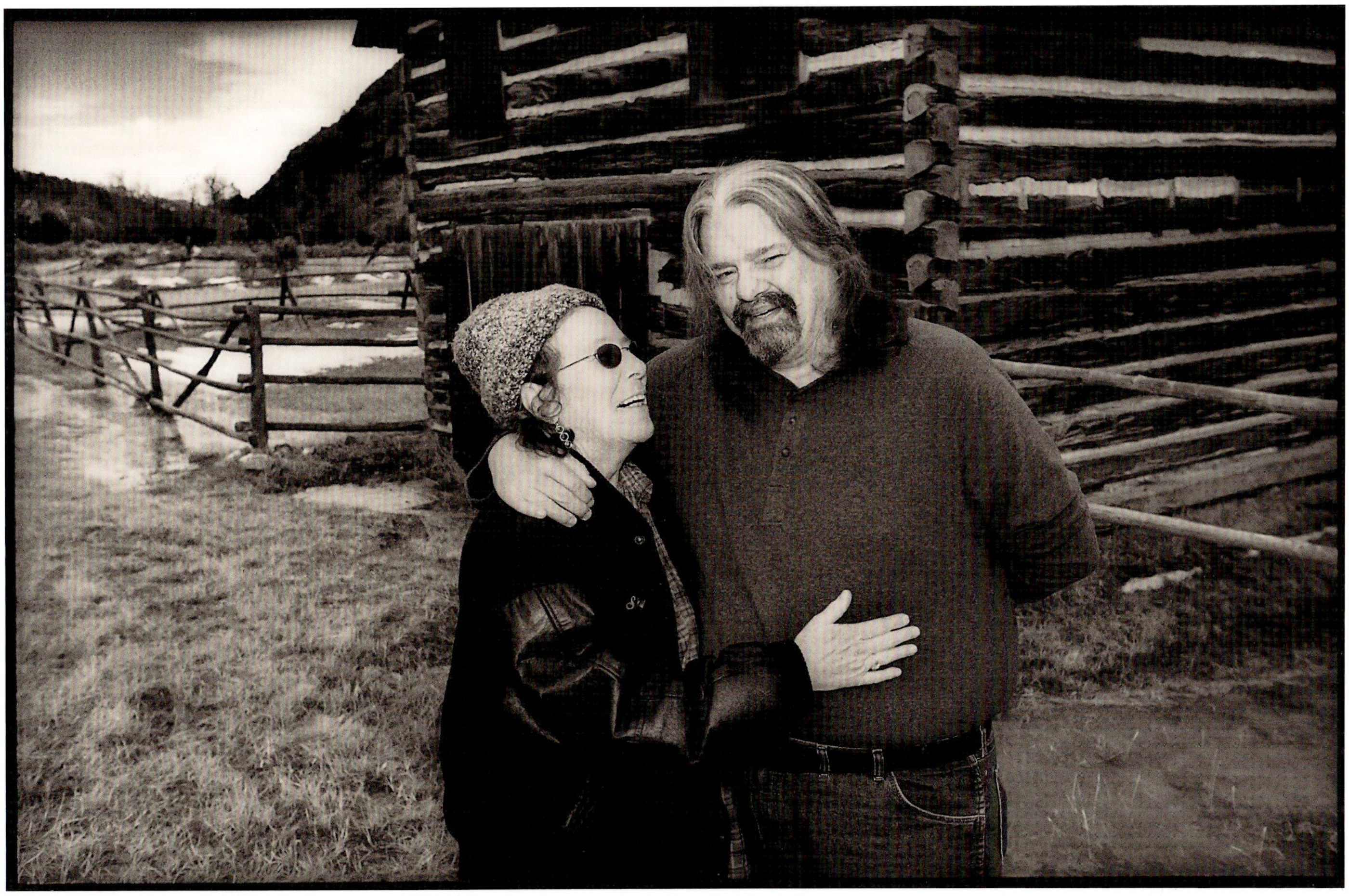

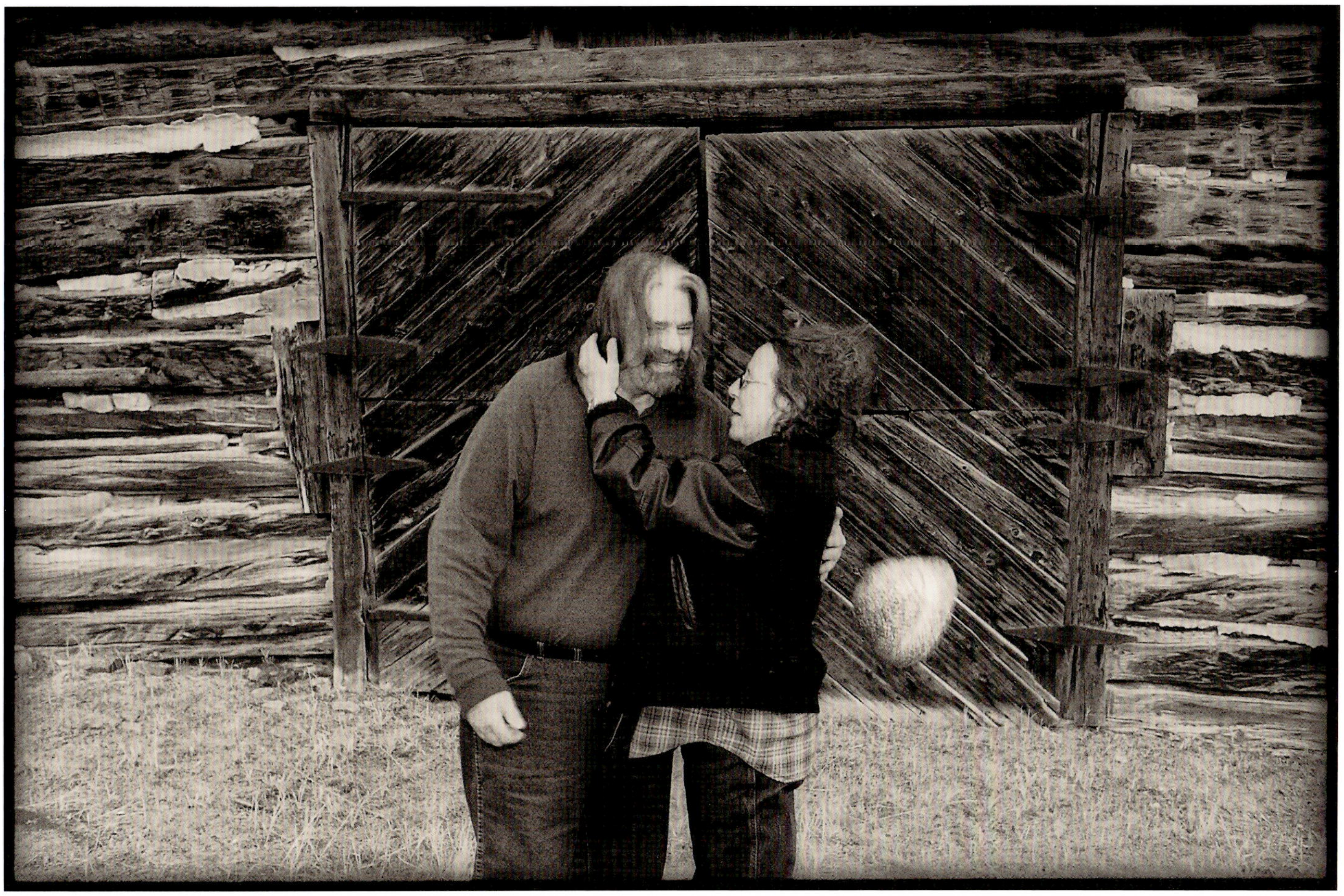

A retired New York cop meets stained glass artist in the mountains of Montana!

"Eighteen years and still dancing!"

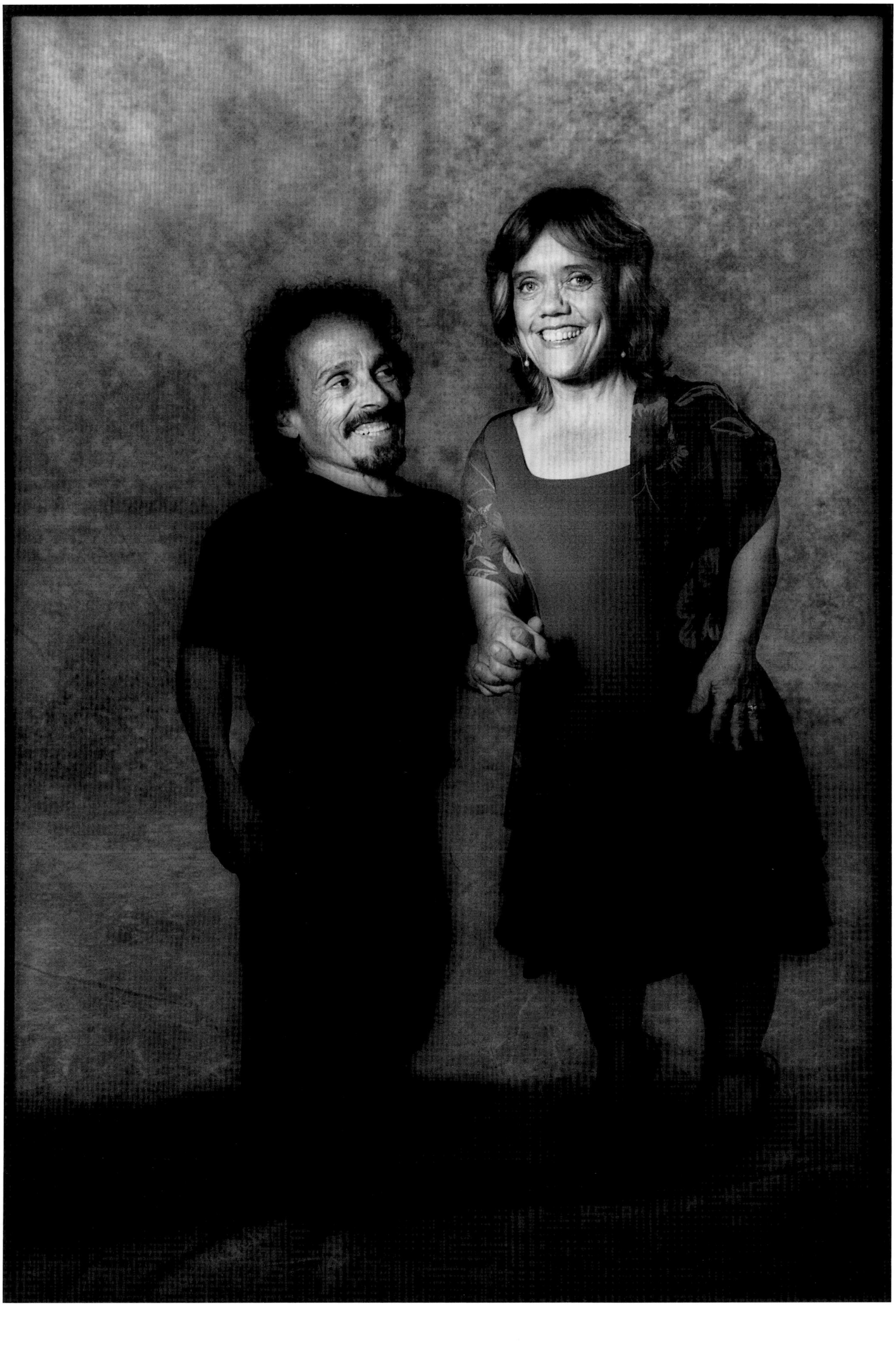

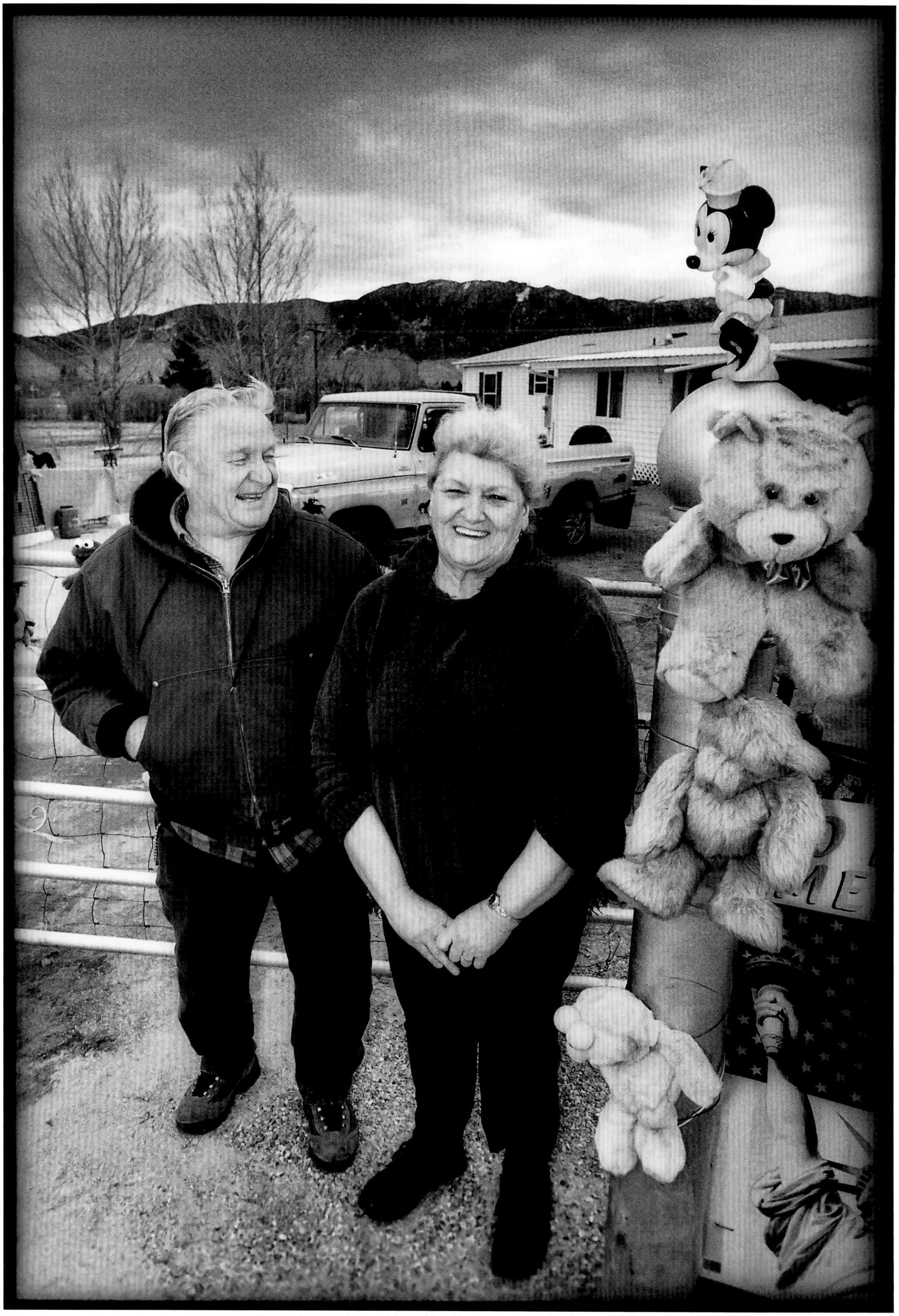

"Projects like our whimsical 'animal farm' keep us young, and makes us smile."

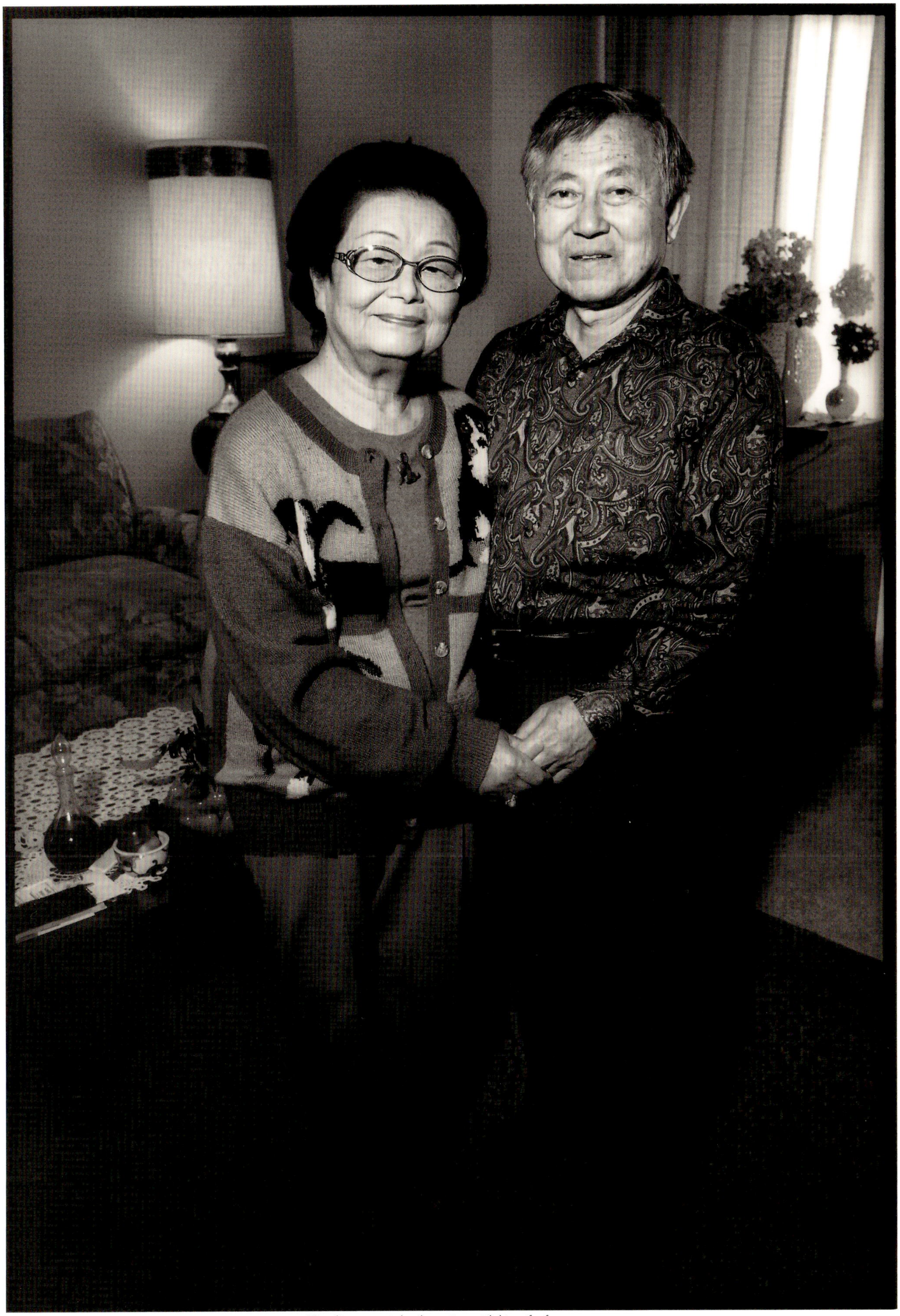

Hiroshima atomic bomb survivor with his wife of 44 years.

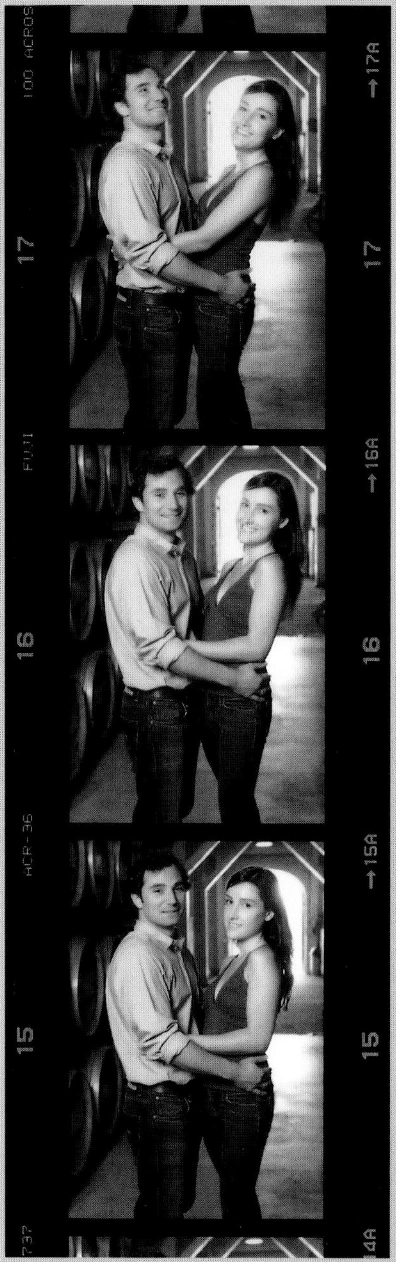

"Under warm California stars, we recently held our wedding reception in front of the old stone winery.
Being third-generation vintners and growers, it felt like a natural site for our friends and family to gather and celebrate.
The music for our first dance still echoes through the wine caves."

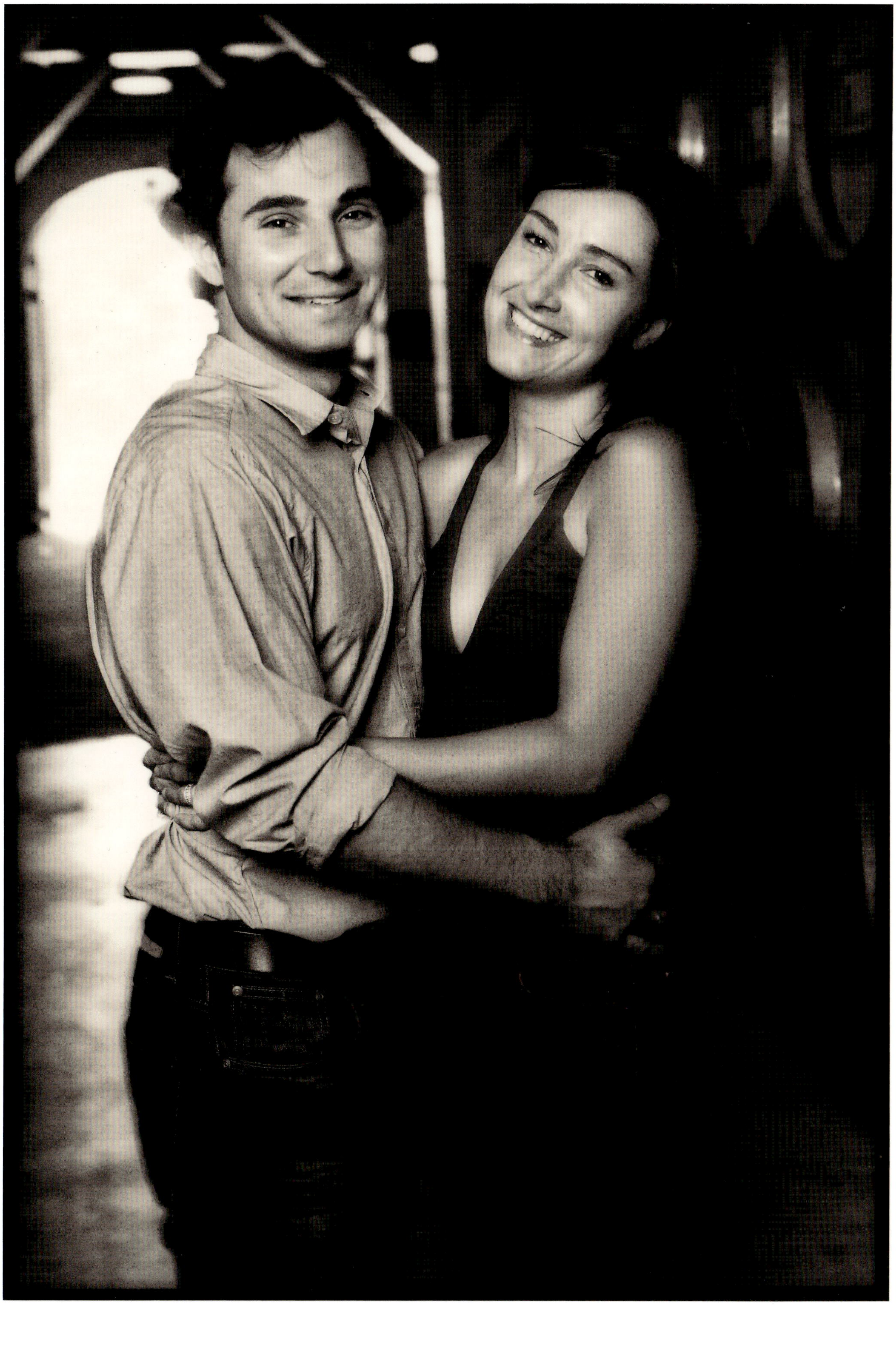

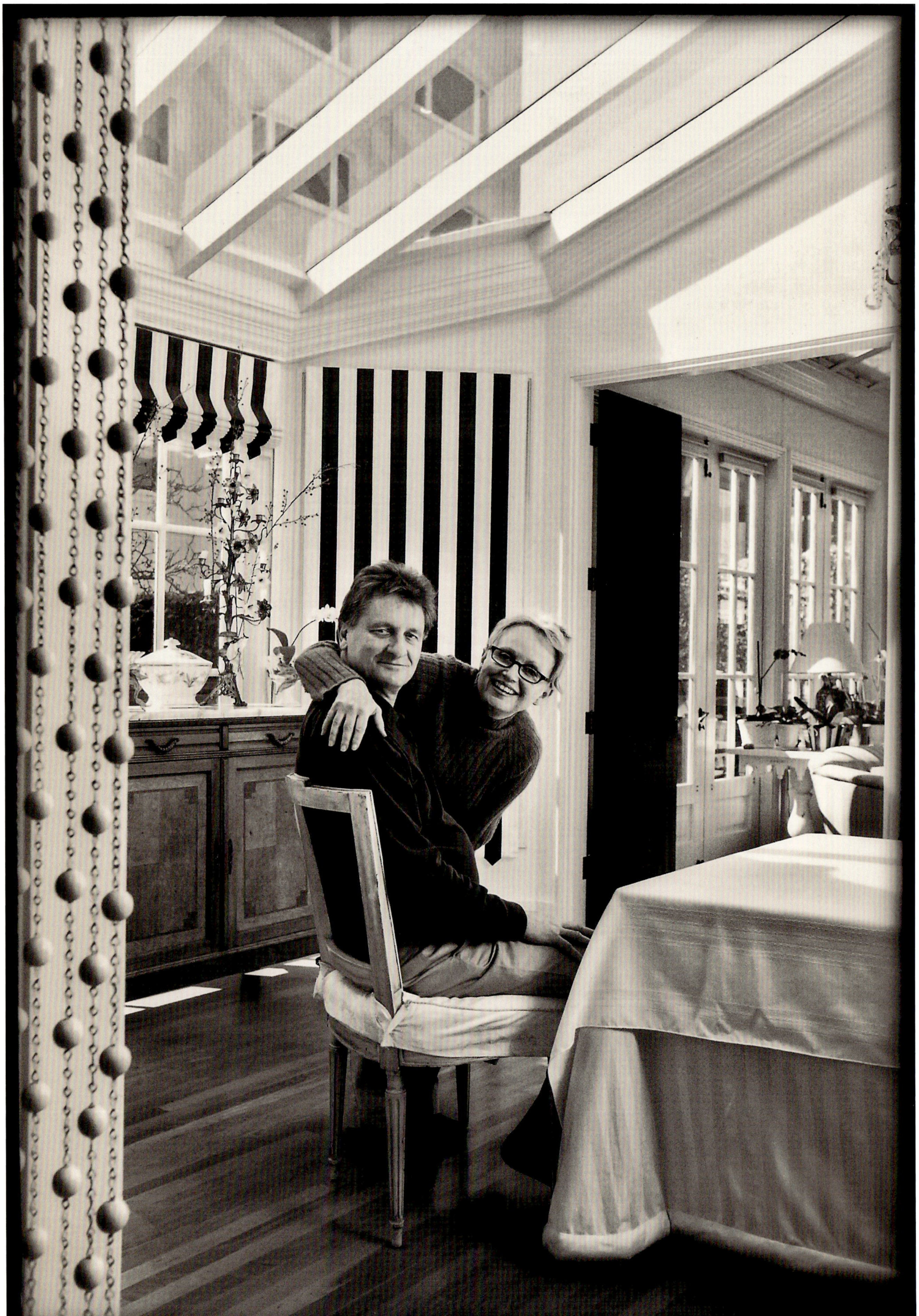

"Common wisdom tells us that each of us can have it all, or be all – but we've found that none of us is 'all.' Our spouses augment what we ourselves are not."

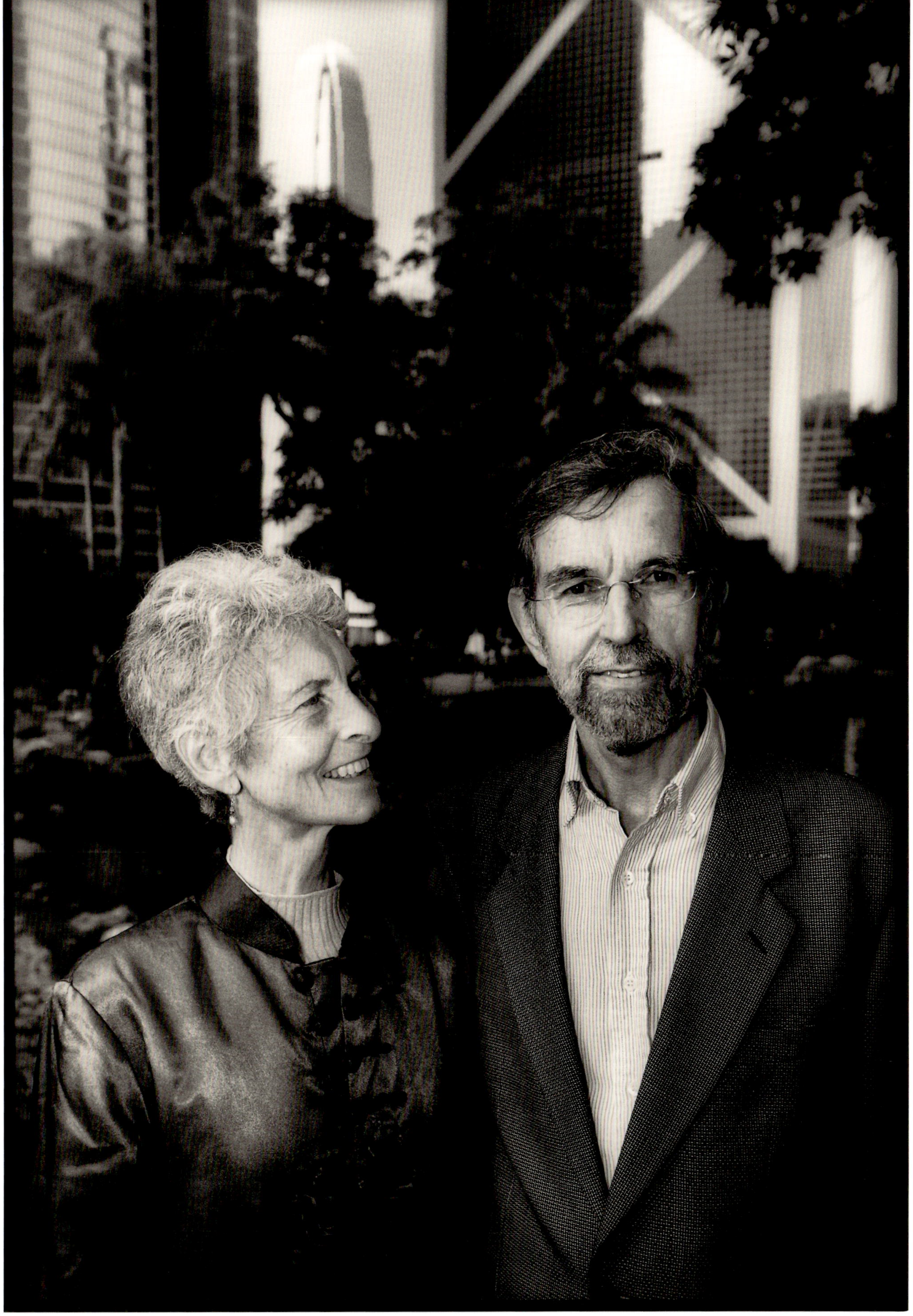

"I'm with you all the way."

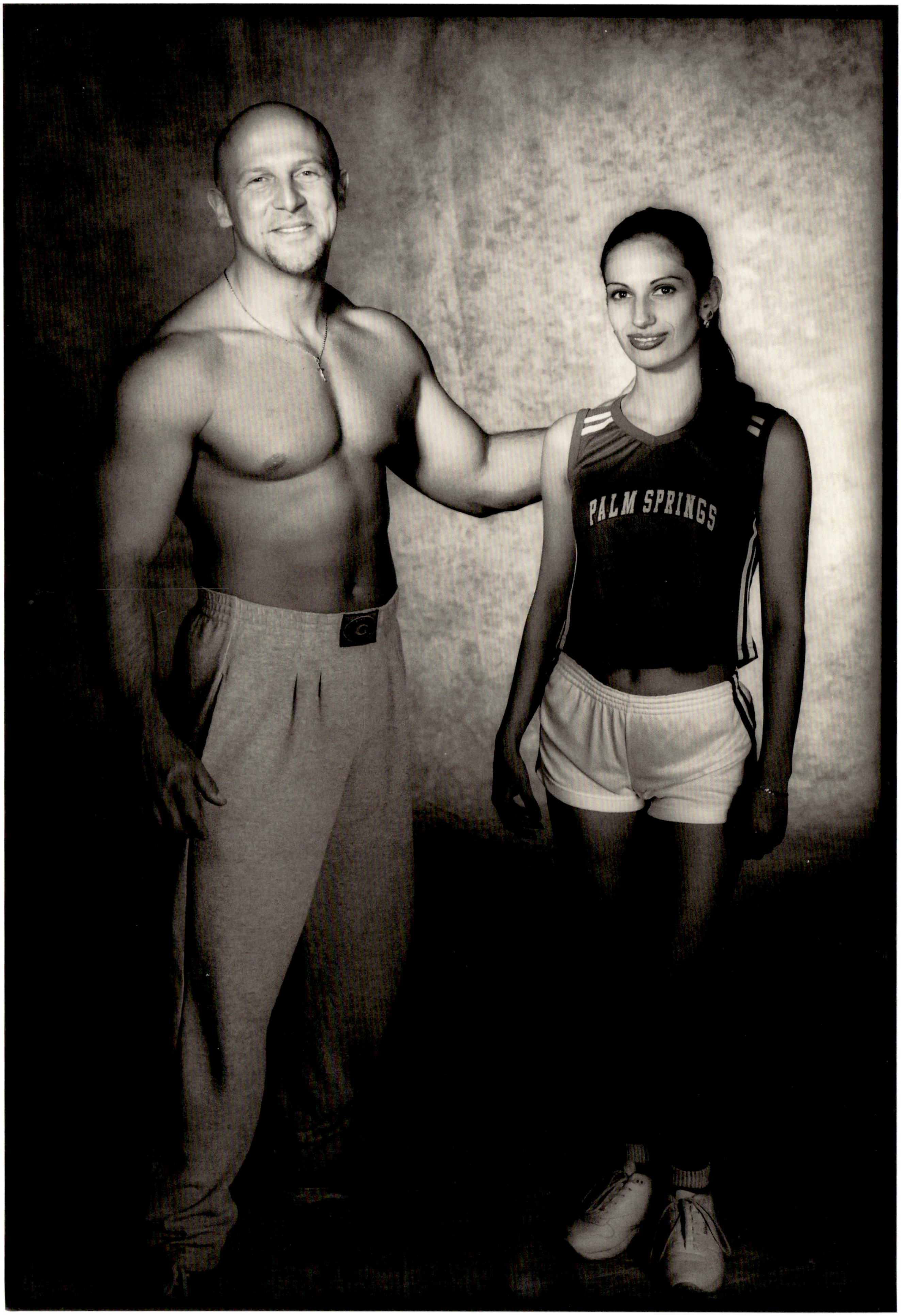
PALM SPRINGS

"A 120-pound difference in weight makes no difference to those in love."

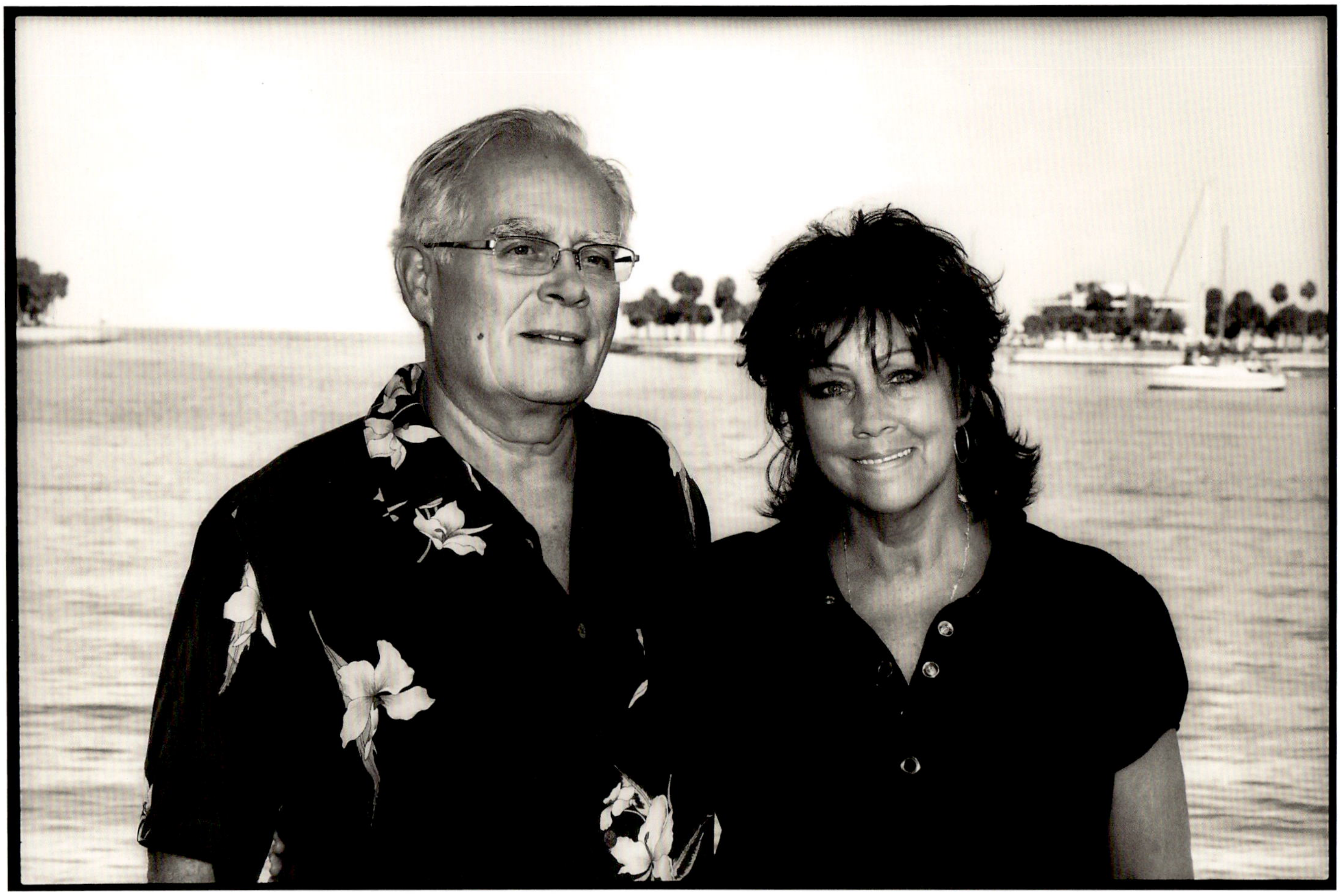

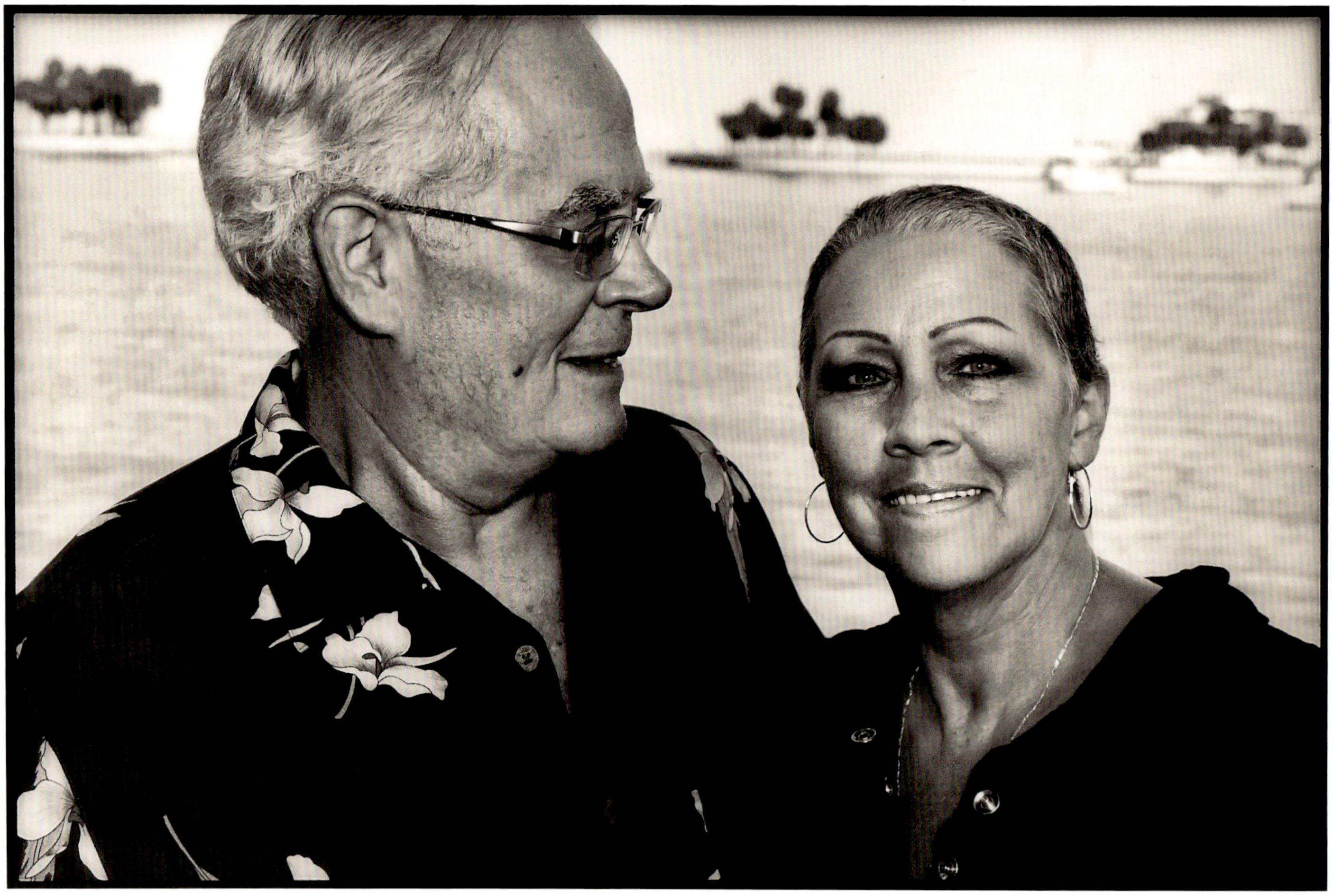

"Marriage has many challenges,

but the true meaning of our love was surviving breast cancer together."

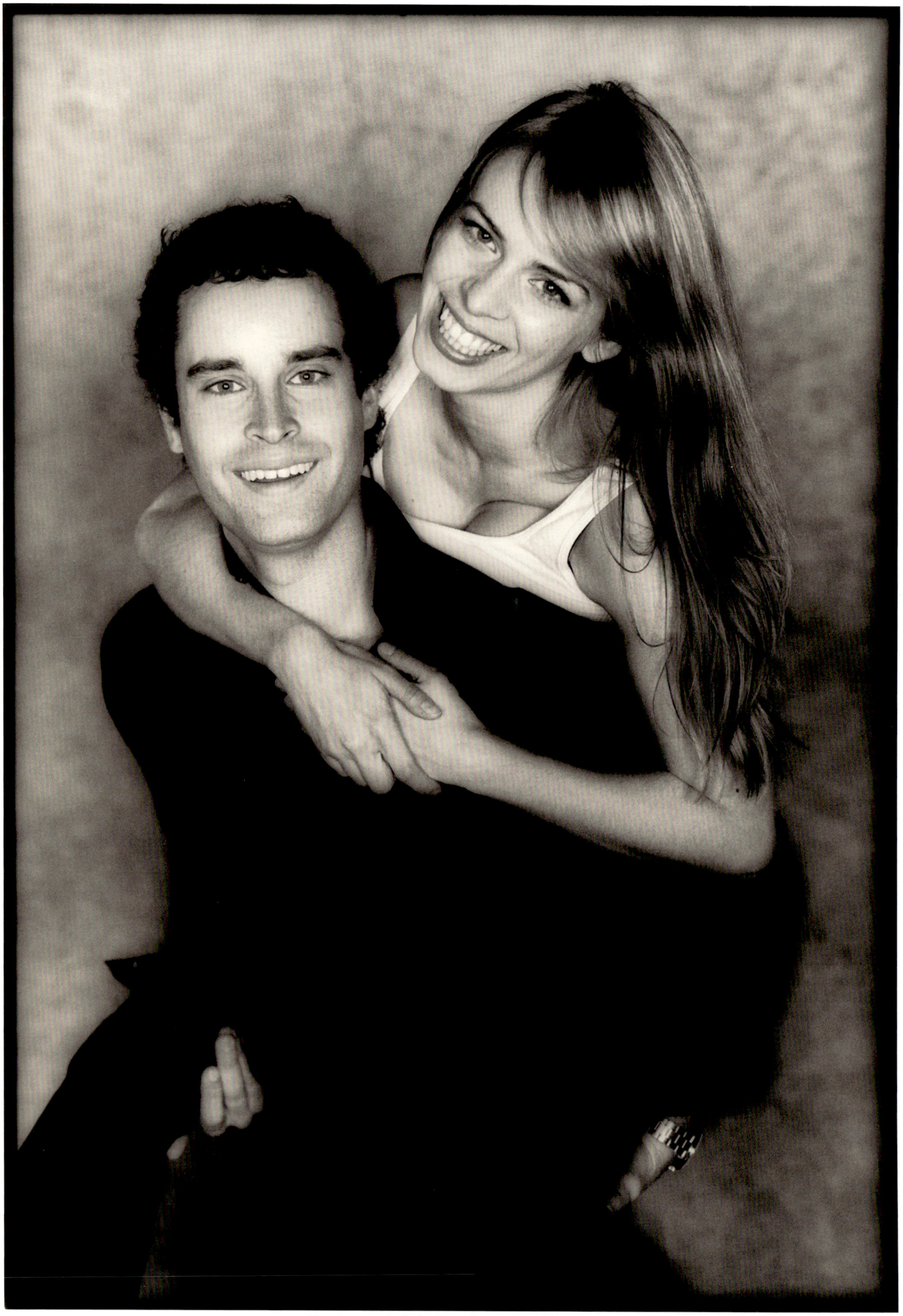

There is no remedy for love but to love more. —Thoreau

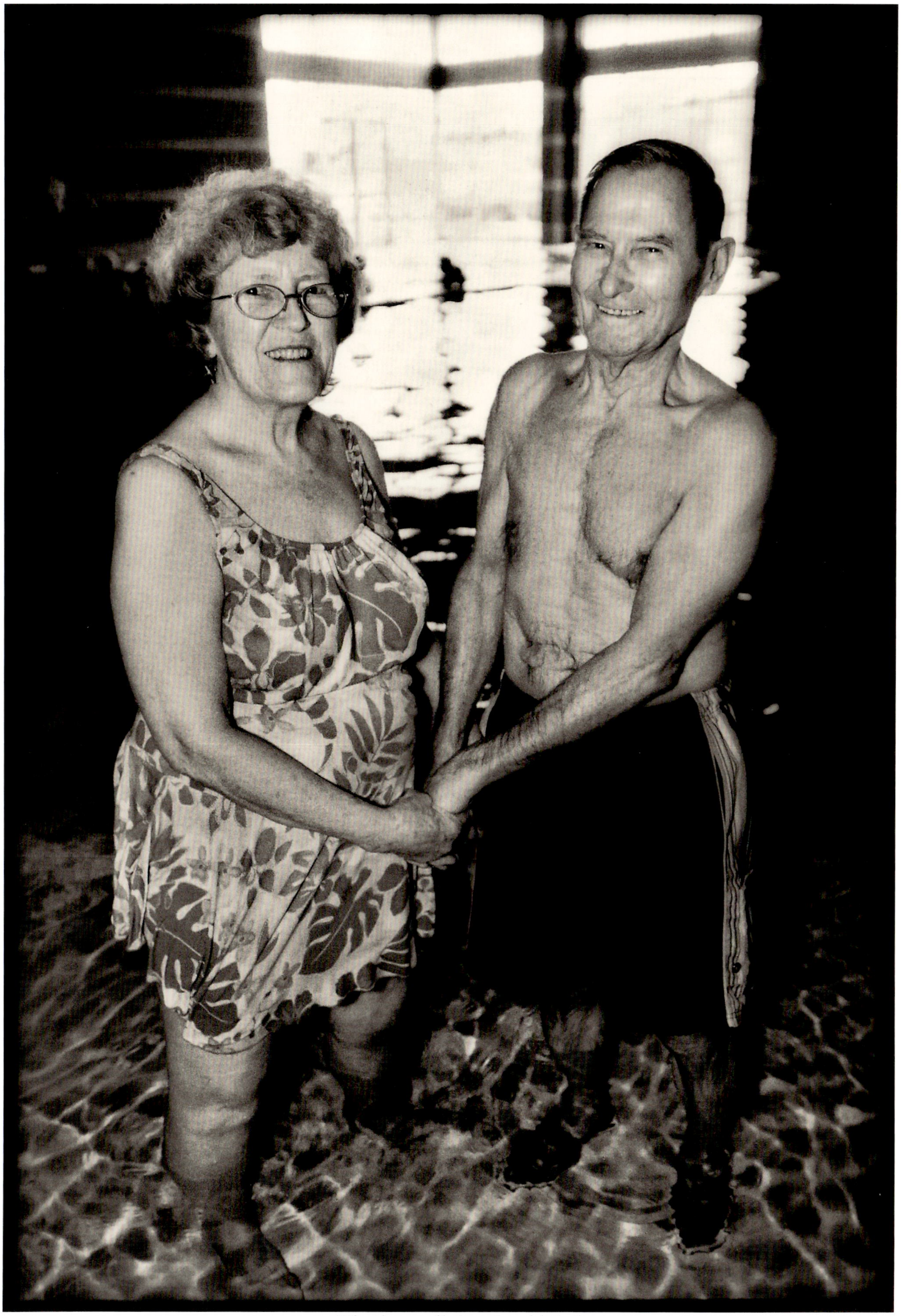

"Fifty- plus years of loving, caring and sharing."

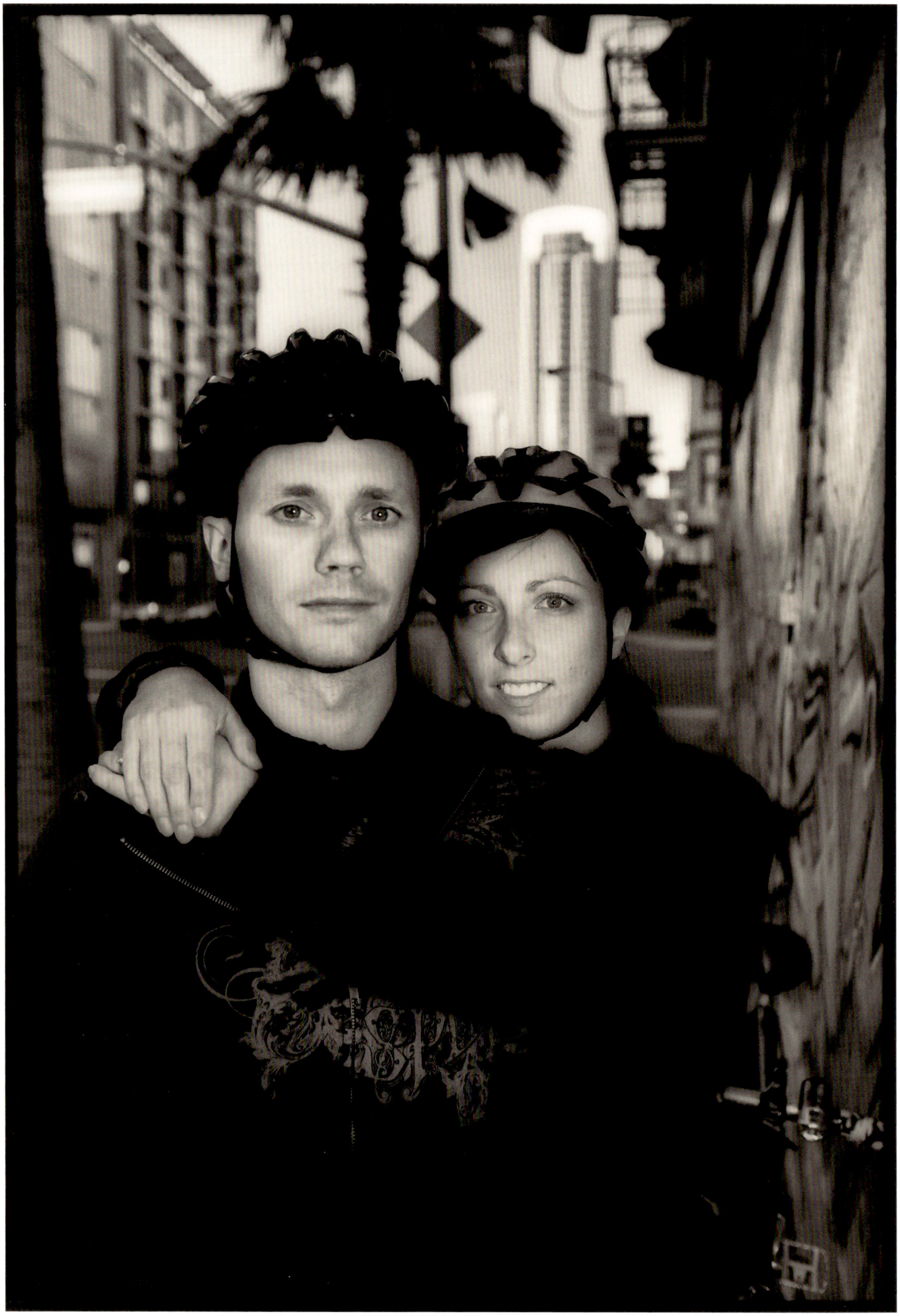

"Coding and decoding, then having analog fun in the City."

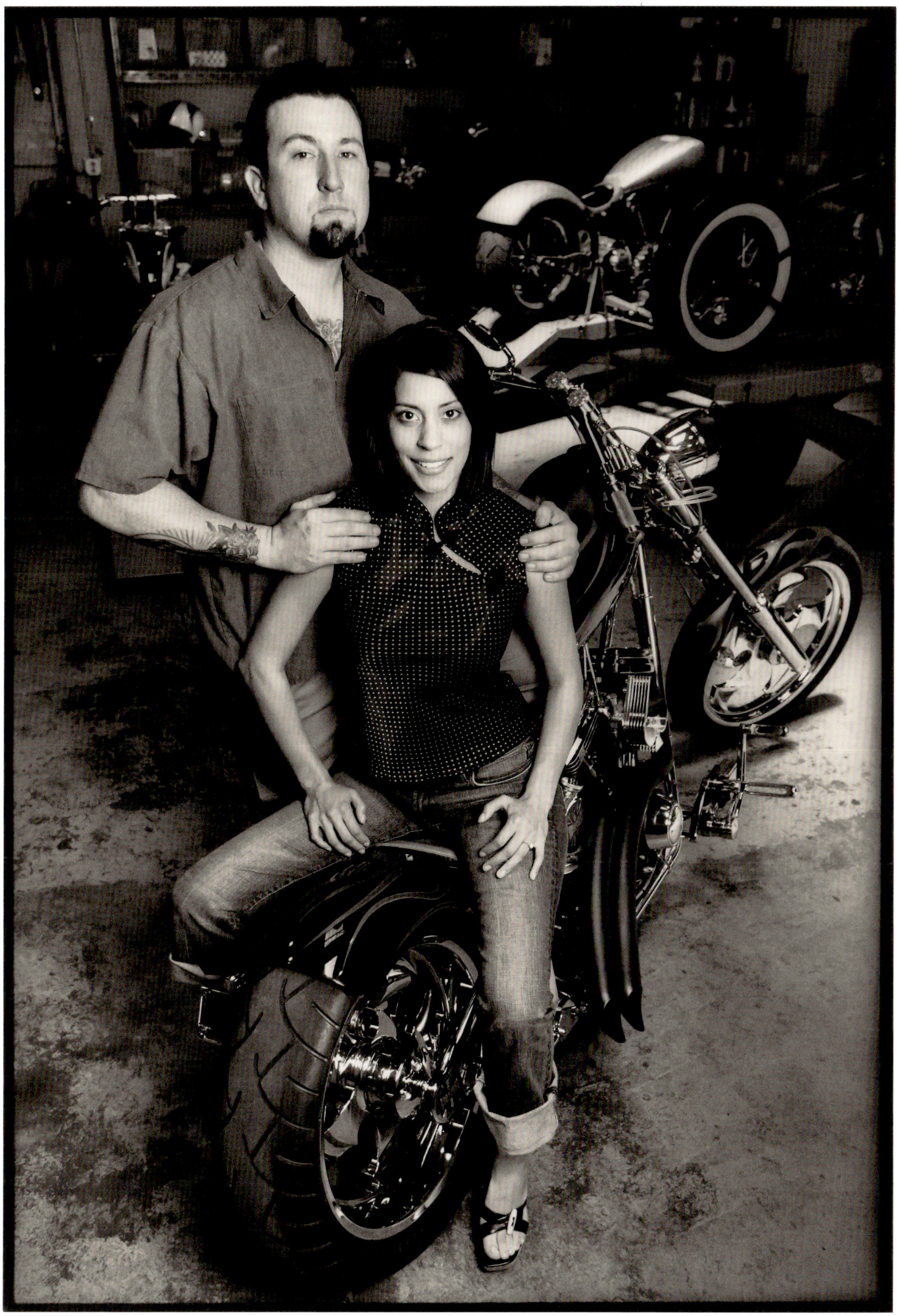

"Fire and Ice."

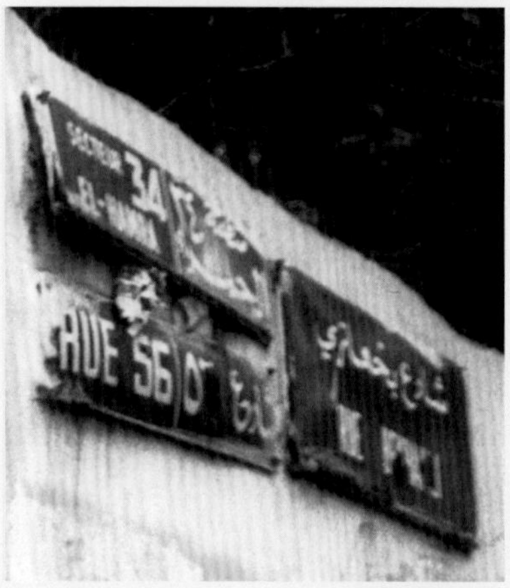

"I speak to her with words, and she replies with her eyes.
To fall for the beauty of a look."

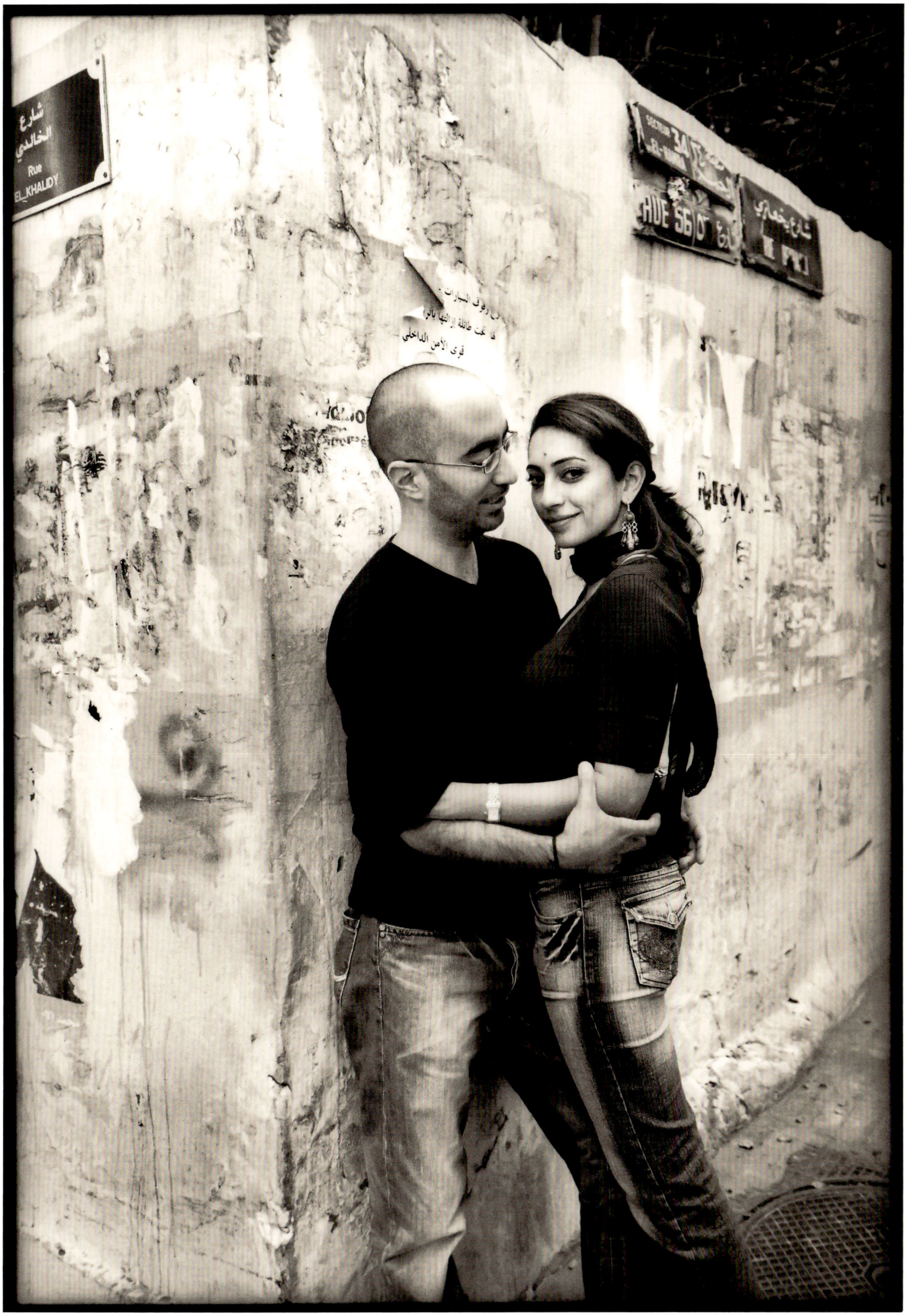
شارع
الخالدي
Rue
EL_KHALIDY

"East meets West."

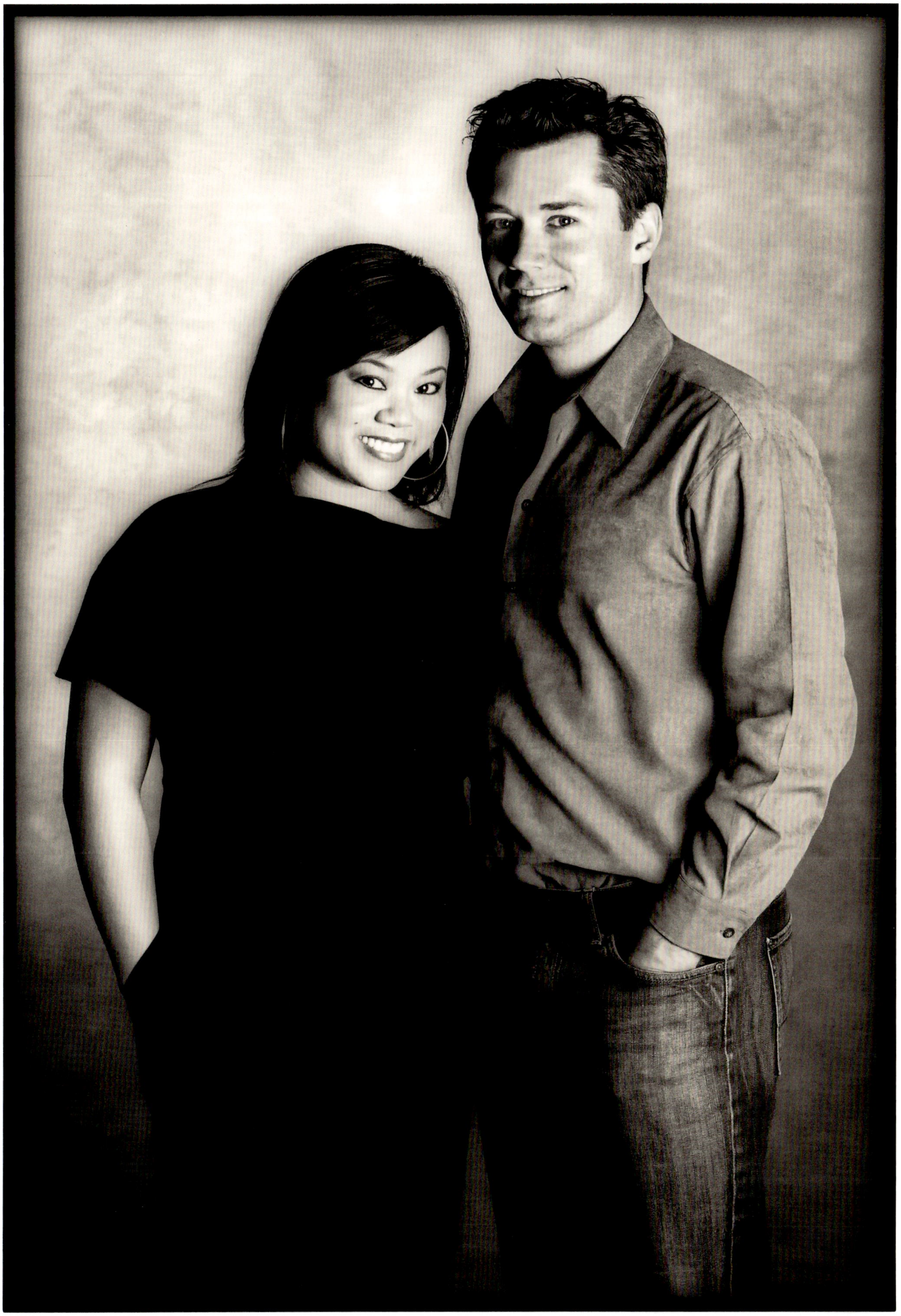

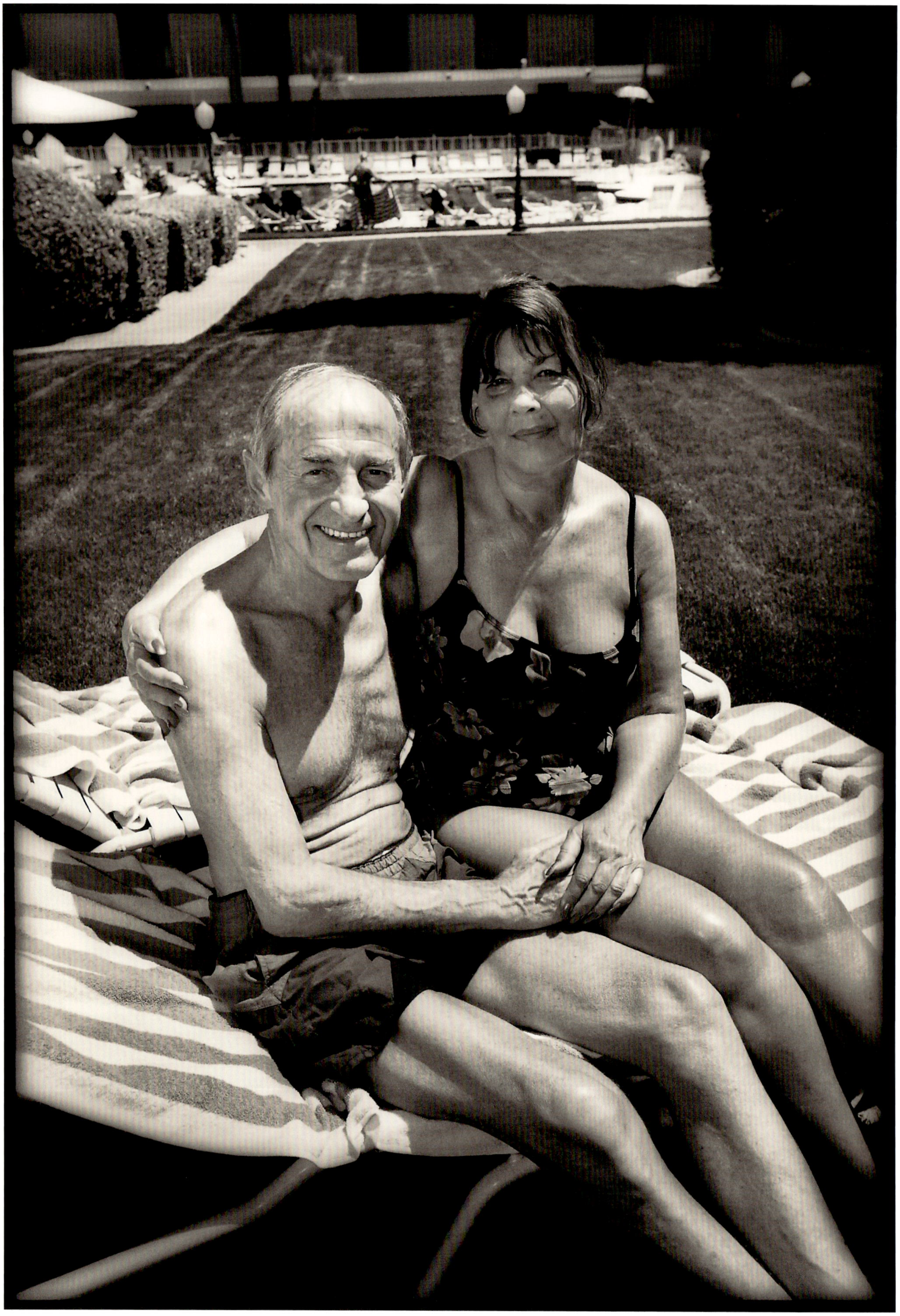

"Our lifetime of loving, sharing and caring for each other and our two sons began here in Las Vegas, in 1969."

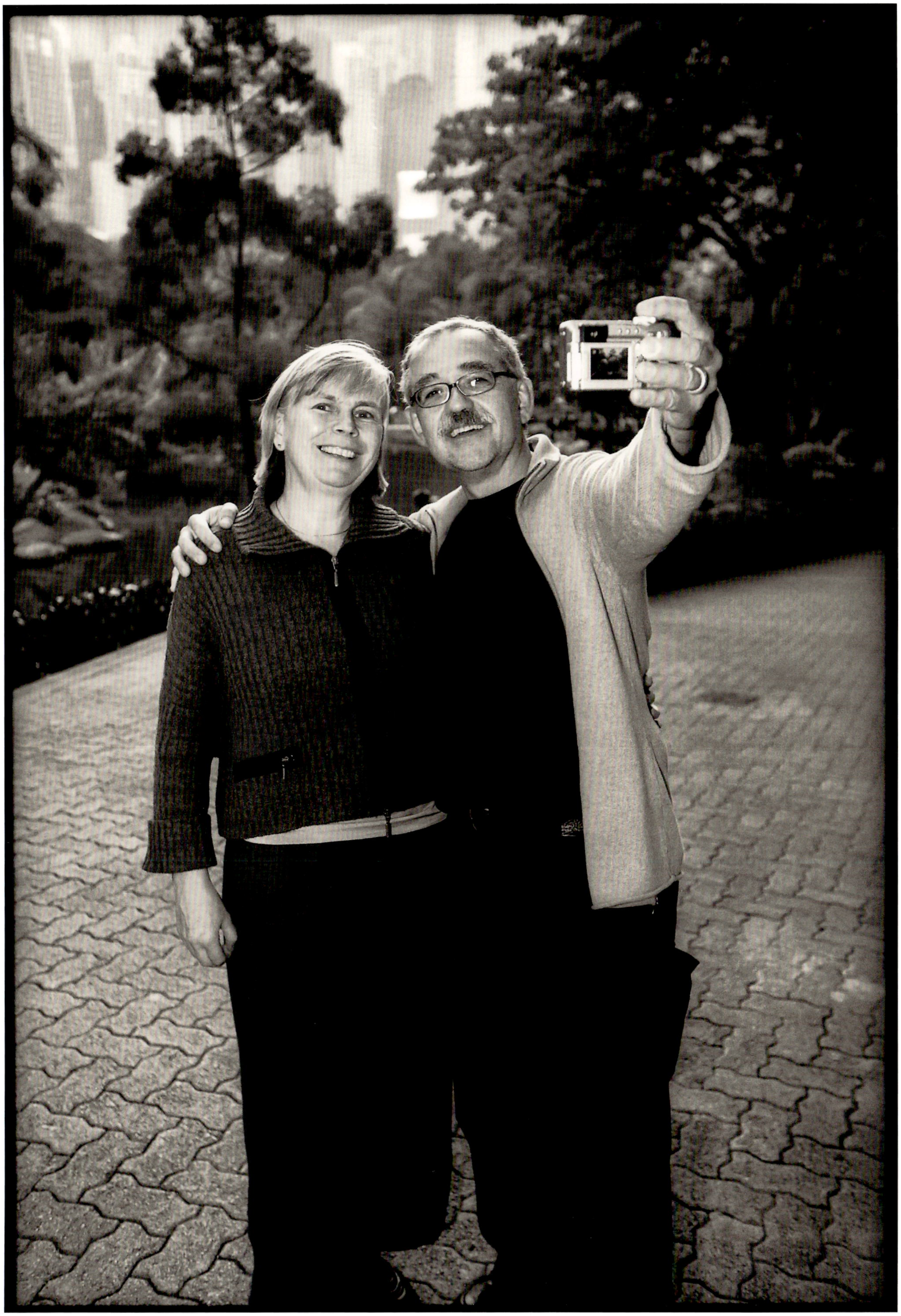

"Our first trip together was in 1989, when we went to Siena, Italy, where we made our first self-portrait at the famous Piazza del Campo. From then on, we did it again and again: in Greece, in the USA, in Thailand, and in many other countries and, of course, at home in Switzerland. It documents not only the places we've been, but also ourselves – seeing how we slowly get older – but happy as ever together."

"Beauty, brains, business, pleasure, sharing and love –
never a dull moment in our Hong Kong."

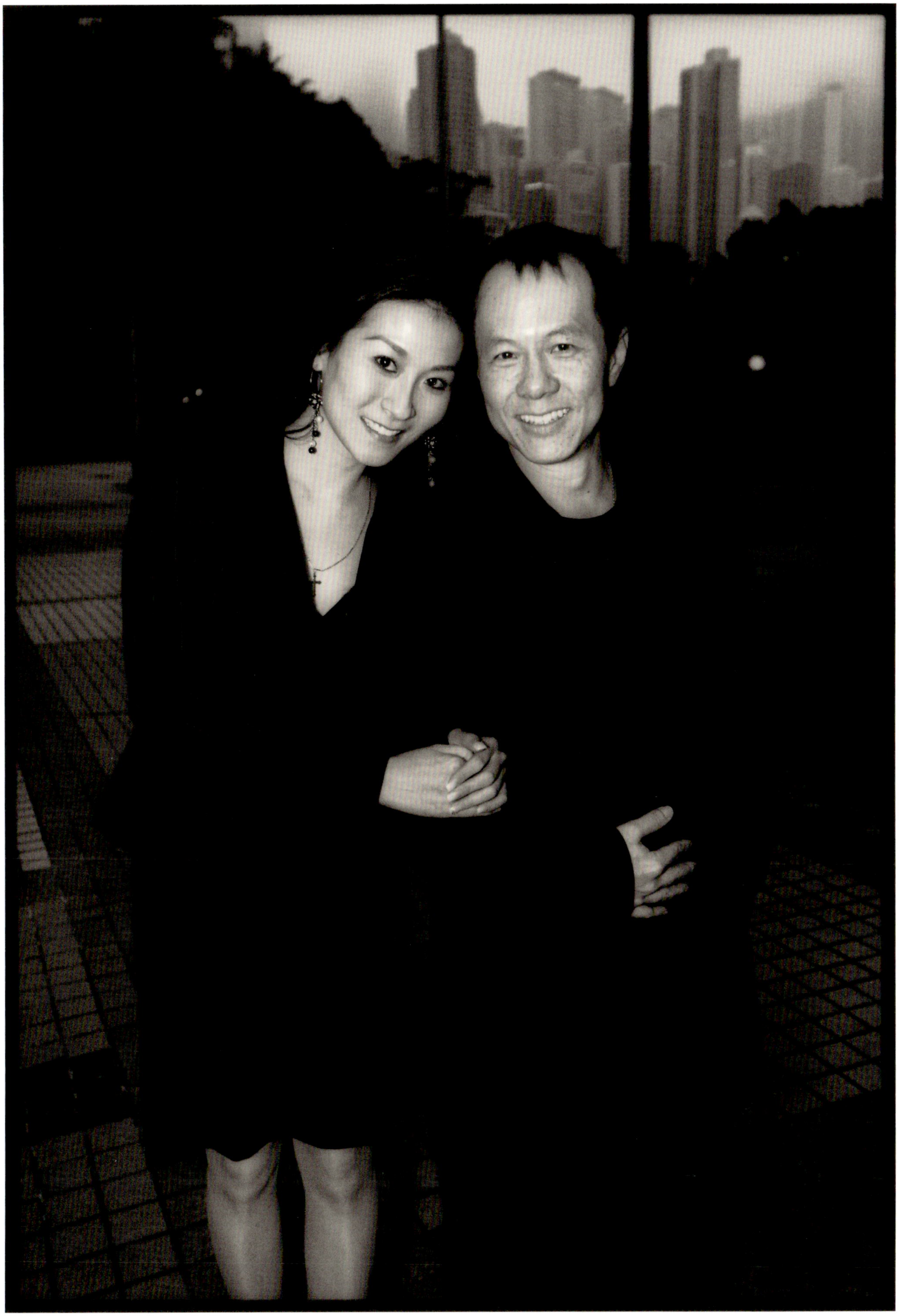

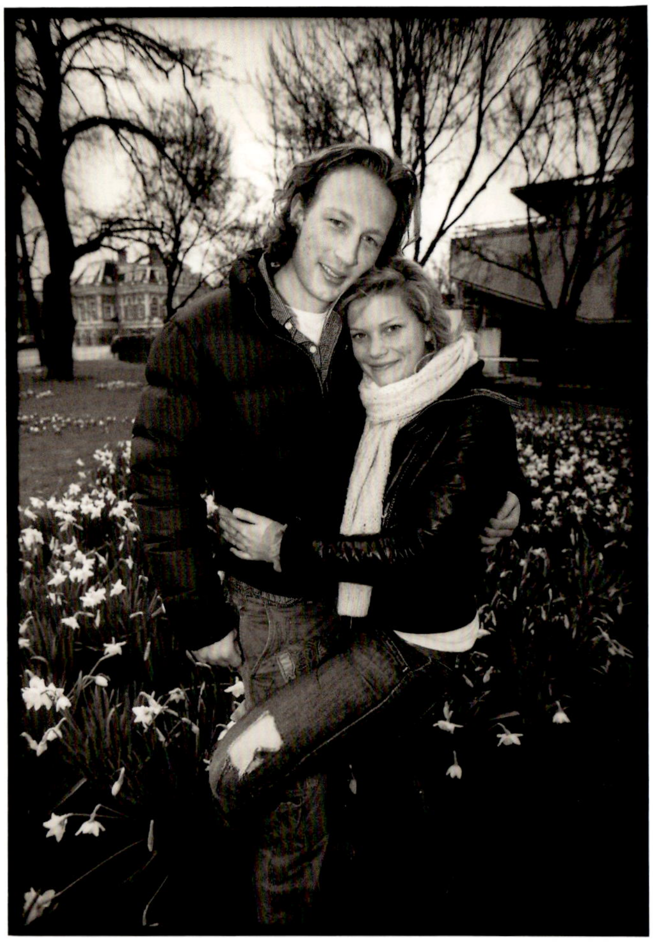

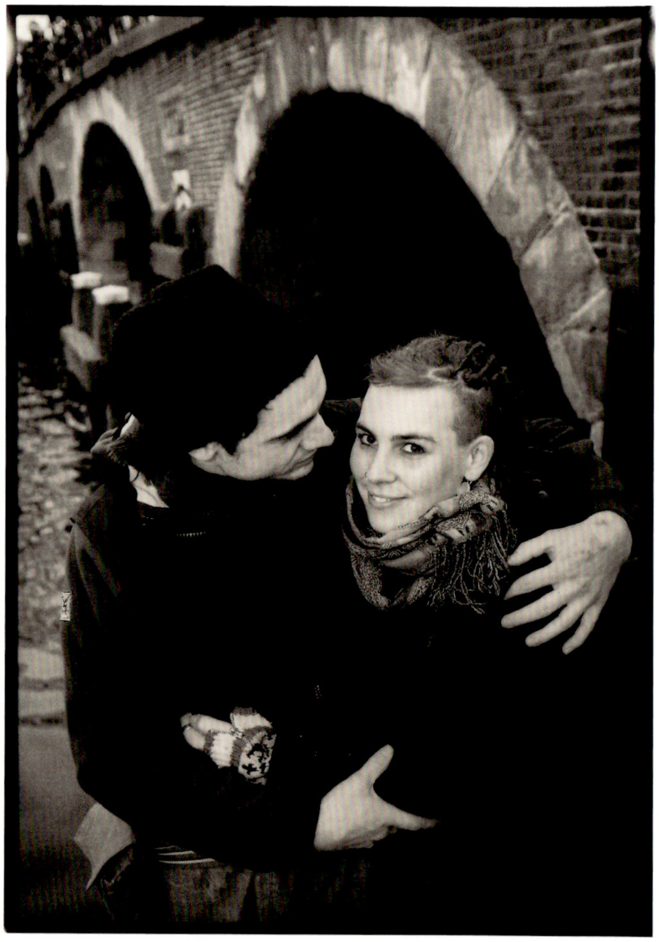

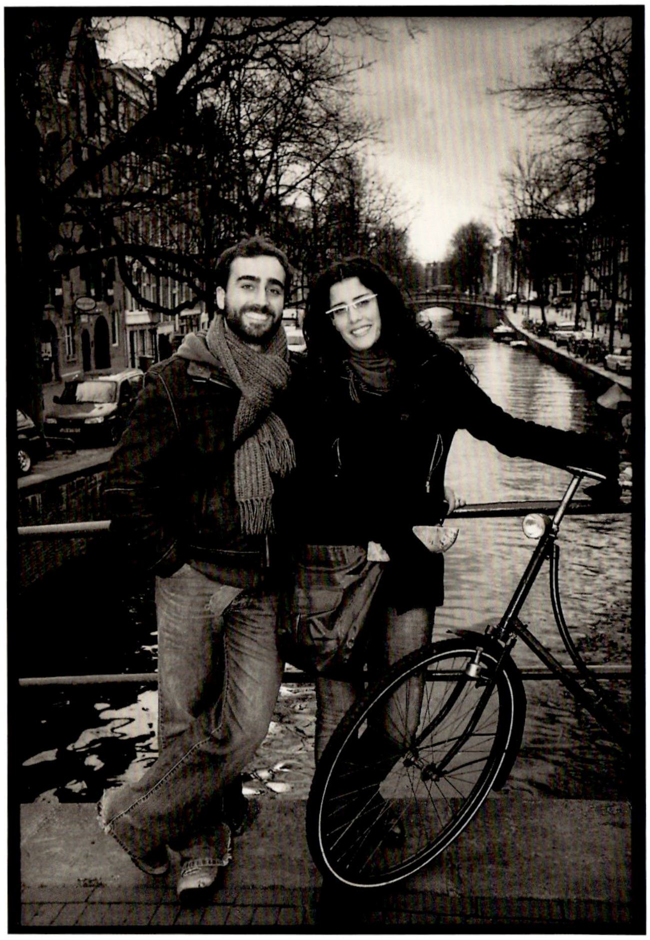

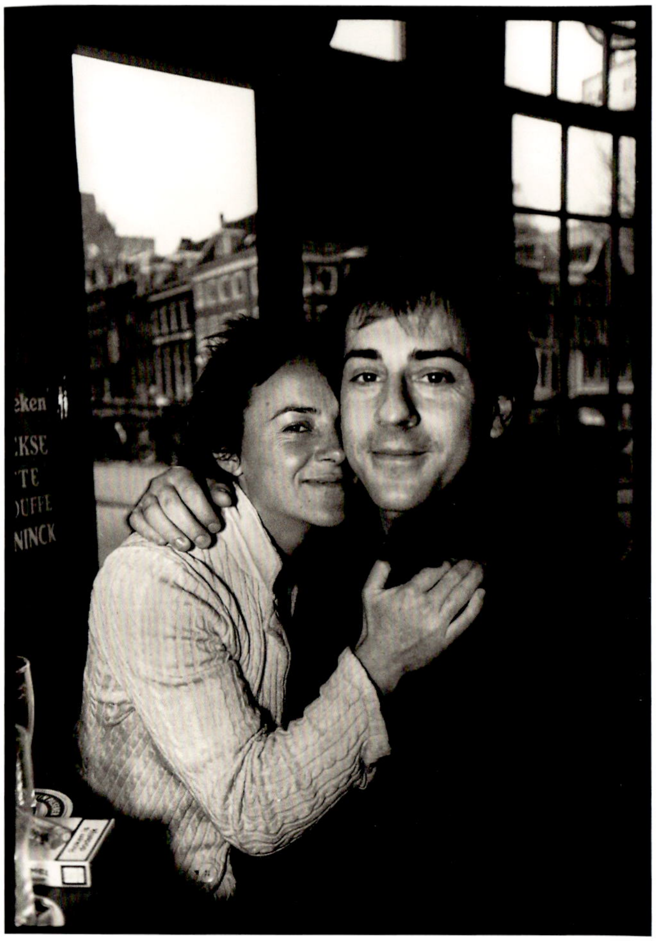

LOCATION

Amsterdam

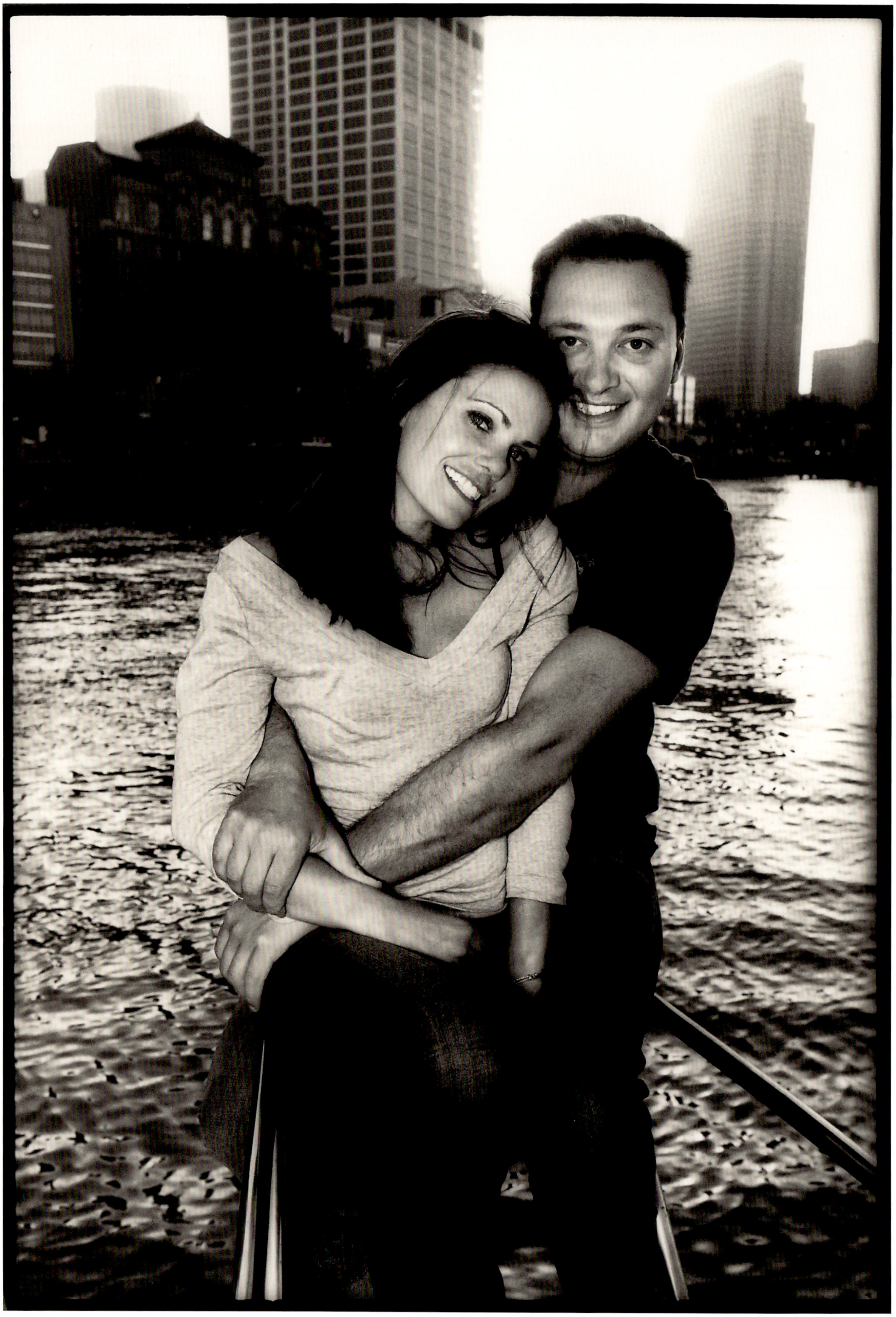

"Fools for love – we met on April Fool's Day"

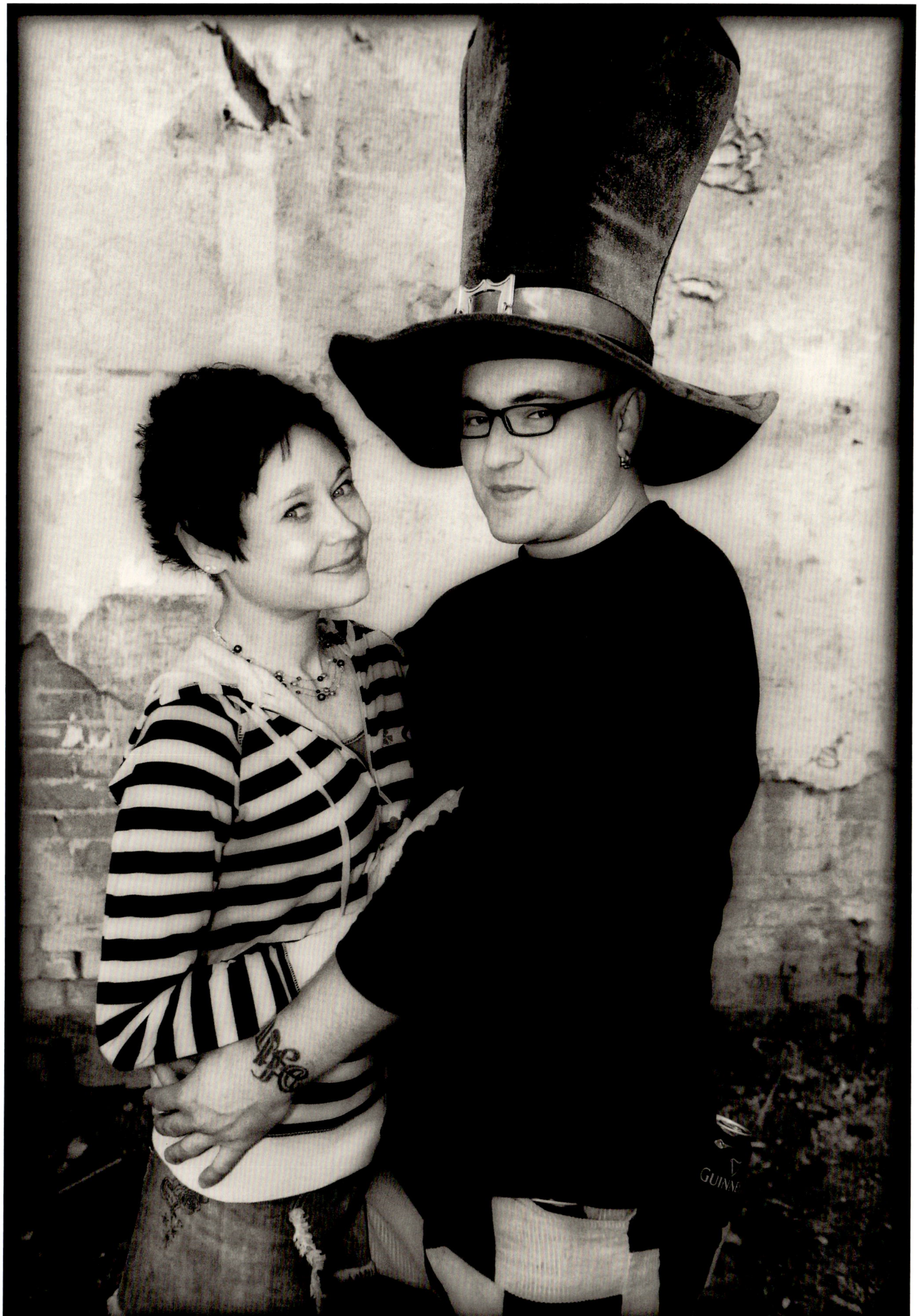

"When Leprechauns dance with Ladybugs, phantasmagorical happens!"

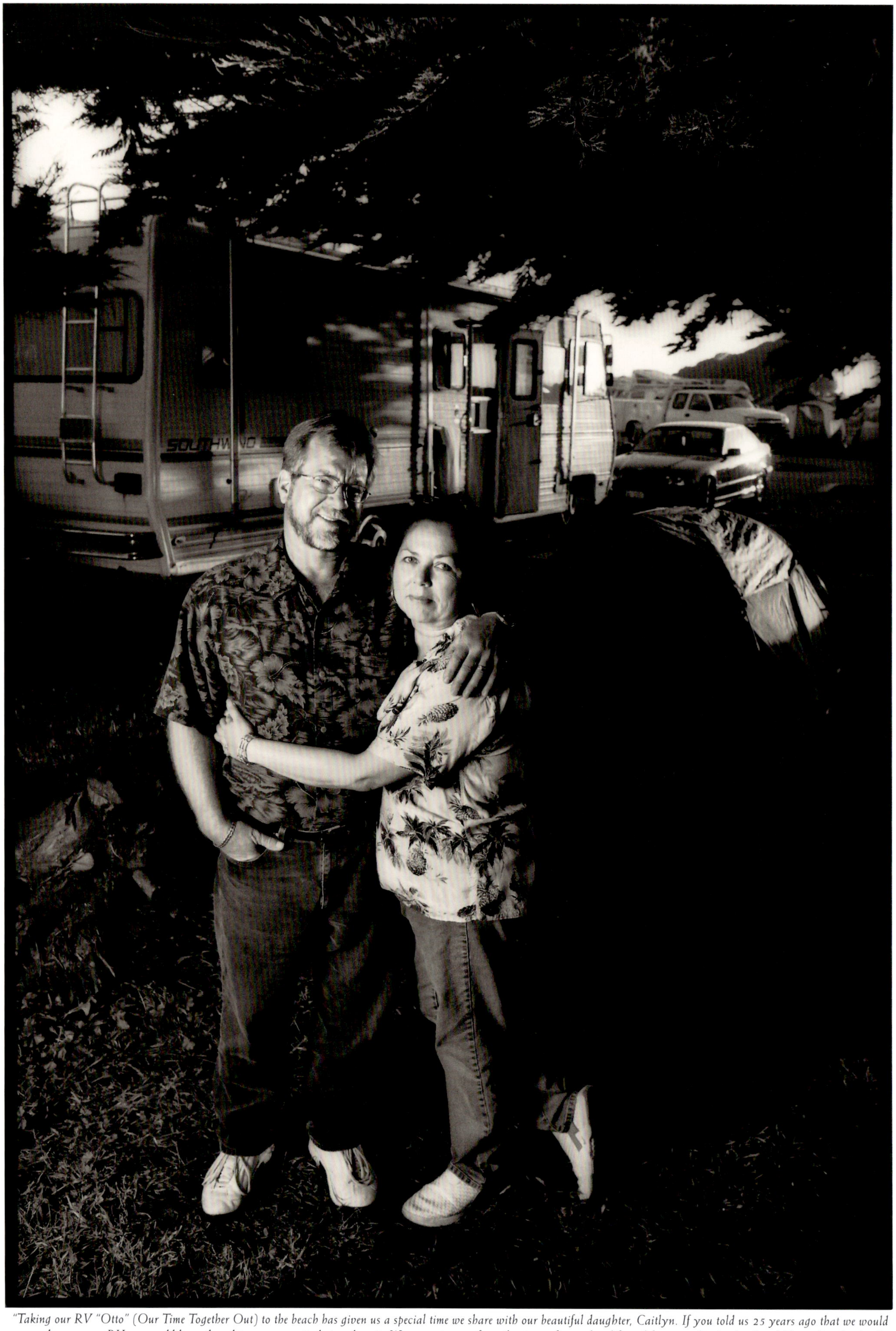

"Taking our RV "Otto" (Our Time Together Out) to the beach has given us a special time we share with our beautiful daughter, Caitlyn. If you told us 25 years ago that we would one day own an RV, we would have thought you were nuts, but we love it. We can get away from the stress of everyday life and focus on the simple gifts of life, and each other."

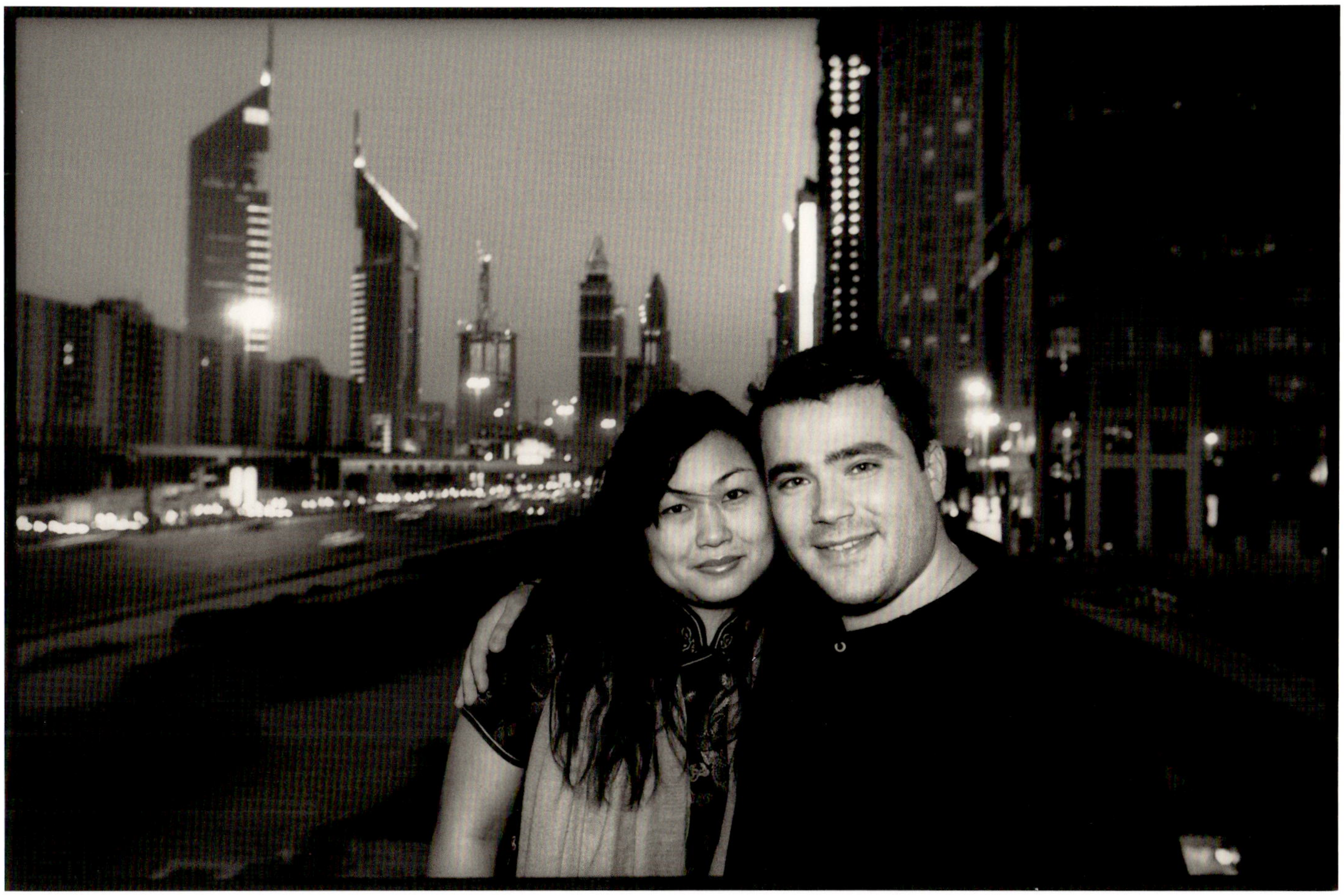

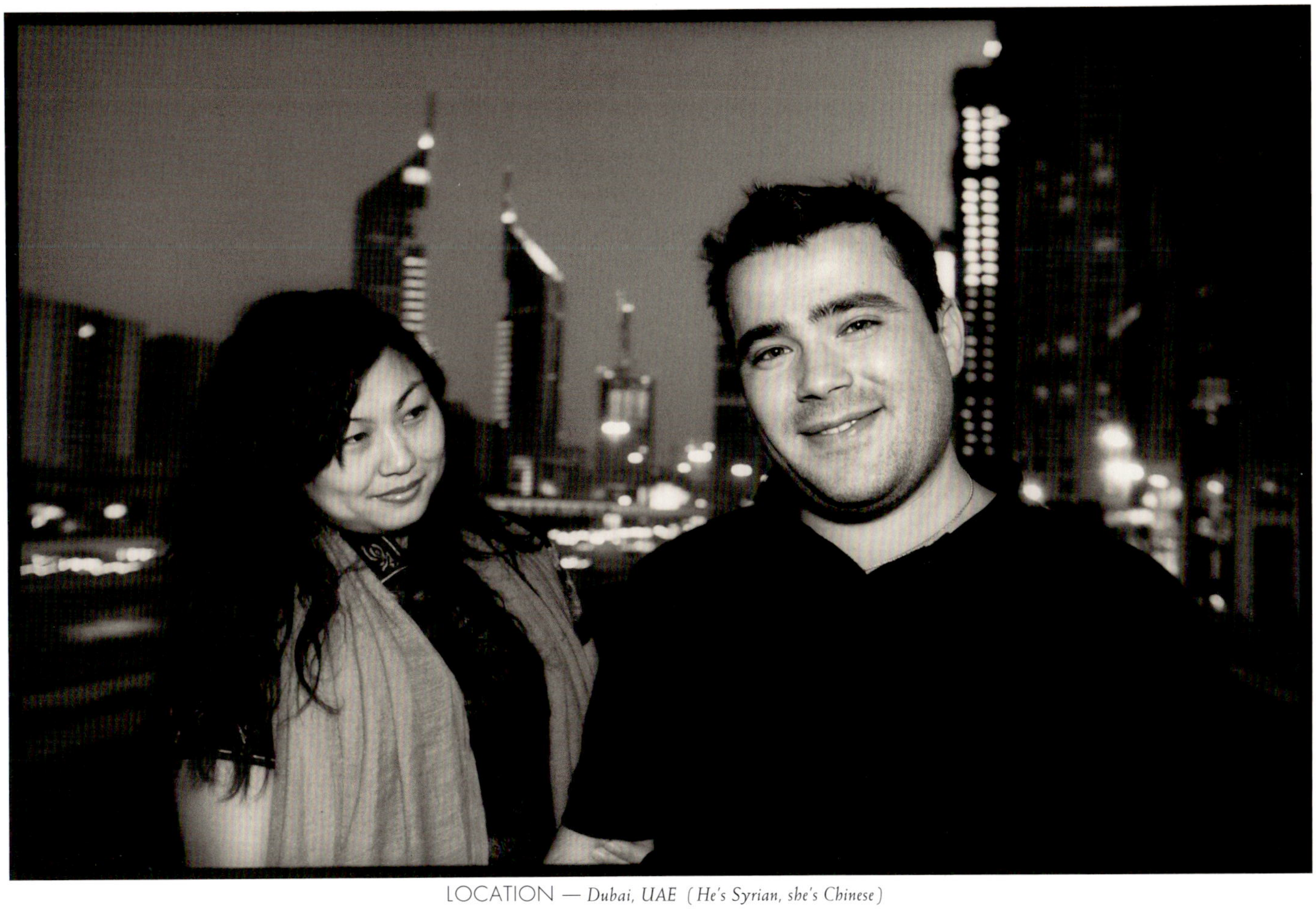

LOCATION — *Dubai, UAE* (*He's Syrian, she's Chinese*)

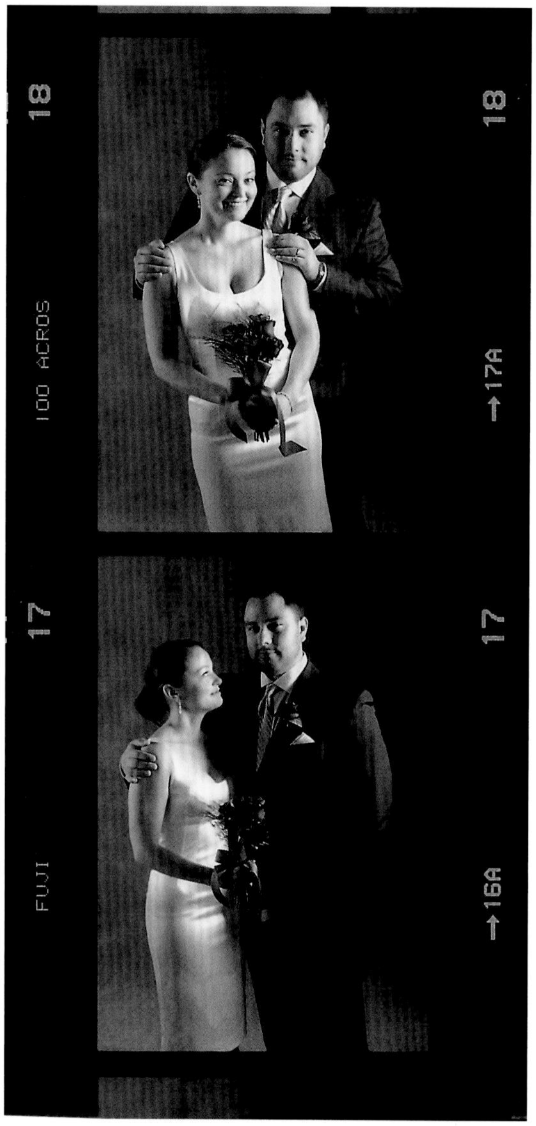

"We didn't want anything to distract us from each other, so we opted for a simple City Hall wedding, with only our parents in attendance."

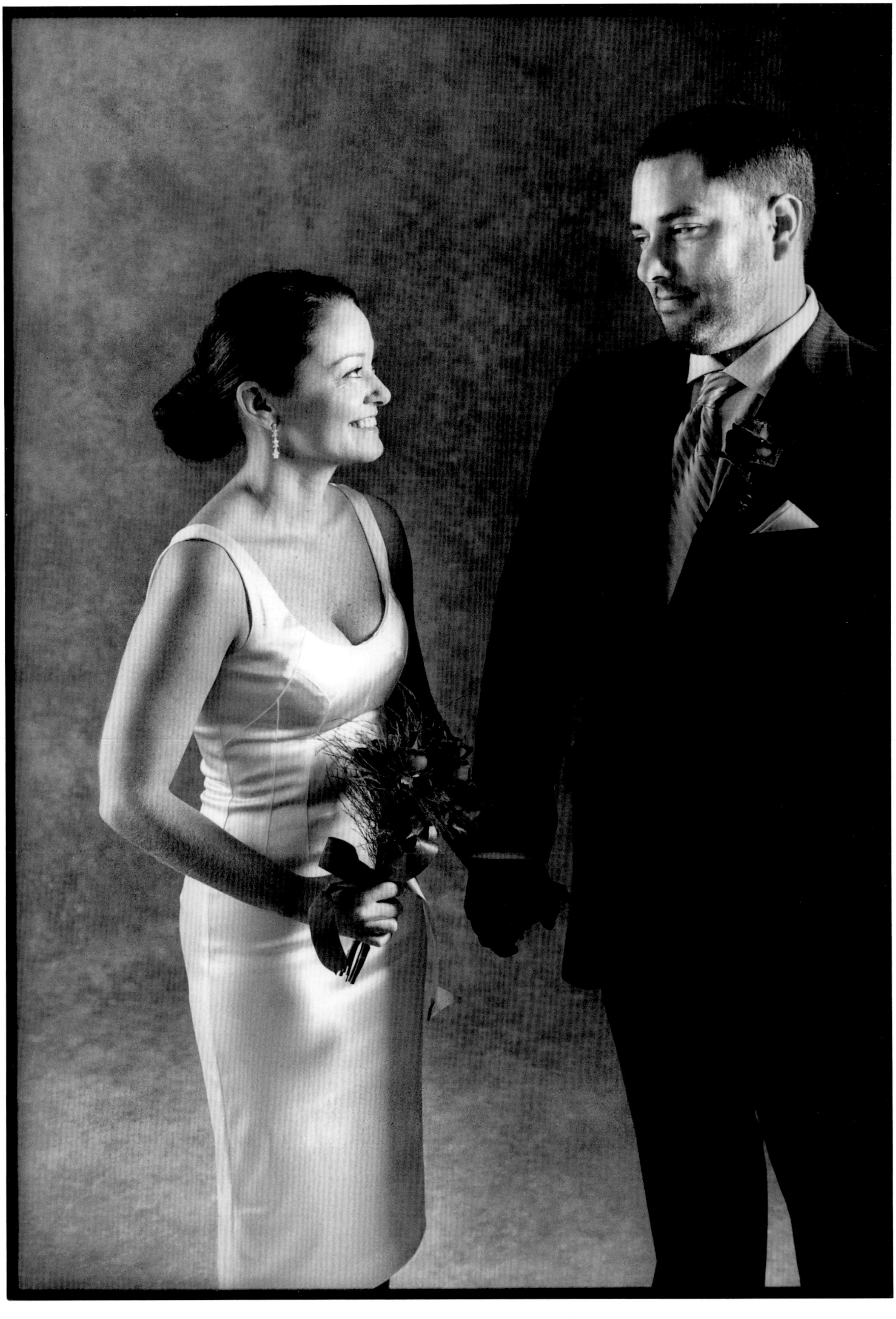

LOCATION

A Berkeley Yoga Studio

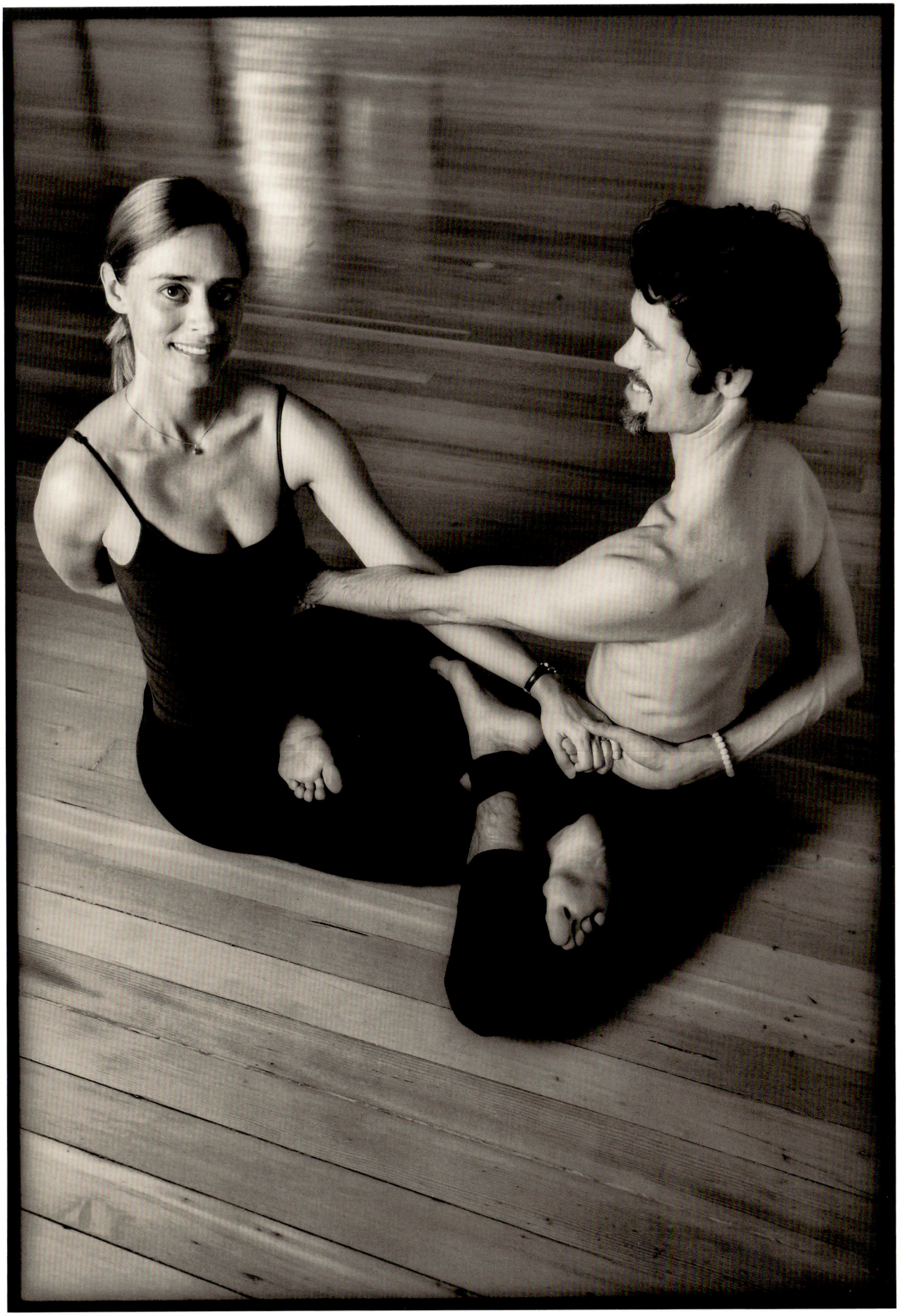

"Let's do the Twist..."

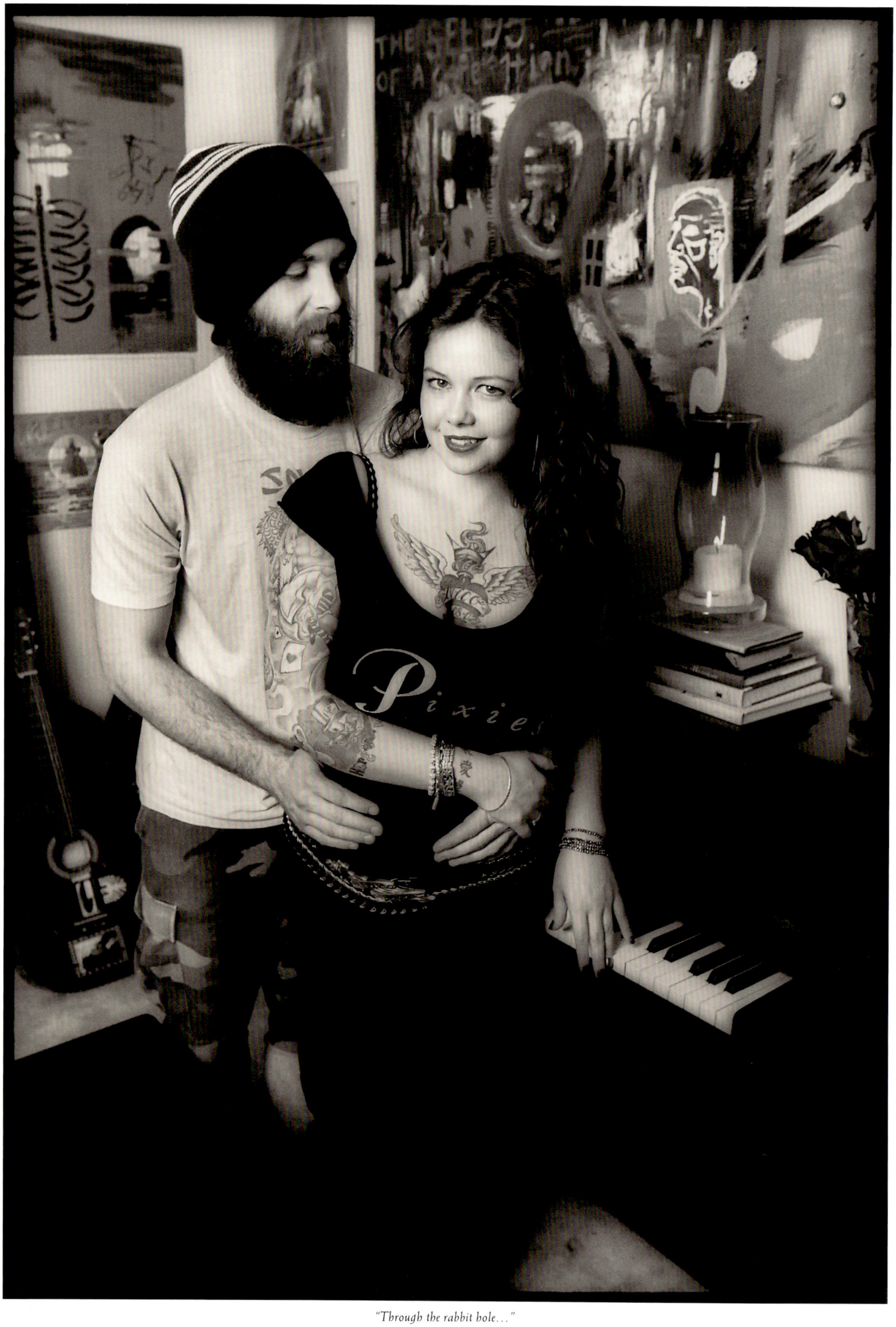

"Through the rabbit hole..."

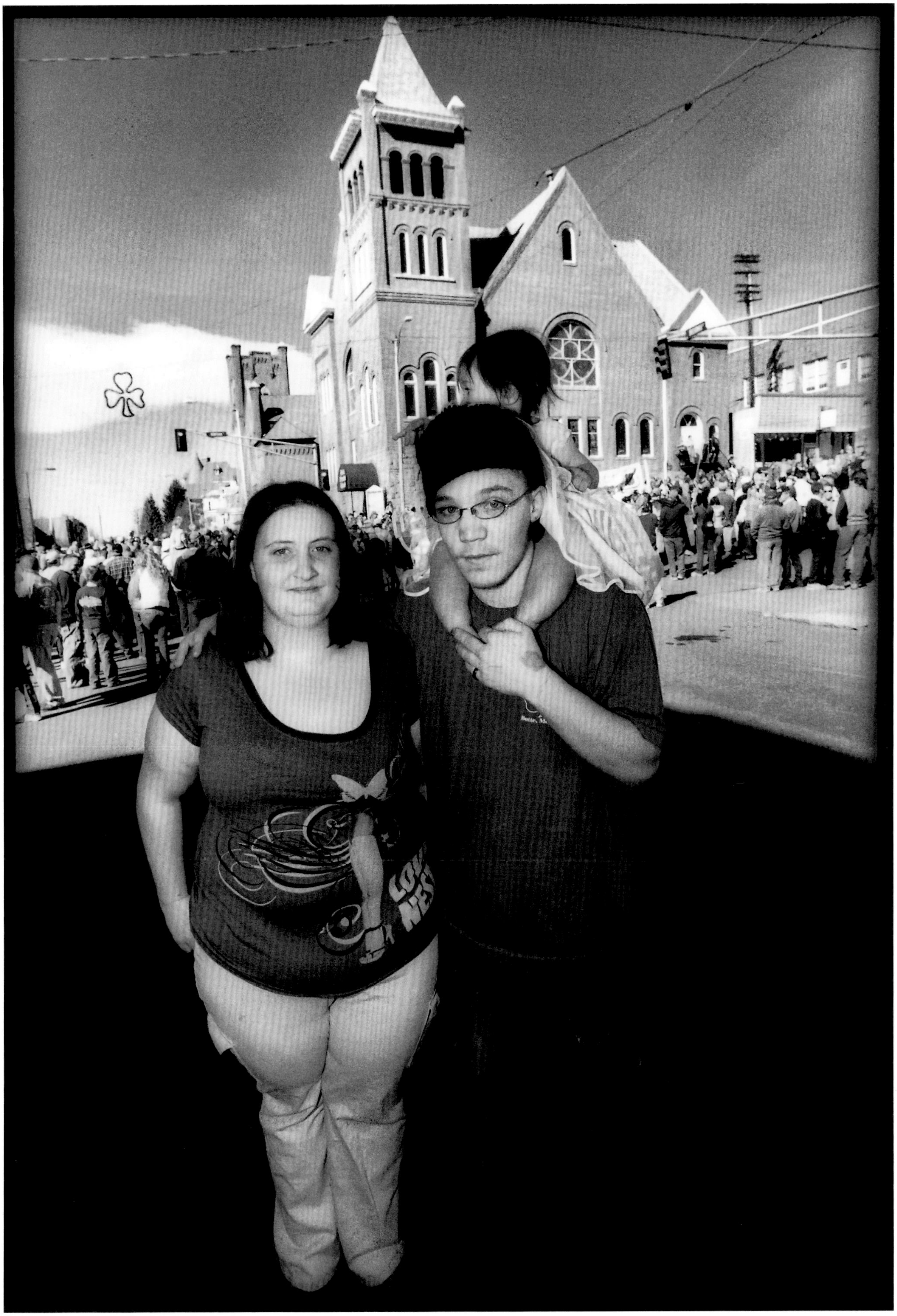

"A beginning to a lifelong journey."

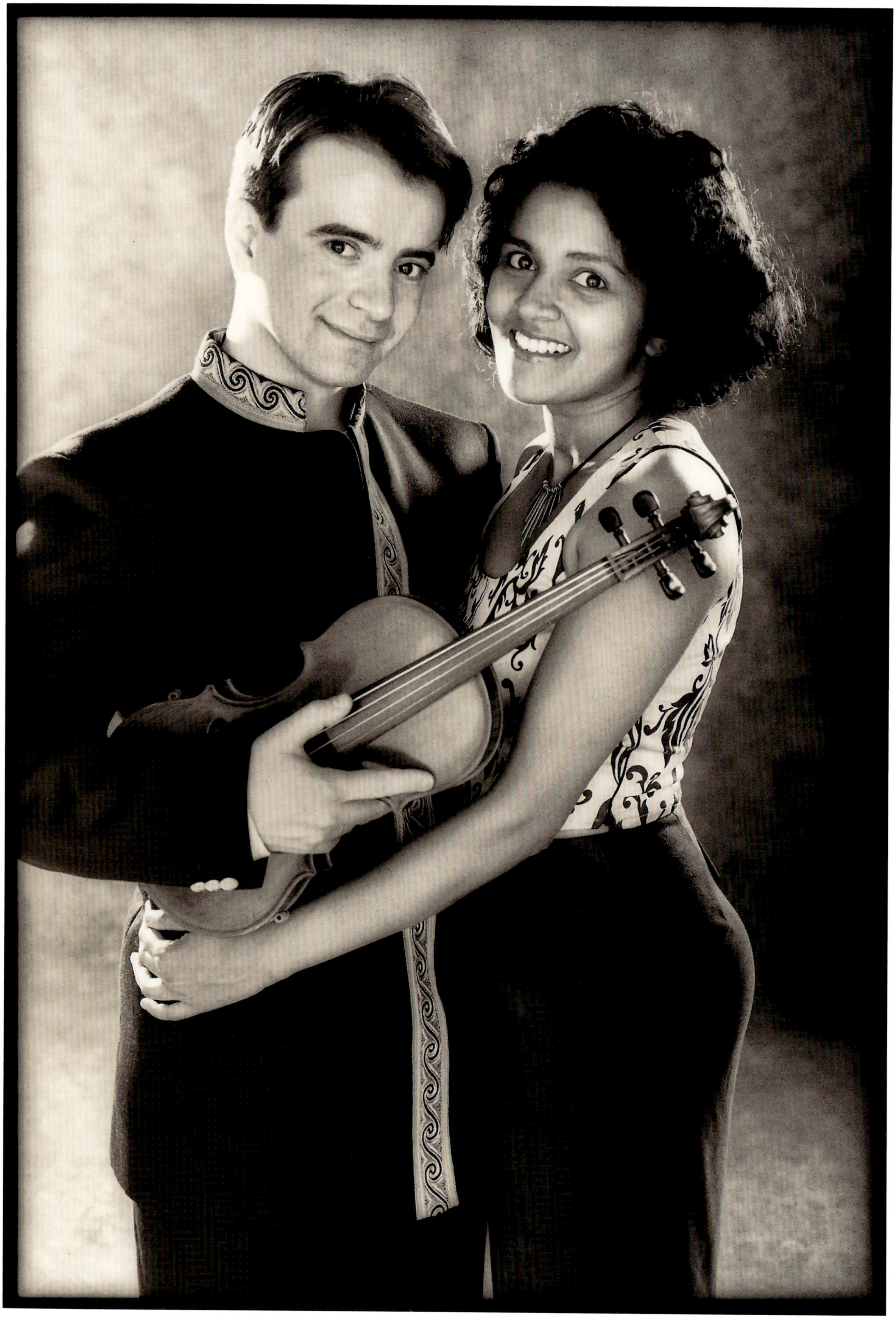

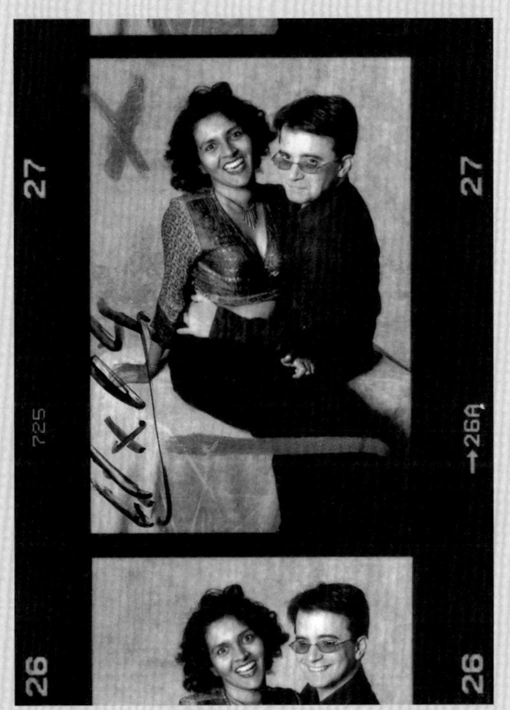

"The Marriage of Words and Music."

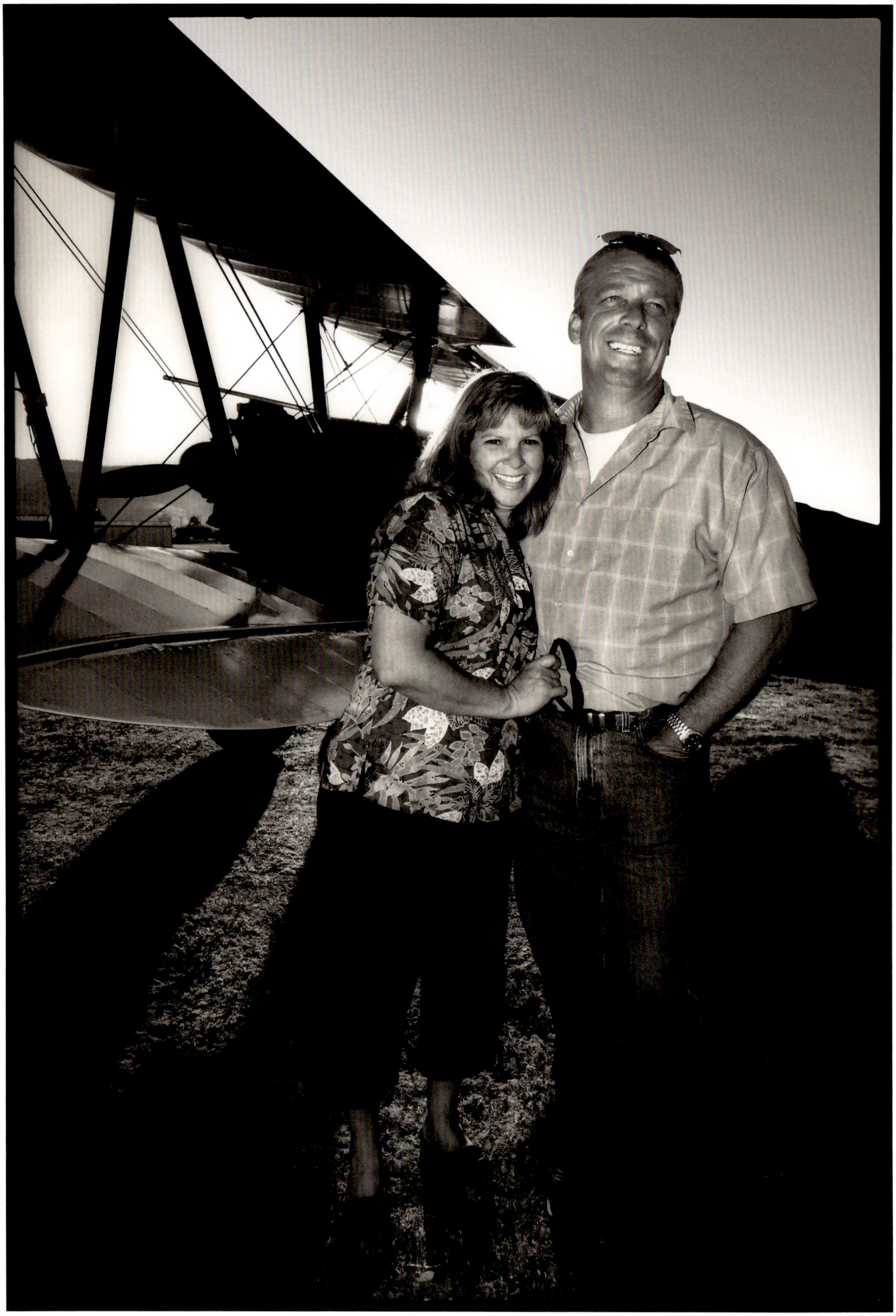

"Fully and richly, completely and absolutely – and fly as much as possible."

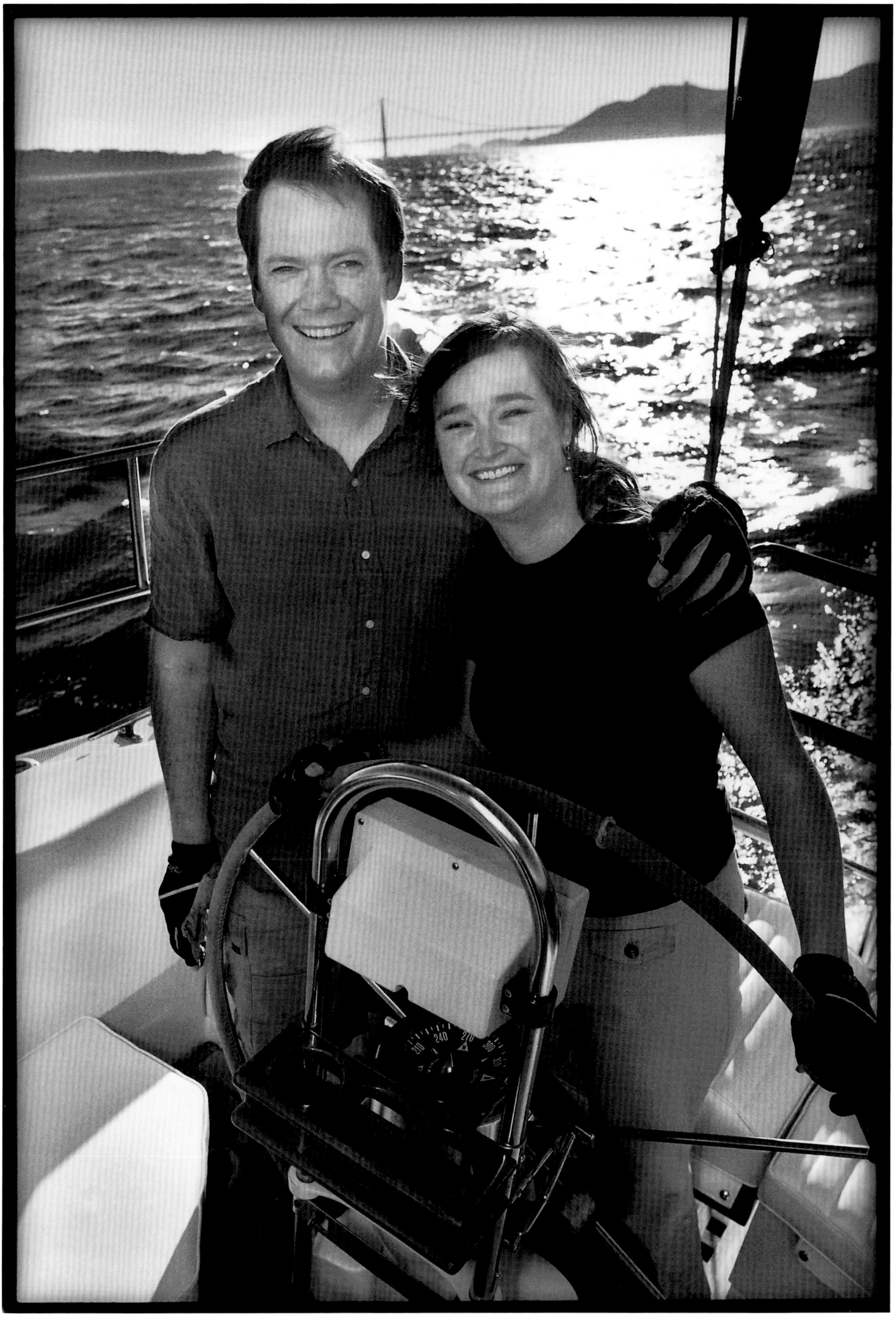

"Sailing taught us everything we needed to know about love: work hard, communicate and have fun."

LOCATION

San Francisco

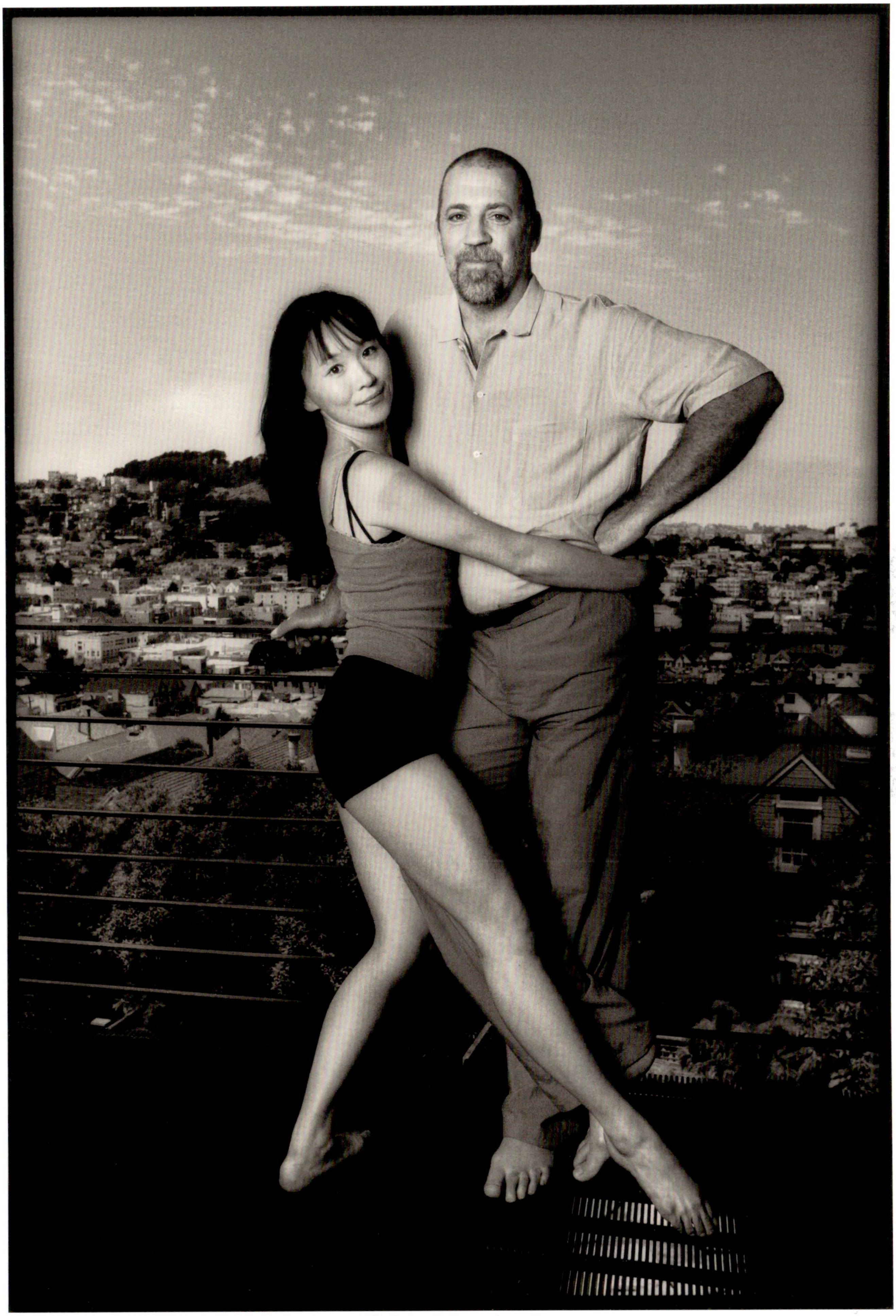

"The Dancer, the Doctor, plus one."

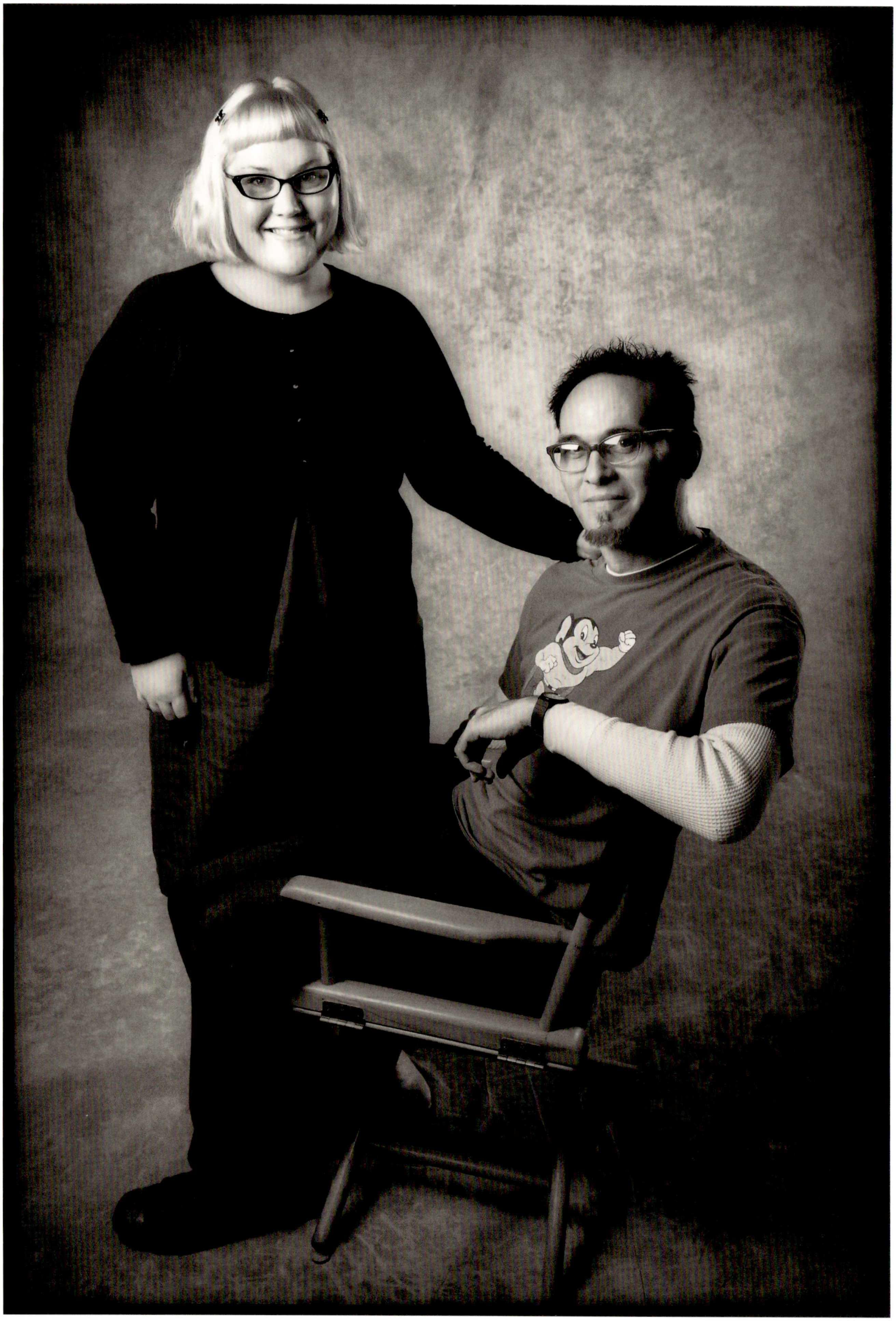

"For the love of food, for the love of life. Bakers in more ways than one."

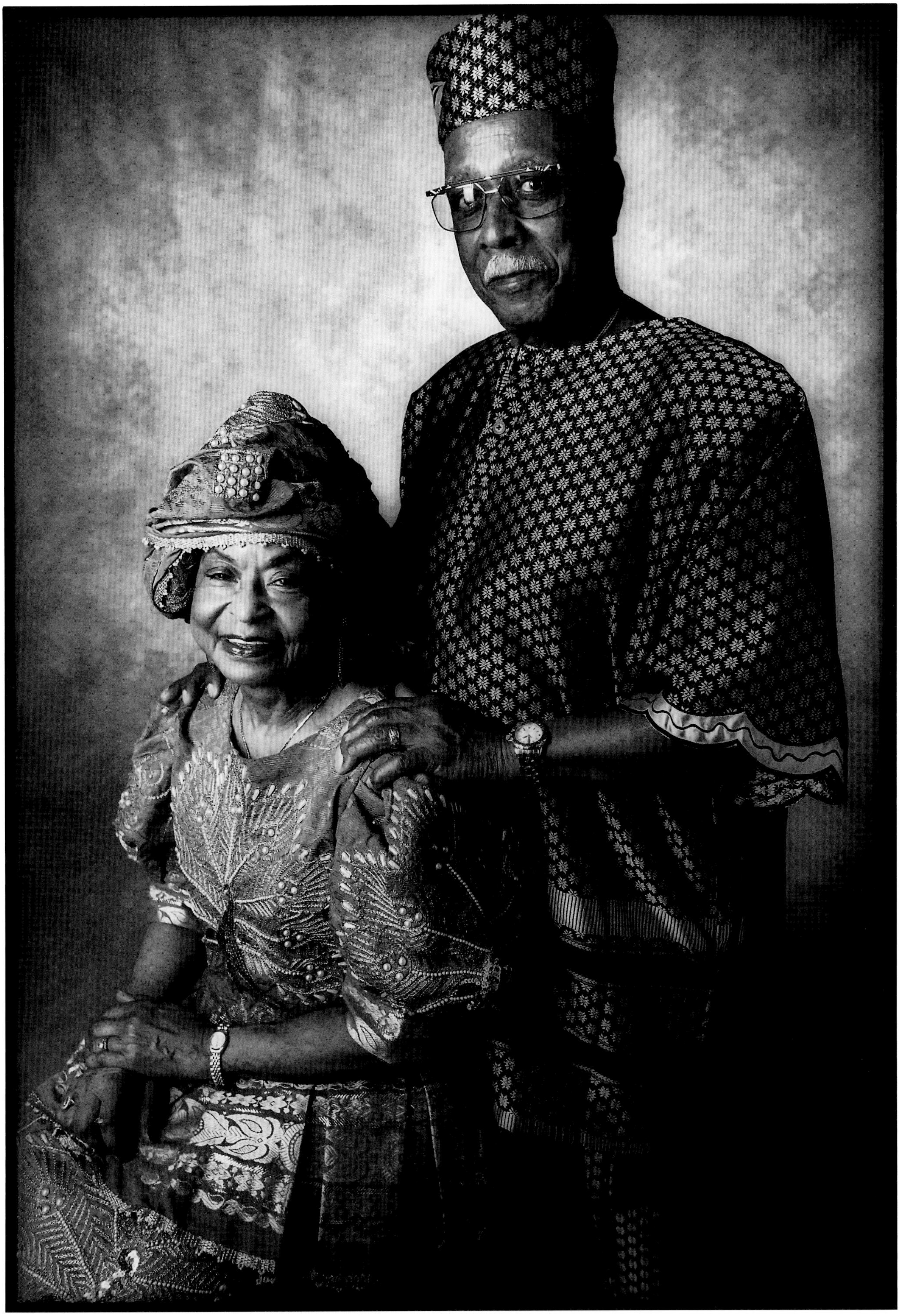

HE: *"It was love at first sight."* SHE: *"I had my doubts."*

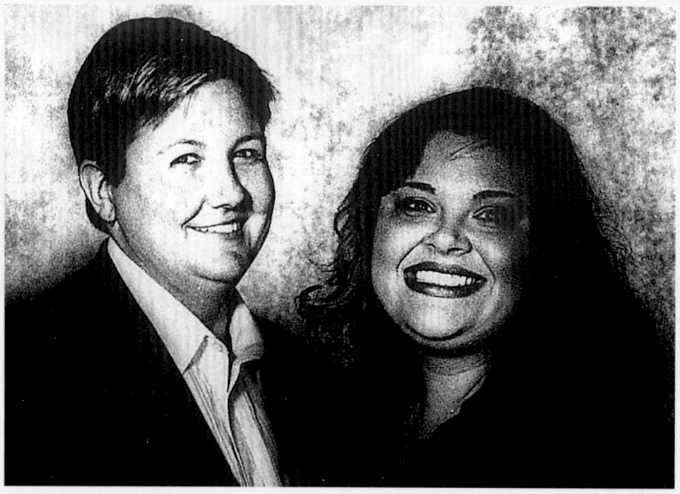

"How do I love thee, let me count the ways... Still counting after all these years!"

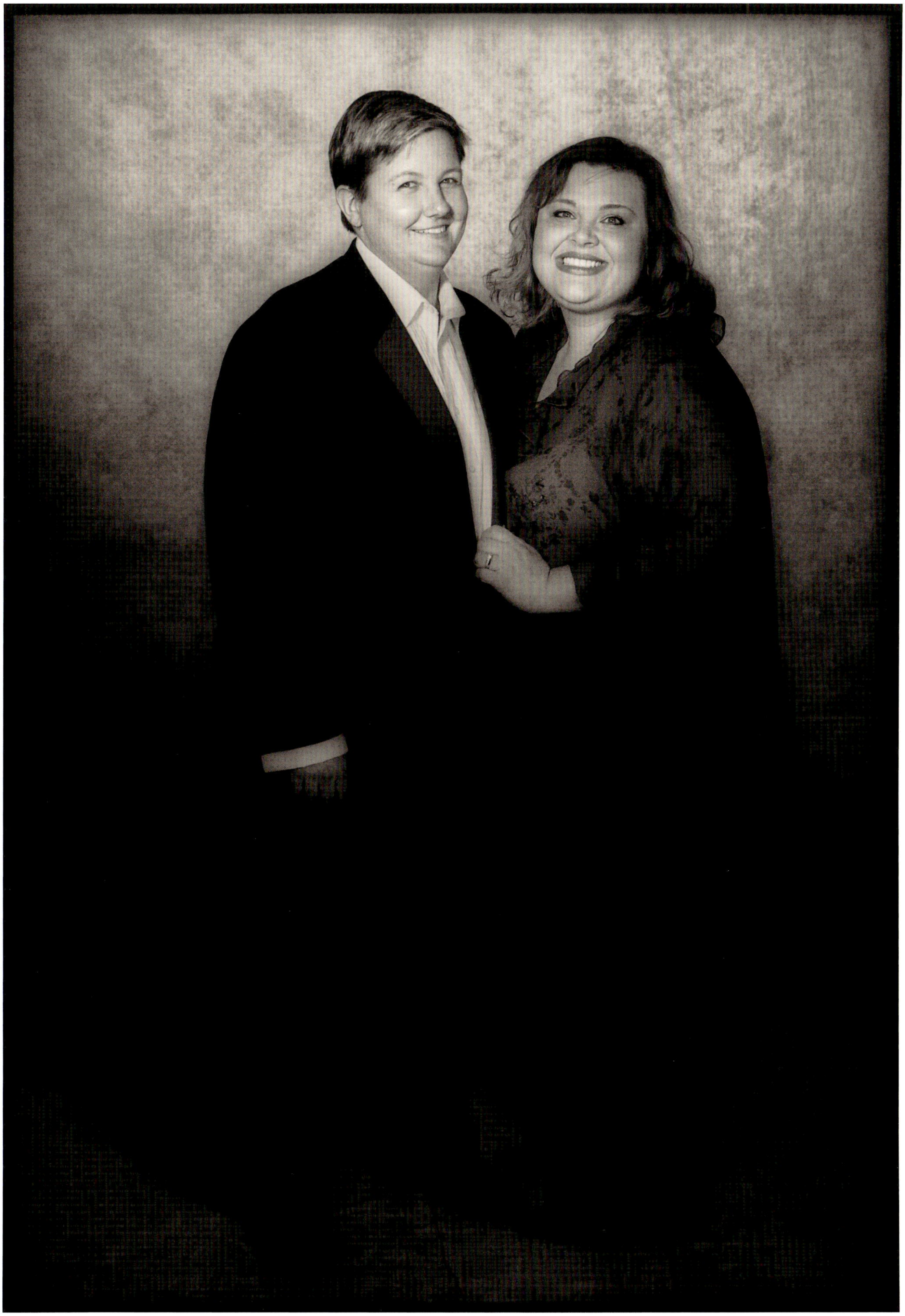

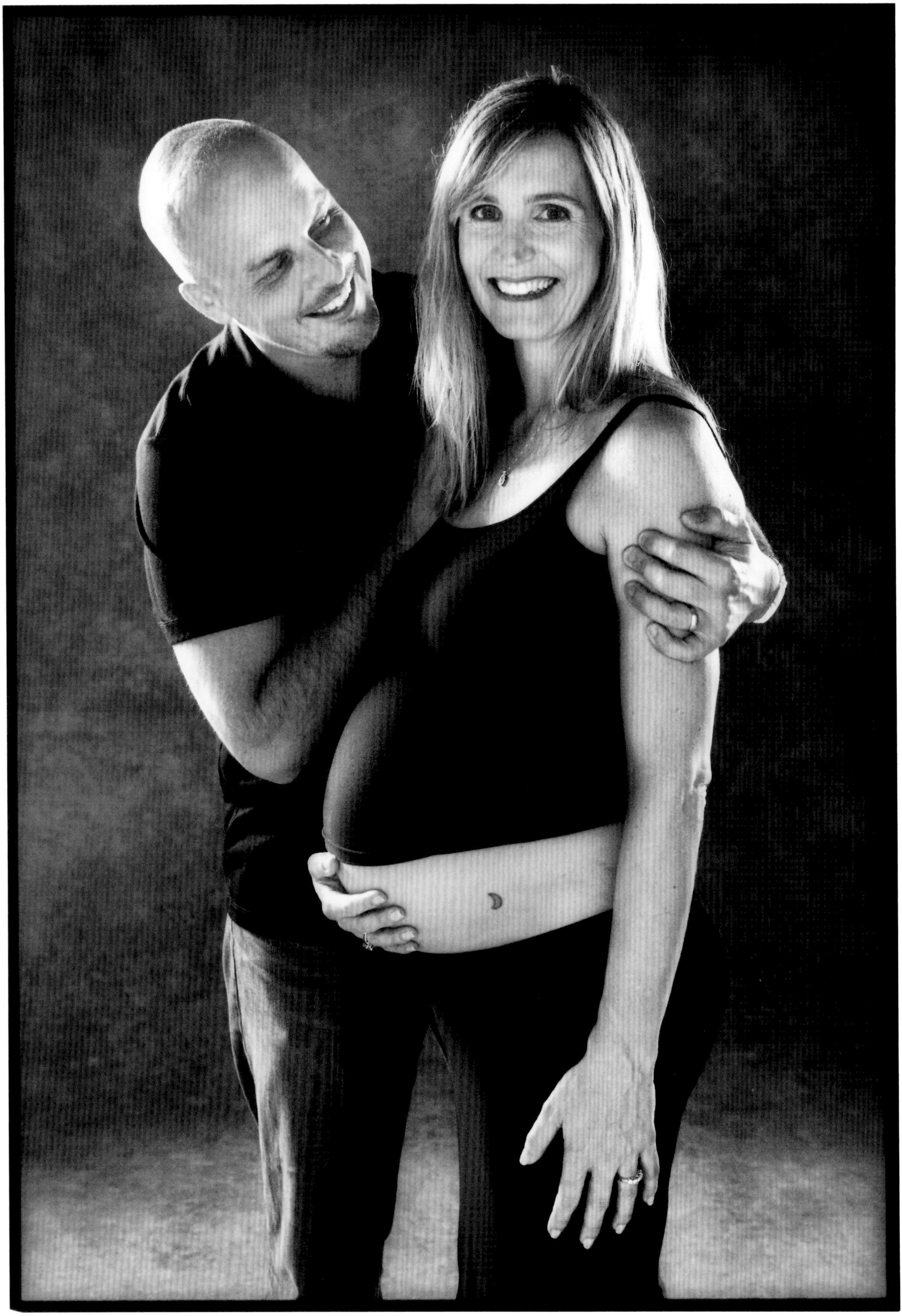

After a yearlong honeymoon that took them across twenty-three countries, on three continents, Joe and Veronica were ready to settle down.

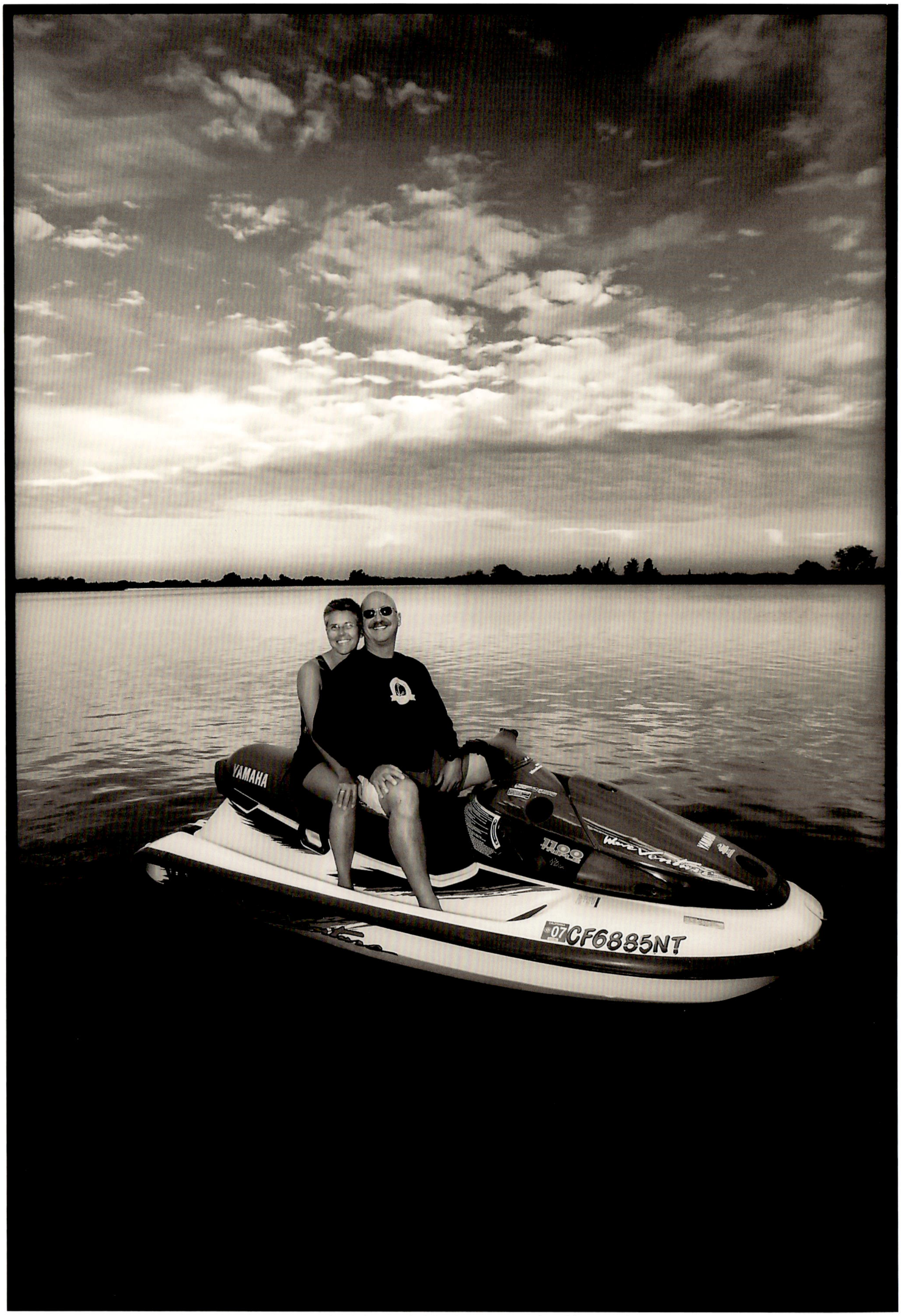

"Sharing together the beauty which has been given to us, for a lifetime together."

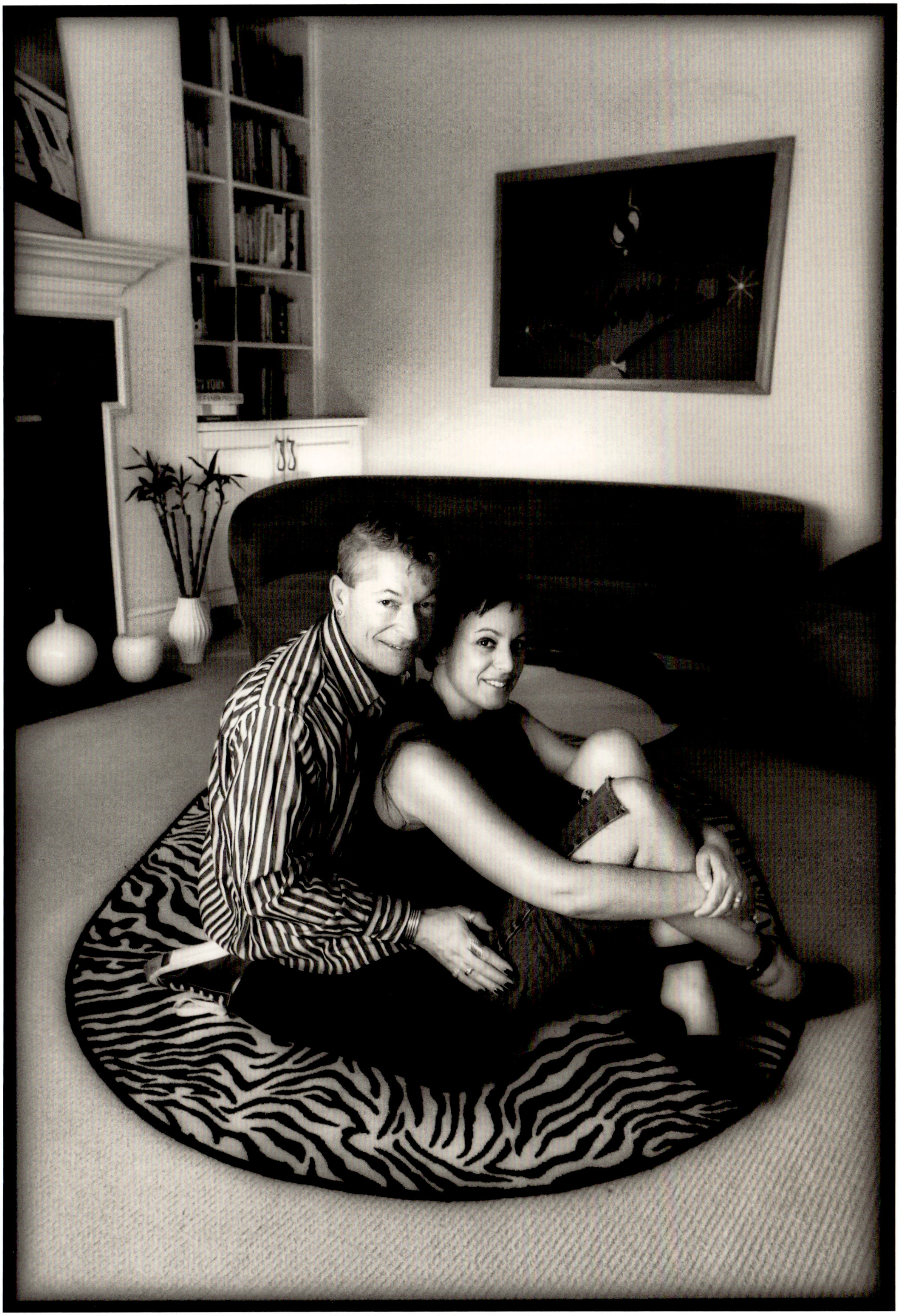

"Some nights we love to sit on the floor and pretend we're tobogganing."

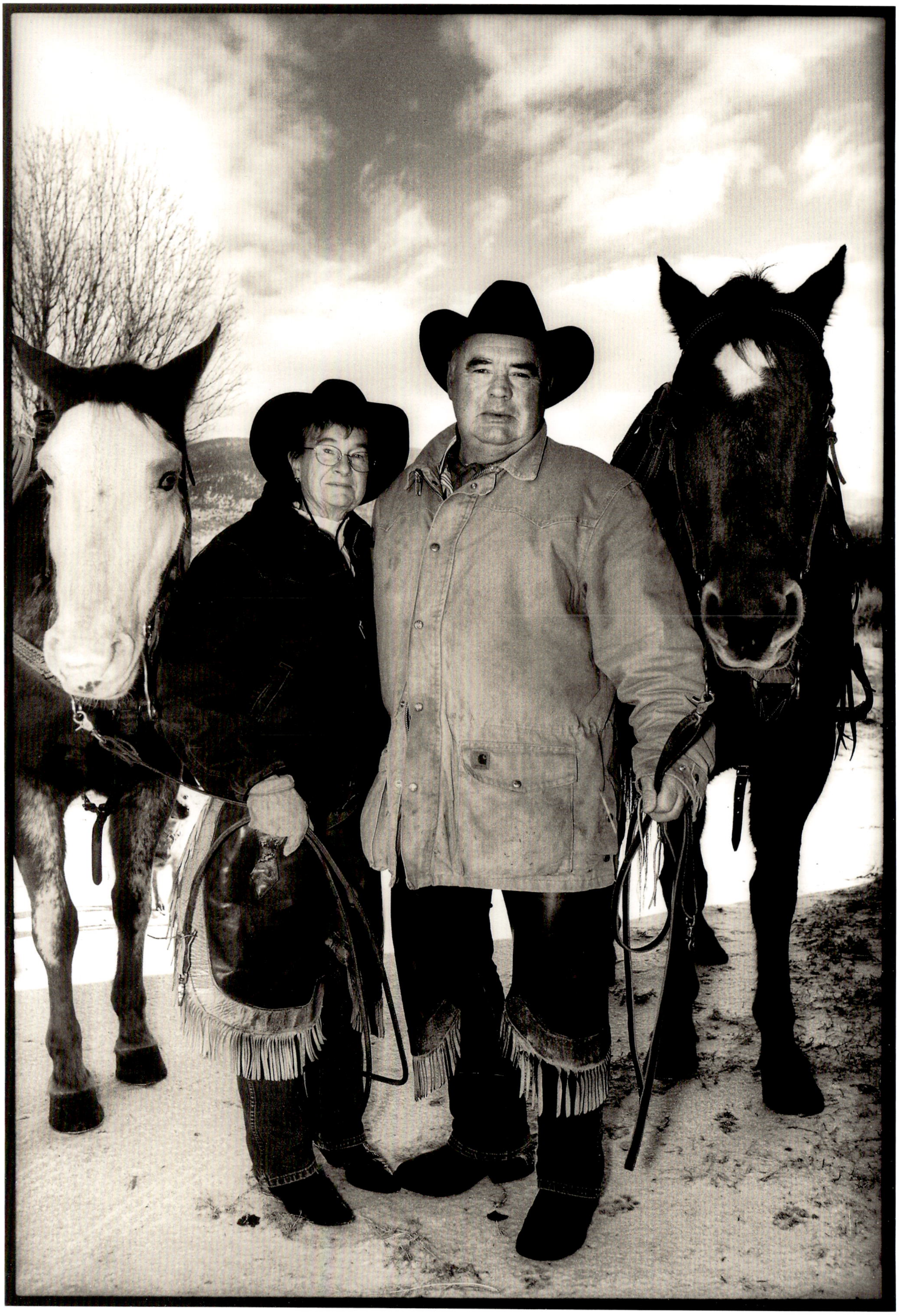

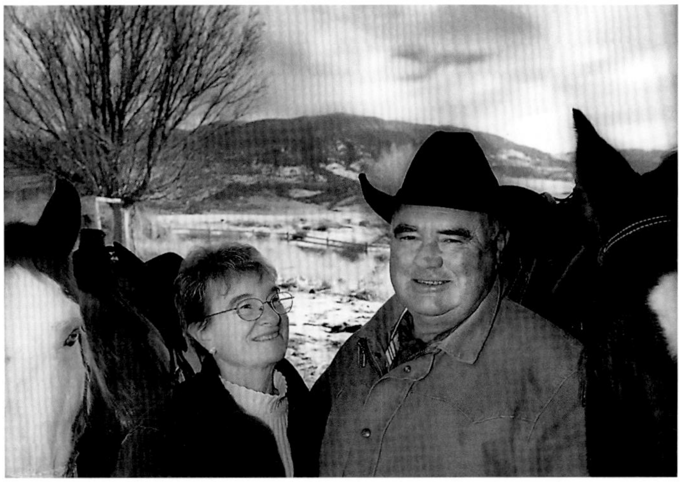

"Laughing, riding, loving – 40 years of ranching!"

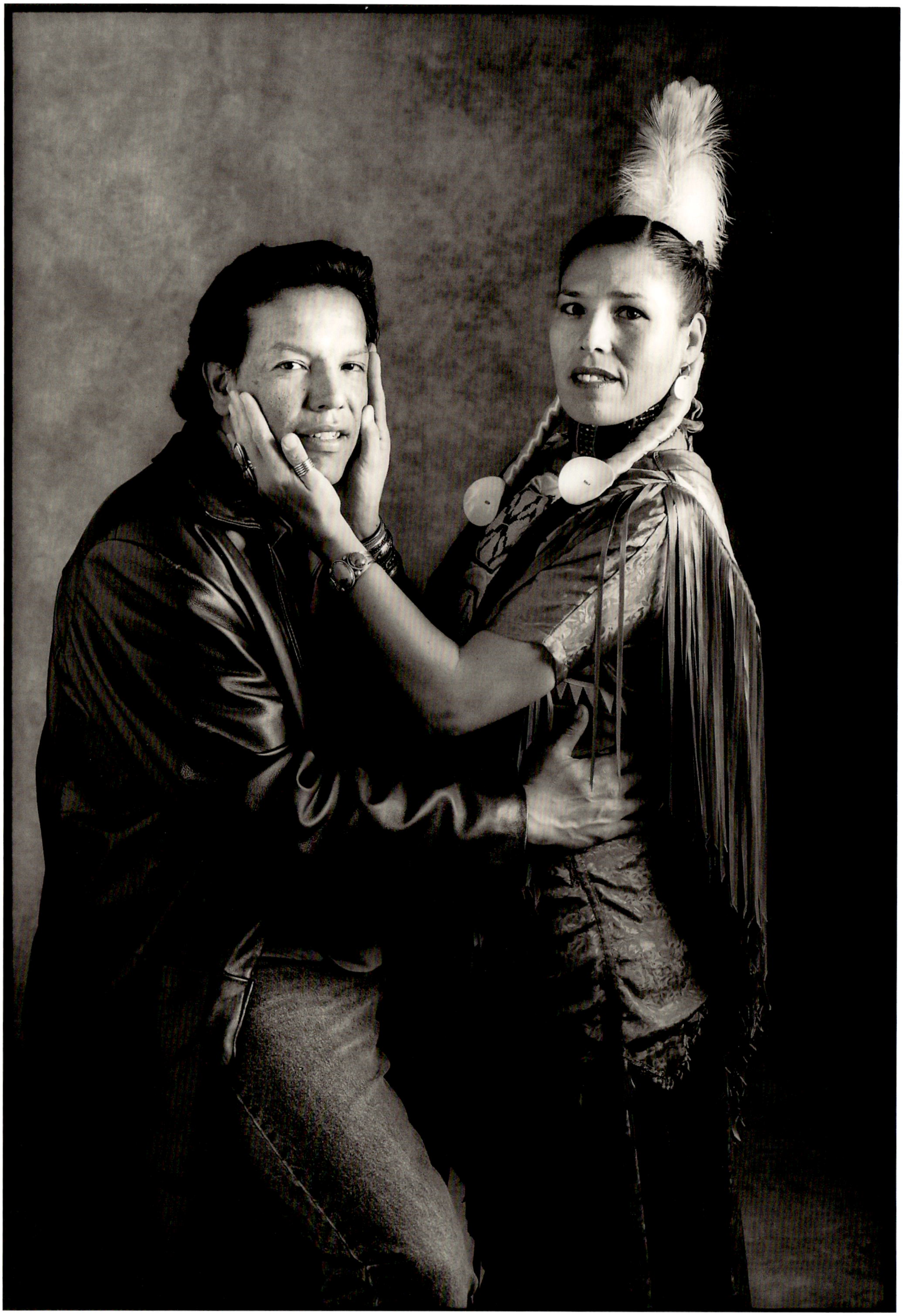

"Mi bigna kin a mitha wichu ki." (*"My husband and my wife."* Lacota Sioux)

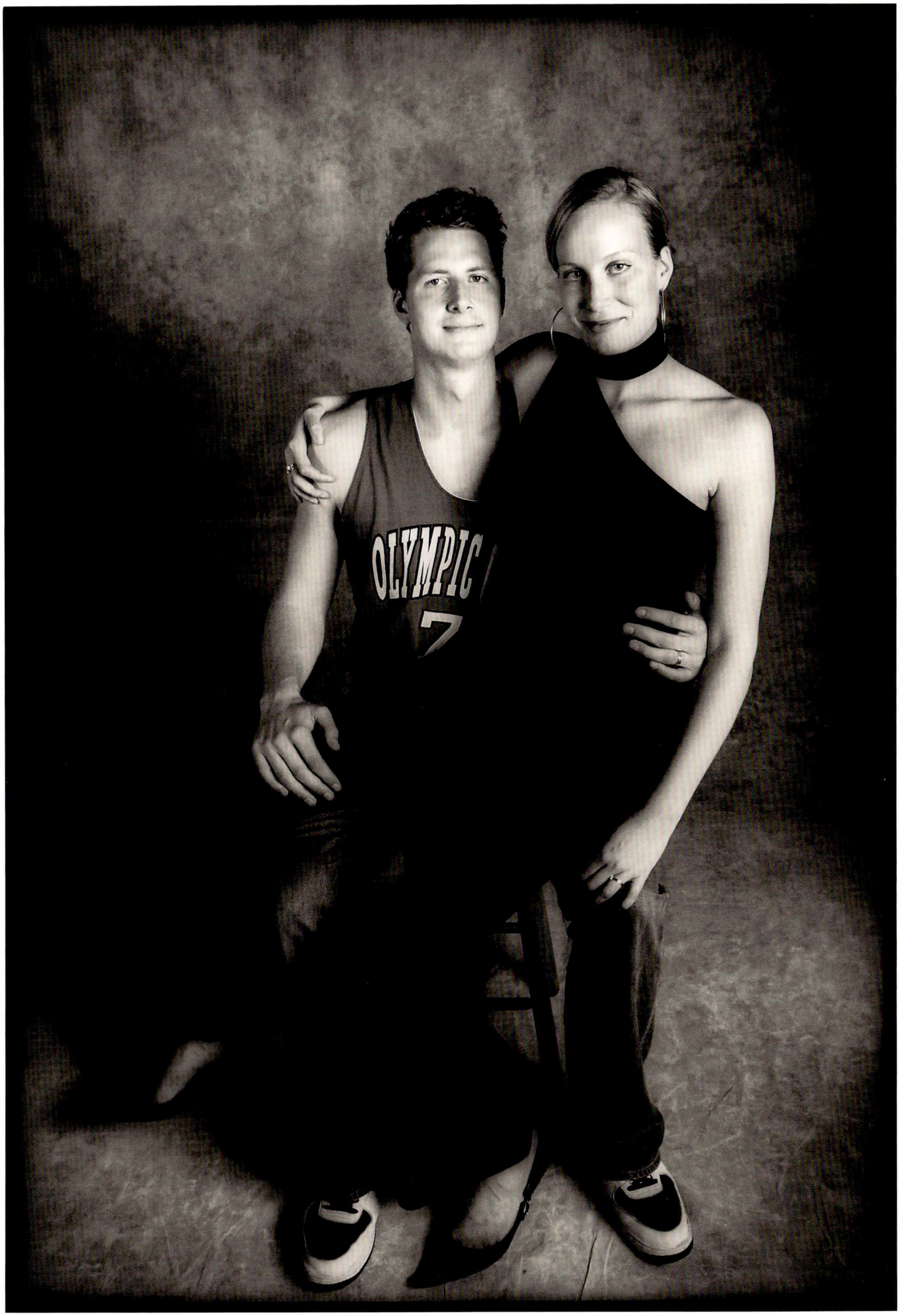

SHE: 6' tall – *"I needed a guy I could wear heels with."* HE: 6'7" tall – *"I needed a girl I didn't have to bend over to kiss."*

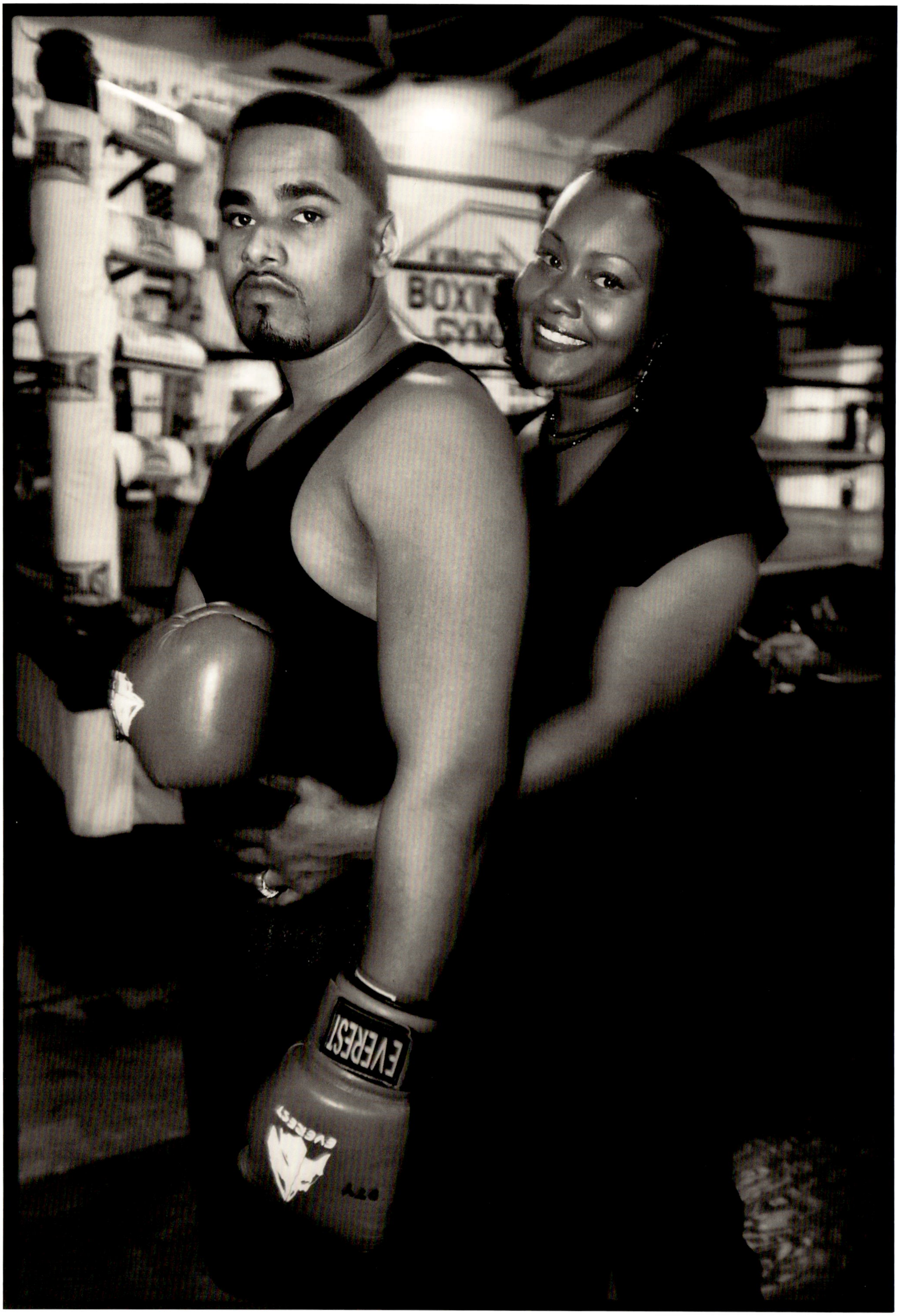
EVEREST

"And in this corner, the winner is: Love, by unanimous decision!"

THE OLD SAYING:

Was it love at first sight?

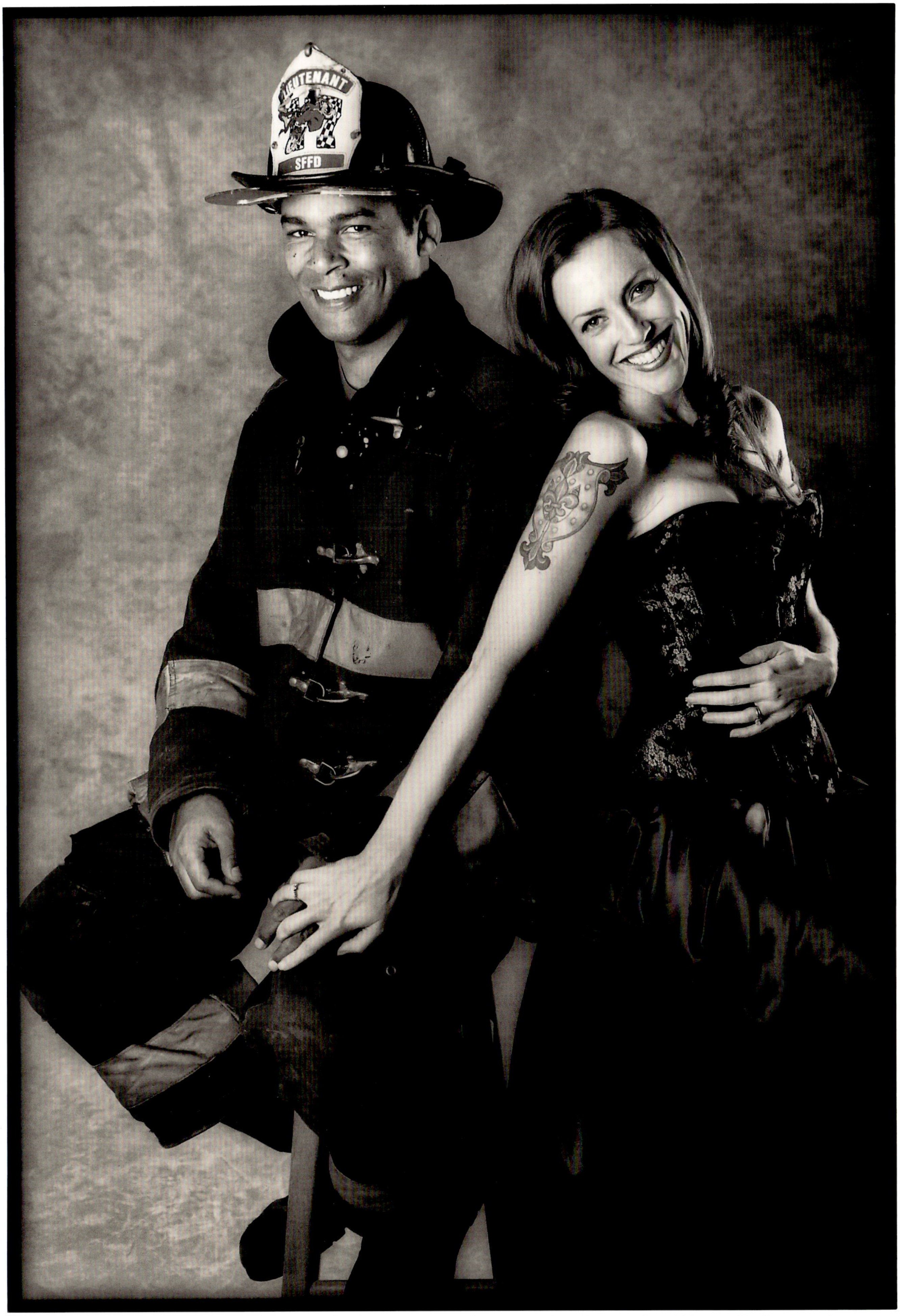

"Engaged after three weeks, married at seven months... happier everyday – still going strong after eight years and two children: my official forever love."

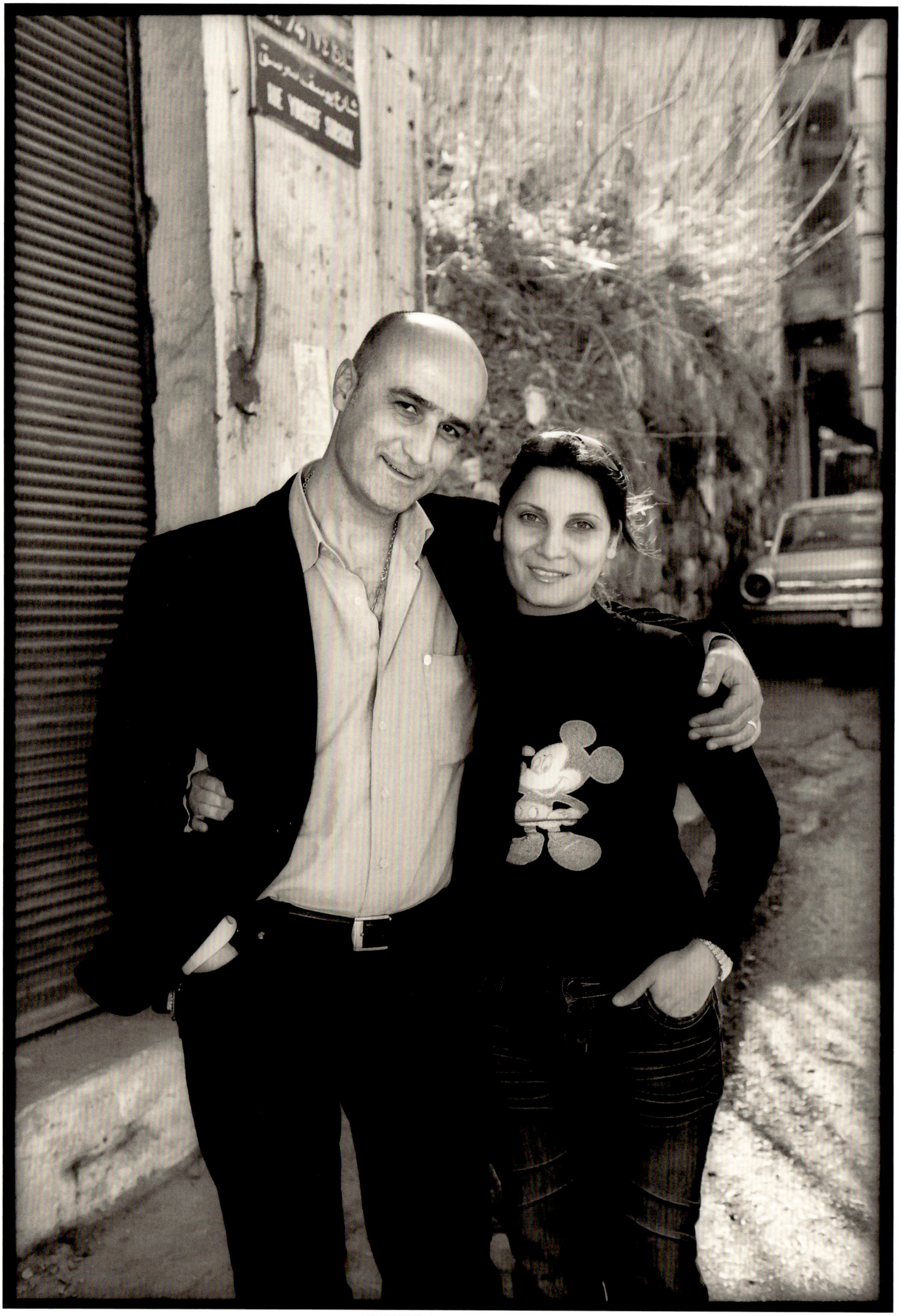

LOCATION — *Beirut, Lebanon*

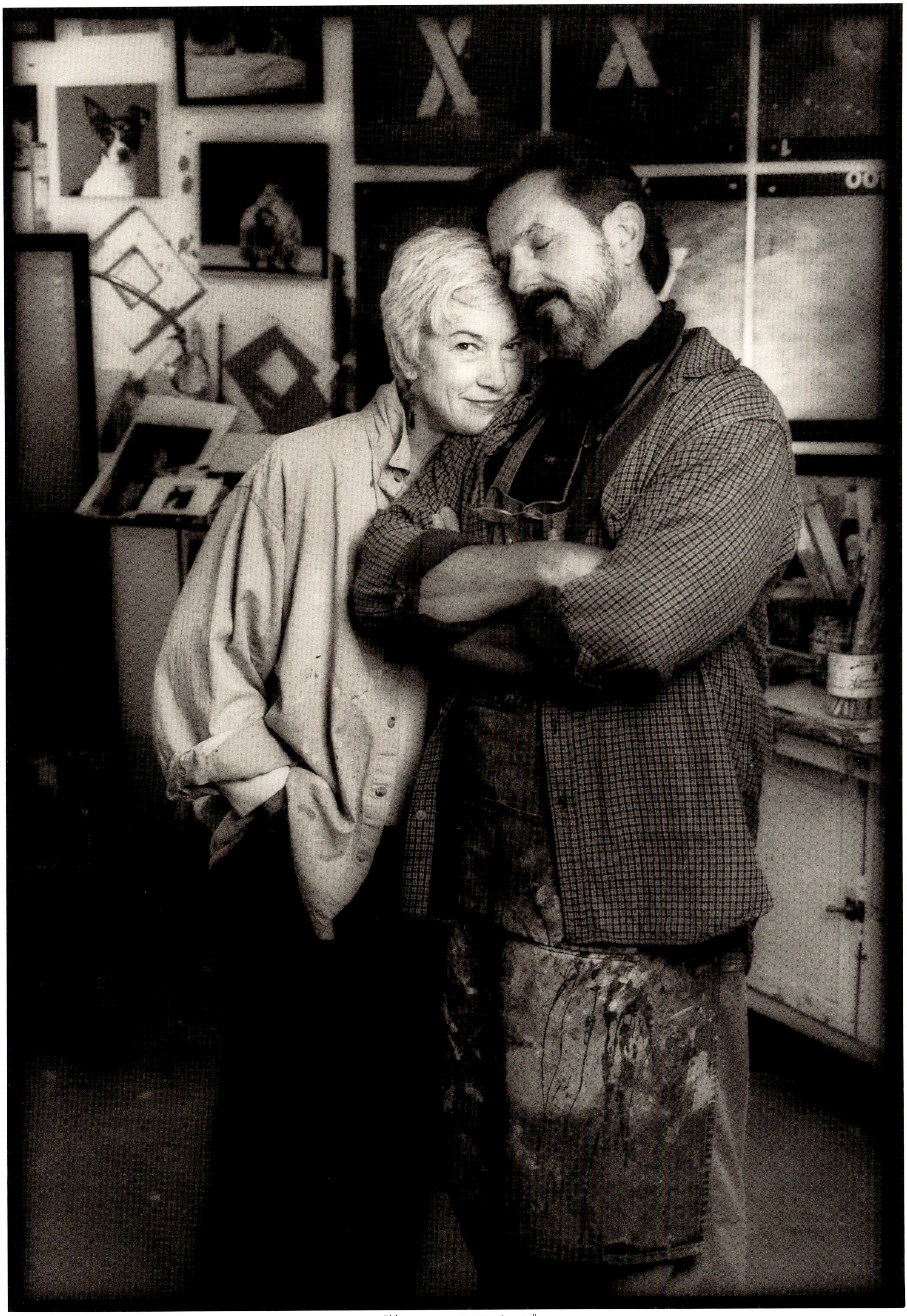

"Never, ever, ever, ever give up."

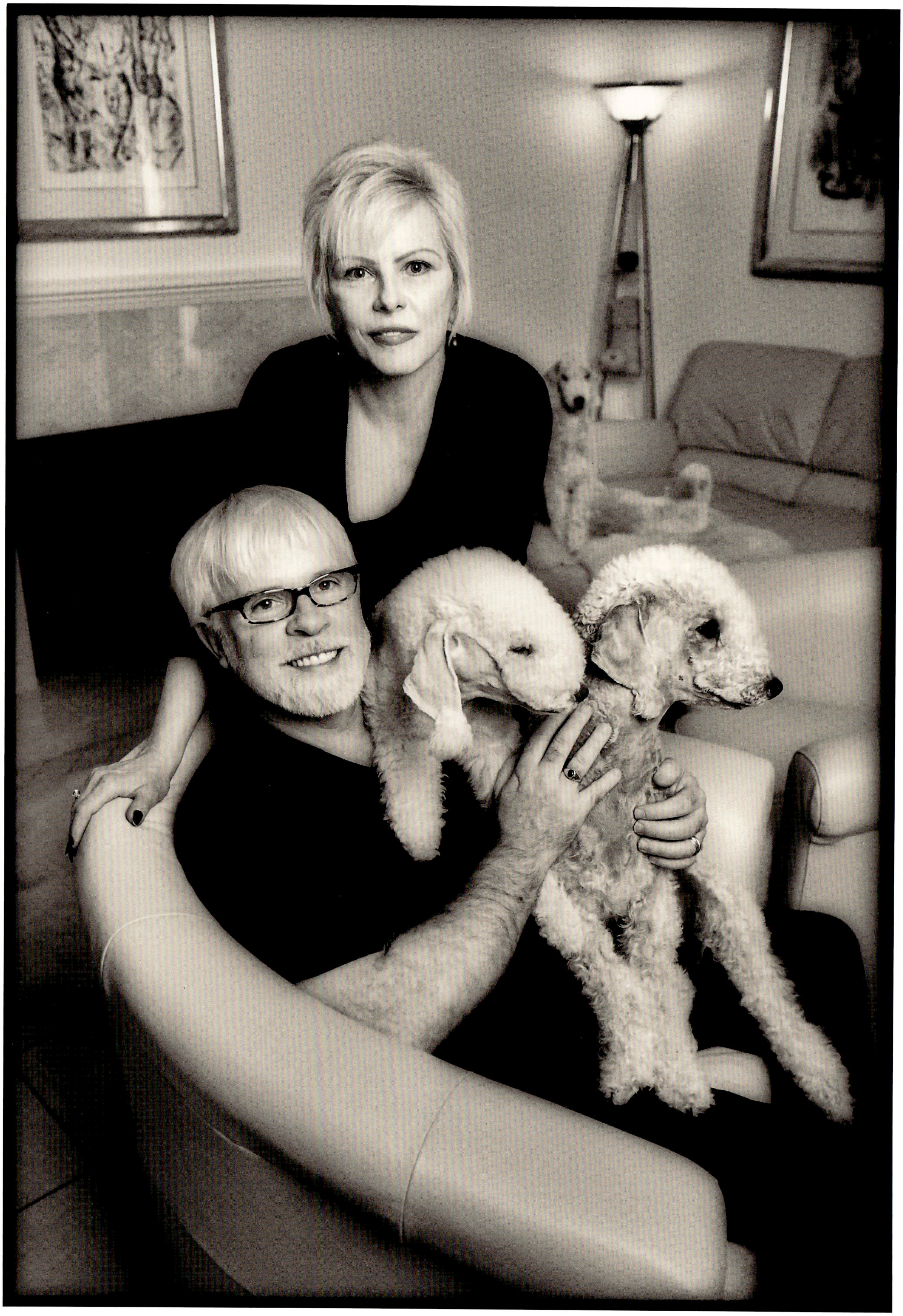

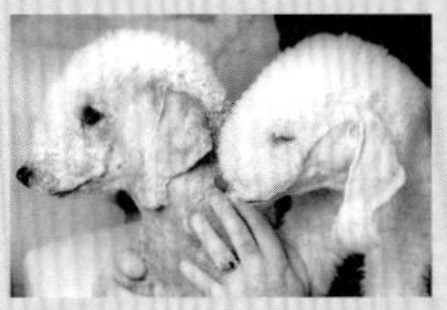

"A passion shared for the rare and beautiful."

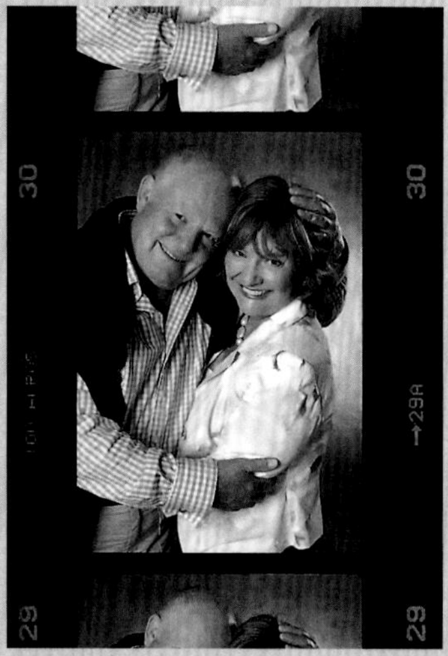

"Still on the road together after 38 happy years."

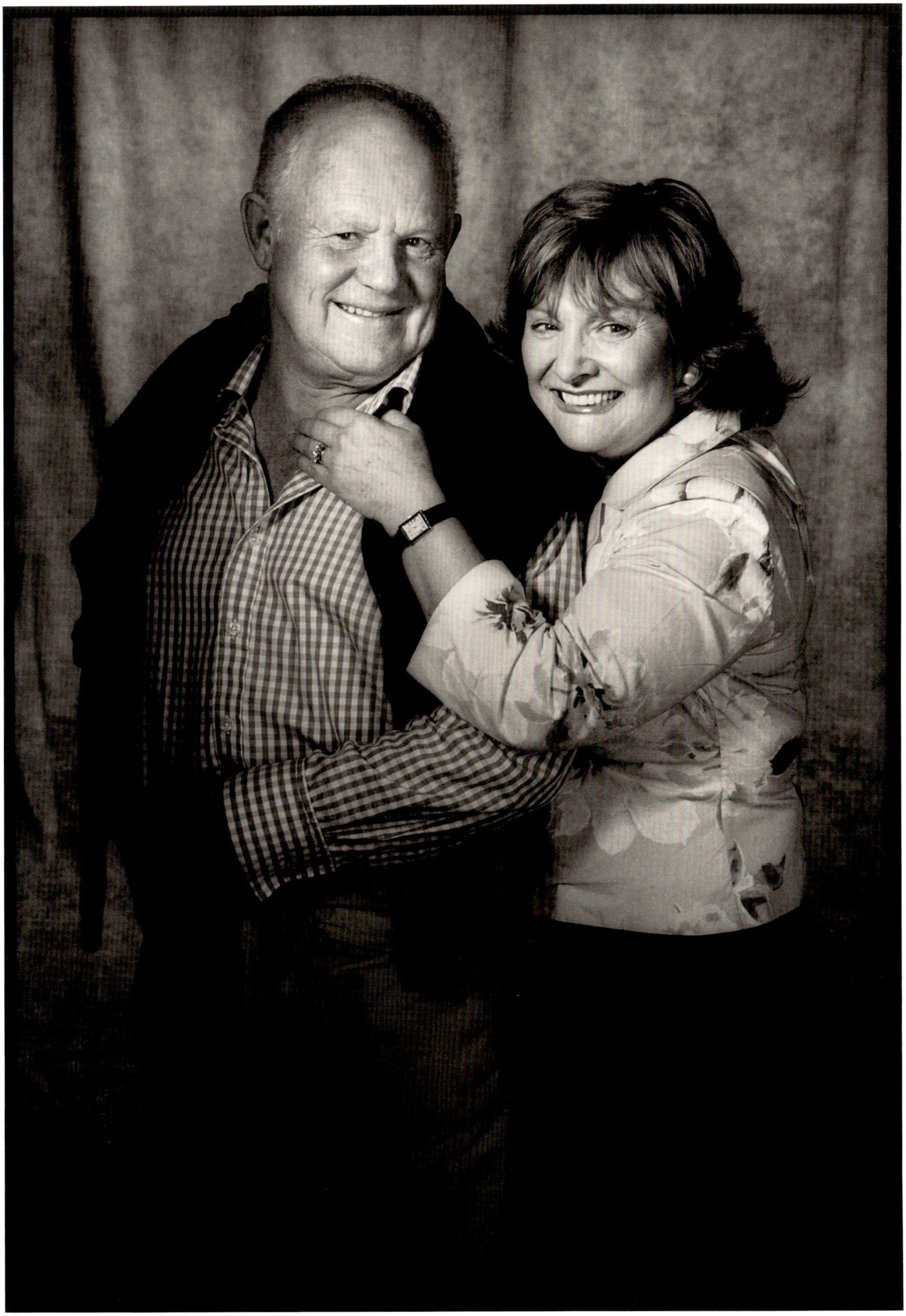

A FEW SUGGESTIONS

On How To

Photograph

A

RELATIONSHIP

Select a Meaningful Location

Set an Atmospheric Mood

Look for a Telling Gesture

Try a Non-pose Pose

Encourage Physical Contact

Record Joy

Try Direct Confrontation

Add a Family Element

Play Up Contrasts

Capture a Revealing Glance

Watch Their Eyes

Keep Shooting